"I Will Fear ...

*Ojibwa-Missionary Encounters
Along the Berens River, 1875–1940*

....

"I Will Fear No Evil"

Ojibwa-Missionary Encounters Along the Berens River, 1875–1940

By Susan Elaine Gray

UNIVERSITY OF
CALGARY
PRESS

Published by the University of Calgary Press
2500 University Drive NW
Calgary, Alberta, Canada T2N 1N4
www.uofcpress.com

Library and Archives Canada Cataloguing in Publication

Gray, Susan Elaine
    "I will fear no evil" : Ojibwa-missionary encounters along the Berens

River, 1875-1940 / Susan Elaine Gray.

Includes bibliographical references and index.
ISBN-13: 978-1-55238-198-4 (University of Calgary Press)
ISBN-13: 978-0-87013-792-1 (Michigan State University Press)
ISBN-10: 1-55238-198-6 (University of Calgary Press)
ISBN-10: 0-87013-792-1 (Michigan State University Press)

    1. Ojibwa Indians—Missions—Manitoba—Berens River Valley—
History. 2. Methodist Chruch—Missions—Manitoba—Berens River
Valley—History. 3. Catholic Church—Missions—Manitoba—Berens River
Valley—History. I. Title.

E99.C6G73 2006   266.0089'733371272   C2006-904005-2

We acknowledge the financial support of the Government of Canada, through the
    Book Publishing Industry Development Program (BPIDP), and the Alberta
    Foundation for the Arts for our publishing activities. We acknowledge the sup-
    port of the Canada Council for the Arts for our publishing program.

Cover design by Melina Cusano. Page design and typesetting by Mieka West.

For W. H. Brooks, who tells me that although my personality is definitely deteriorating, I am getting better looking with age.

Contents

Foreword

··

When I had a conversation with Susan Gray about her research and writing on a period of missionary history along the Berens River, I was very interested. My great-grandfather Joseph Everett was from Berens River and that was a connection for me. Even more important was my lifelong involvement in the work of the United Church and a desire to have a greater understanding of the historic developments in the church. Susan asked if I would be willing to write the foreword to her book. I replied, "Send me the manuscript and we shall see what is possible."

The reading of the manuscript has been exciting. Susan Gray has demonstrated the remarkable discipline that is required to focus her writing on a fixed period of history. The limiting of her book in this manner is especially notable because she was interviewing elders who would often wander beyond this period of history in the natural process of storytelling.

The preface is a valuable contribution to cross-cultural understanding. Susan Gray had a plan in place before her visit to Berens River but it was not the "people's plan." The learned patience and the testing of motives explains the requirement for building right relationships with the Ojibwa of Berens River. The testing of intentions was a part of treaty negotiations a century before Susan visited Berens River and it is the continuing tradition.

The project built momentum when it was understood that it would be a means of giving voice to the elders. The process with each interview had a pattern which also was about building trust. The elders of Berens River have been questioned by academics before now, but this was different because they were being encouraged to reflect on mission history from their perspective.

The recorded interviews are valuable and the elders obviously felt they were respected. The growth of confidence, knowing that they could contribute helpful information, is obvious. The elders used the oral tradition to pass on teachings about spiritual and philosophical insights. Equally significant is the sharing of laughter with memories of life on the Berens River. They spoke openly of their dreams.

The elders interviewed shared their memories of how it was, an awareness of how it is now, and hints of their concern for how it will be. The stories of the church working to make conversions and of the competition between Catholics and Methodists for the winning of souls reflects the level of misunderstanding which existed in those times. The Shaking Tent ceremony continued but Ojibwa people were called on to make a choice between their traditional practices and membership in a church.

The historic context is a challenging backdrop as many issues arose. There was a problem with fishery management as the movement of commercial fisheries entered the area and hunting was less dependable. Chief Jacob Berens requested that the commercial fishers leave the area but depletion of resources continued. Children were being taken to residential schools and flu epidemics impacted the community.

The struggle to maintain self-sufficiency was a major challenge by 1930 and Chief William Berens was prophetic in his resistance to the people becoming dependent on rations from the government. Susan describes the mission history as the Ojibwa were moving from a bounty of food to a period of hunger. There was a political link between illness and hunger which resulted in more "conversions." The two denominations certainly "kept score" as they counted their members and reported them in letters to regional church offices.

This research offers insights into the unfolding of the history of mission. From ceremonies of life on the land, there was a movement to settlement on the banks of Berens River, with schools and churches. It was a situation of conversion and compromise but Susan maintains the Ojibwa kept a vision which is their own. She defends the concept of "a fusion of cultural traditions" which she describes as syncretism. Her conversations with the elders indicated there were "strong roots" with the mission churches but that they also valued their own traditions.

The challenge of this important historical research is how to apply the learnings to the present context. Virginia, Percy, and John were the last generation of Ojibwa to live self-sufficient lives on the land along the Berens River. Their strong self-confidence and identity as Ojibwa elders was grounded in their knowledge of their language and the traditional cultural teachings. Over the past fifty years they had watched the development of a growing dependency on social assistance and the acceptance of a concept called "unemployment," something that they never knew. Now the Ojibwa along the Berens River have many more chapels built by religious denominations which add to the historic Catholic-Methodist tensions.

As you read this book you will be guided through a significant period of Canadian history as experienced by a small community of Ojibwa. The focus on spiritual and philosophical reflections gives a depth to the stories which is not often available to Canadian readers. I am encouraged by it.

I pray it might be used to lift up discussions about our relationships in Canada – past and present – so that we may learn more of the teachings of respect for diversity. This book has much to offer to those who study missiology, and the material might engage students of history in creative reflection. Most importantly it may open doors for First Peoples as we seek to understand the influence of missions on our lives.

The Very Reverend Dr. Stan McKay,
Past Moderator of the United Church of Canada

Preface

On my fourth Christmas I went with my family to visit my grandmother, Anna Mahase, in Trinidad and Tobago. In 1919 she had qualified to become the first East Indian woman teacher on the island. Her mother, Rookabai, had been converted by Presbyterian missionaries who found the twelve-year-old Brahman stowaway hidden in a boat that had carried her to Trinidad from India – away from an arranged marriage to a man she considered old and ugly. Anna, who was raised as a Christian, married Kenneth Mahase, the first East Indian school principal in Trinidad, in August 1919.

Kenneth Mahase came from a wealthy Brahman family that had no need of and little respect for the Presbyterian Mission. Young Mahase converted, however, so that he might attend the Naparima Training College and the jubilant missionaries bequeathed upon him the Christian name Kenneth. It is to be questioned how much jubilation was felt by Mahase's family who subsequently named their dog Kenneth.

On my Christmas visit, Anna had been a widow for almost a decade but still lived in the family home in Sangre Grande, Trinidad. A deeply committed Christian, she was the treasurer of the community's Presbyterian church. On the night of our arrival, as we sat in her large living room, a huge, many-coloured moth flew through the doorway and drifted to my mother, hovering for a few magic moments in front of her face. It then wafted to each of the newcomers ending up at my father who began swatting at the creature. In an instant, the pillar of the Presbyterian Church looked at him and said quietly, "Don't do that, that's Susan's grandfather." She explained that whenever any of the Mahase children came home from overseas for a visit, the moth, a reincarnation of my grandfather, entered the room and greeted the travellers. This never-forgotten incident underlies my interest in encounters between world views.

The histories of North American native peoples embody varied and fascinating dialogues and debates among native people and missionaries. Ojibwa people living along the Berens River of Manitoba and northwestern Ontario between 1870 and 1940 interpreted conversions, and the taking on of Christianity had multi-dimensional meanings in a myriad of different ways. They responded to the Methodist and Roman Catholic missionaries by integrating Christian rituals and practices into their world view in ways that they controlled and found meaningful. Today, people who grew up when the missions were most active continue to interweave both Christian and Ojibwa ideas. Both strands hold power, meaning, and sincerity. The faith and scriptures of Christianity strengthen many in their daily life, and it is equally true that many of the same people's beliefs remain grounded in such Ojibwa concepts as the Thunderbirds, the power of medicine men and conjurors and the use of dreams as vehicles of prediction, guidance, and foreshadowing.

The Berens River Ojibwa often describe themselves in English as Saulteaux. When the French first encountered the early ancestors of these Indians at Sault Ste. Marie, they referred to them as *Saulteurs* (a term which later became *Saulteaux*) and *Outchibouec* (which later became *Ojibwa* or *Chippewa*). Interactions and intermarriages within the French fur trade blurred distinctions between local ethnic groups and fostered the spread of *Saulteaux* and *Ojibwa* to name generally many formerly separate peoples who had been connected to the Outchibouec and Saulteurs through trade relationships and kinship. Some Aboriginal people reject the term *Saulteaux* as a European word.

A word must also be said here about the use of the terms "medicine man" and "conjuror," terms that are still used at Berens River when people speak in English. Some scholars have reacted against the use of these terms, seeing them as embodiments of ethnocentric and judgemental thought. I, however, incorporate them because they are the terms of choice used by my Ojibwa friends and informants living along the Berens River. In trying to make this story as true to their stories as possible, I have made a point of not superimposing academic judgements over the judgements of the players. Out of respect to the Ojibwa women and men who opened themselves up to me during my fieldwork, I have chosen to adopt their terminology in this book.[1]

Ojibwa people along the Berens River experienced and still live a deep, dynamic, and complex religion based on the power of belief and yet which is adaptive and flexible. New ideas arriving in their midst – such rituals as Fair Wind's Dream Drum Dance (along the upper Berens River) – have often been welcomed if they appeared powerful and valuable.[2] Contrary to the assumptions of generations of westerners, the Saulteaux employed empiricism and critical thinking at deep levels. The ability to incorporate outside ideas into an existing world view does not imply that their beliefs were superficial.

Beginning in the 1870s, Berens River encounters with Christianity became both commonplace and locally intense. During this time, many Ojibwa in this area actively took on and participated in Methodism or Roman Catholicism, adopting and adapting a number of beliefs and rituals into their world views.

Native people who responded positively to Christianity were influenced by many factors. These included a wish for literacy and Western education and technical resources, a desire to understand the Bible as a source of potentially helpful and beneficial messages, added divine protection from illness and other crises, protection against bad medicine, access to Western medicine, and the enhancing of existing powers derived from traditional dreams and rituals.

Mission successes in these communities usually depended on the sustained presence of a devoted missionary who stayed long enough to achieve respect and earn trust. By the late nineteenth century, many Ojibwa at the mouth of the Berens River were second-generation Christians; the new tradition and loyalty had firm roots in many families.

Christianity, however, was not accepted out of hand. Lack of empathy from missionaries, lack of agreement with the lessons taught to children in schools, lack of a felt need for a new religion, or lack of respect by a missionary for sacred Ojibwa rituals could all be reasons for rejection. Clearly, native people were in control of making choices here; it was they who decided when and how they would or would not accept Christianity.

Until recently, historians have written about Christian missions largely from European perspectives, using ethnocentric criteria for evaluating their success and failures. Native responses have received far less attention than the goals of the missionaries; often, in fact, the diversity of Native responses has not even been perceived.[3]

Church historians have tended to write glowing accounts of missionary endeavour, glorying in native conversions and the usurping of "paganism" by the stronger, more legitimate and dynamic Christian faith. These uncritical hagiographies celebrate the successes of their denominational missionary heroes and are conspicuous in their lack of attention to the perspectives of native people. Their renderings portray the trees' leaves but not their branches, trunks, or twigs – those very things essential to structure and depth.[4]

Another type of interpretation presents missionaries and government agents as cultural murderers, bent on smashing traditional lifeways. The only "real Indians" were pre-contact, and native groups which experienced change through contact were seen as weakened victims who existed in a state of suspension, being neither Indian nor white.[5] Conversions, according to this model, were blind-deaf-and-dumb affairs with confused natives merely going through the motions. Though marred by contact, their minds were sufficiently Indian to ensure that they would never truly succumb to the foreign, lethal white religion. This view reflected the romantic hopes of many scholars that a primitive or traditional consciousness survived. The compulsion to patronize native intellects and condemn Christianity and missionaries as agents of the dominant society, however, too commonly does not do justice to any of the cast of characters: Indian or white.

The best new writing recognizes that native perspectives are crucial to a full understanding of mission history. Recently, scholarship has made exciting advances in studies of syncretism (creative ways by which Christianity and traditional native religions met, mixed, and blended ideas) and integrations (ways in which Christianity and traditional religious world views coexisted as interlocking sets of ideas within individuals). Native people had many reasons for acceptance or rejection of Christianity. Many outside ideas, once thought to have been forced on unwitting native victims, were actually filtered and moulded to suit native cultures within native frameworks. An understanding of these processes comes only from studying individual native communities and missions with as open a mind as possible. The careful tracing of individual native perspectives and responses over generations can help to place indigenous perspectives at centre stage among the other voices that have too long dominated these conversations.

In the North American context, a small but growing body of literature on syncretism and Christian missions provides a useful context for this study. Raymond DeMallie has studied the influence of Christian teachings on Lakota culture in this century through an in-depth look at the life of Black Elk.[6] In the western subarctic, Jean-Guy Goulet learned from Athapaskan Catholics that these Dene have two religious systems available to them, experiencing both Aboriginal and Christian ideologies as "socially available and meaningful."[7]

As well, closer and more balanced scrutinies of individual missionaries – their personalities, backgrounds, motivations, knowledge of Aboriginal language and culture, sensitivity to native values, and their interactions in the field can etch pictures that, as Ann Fienup-Riordan puts it, are "subtle and full of nuance."[8]

The history of Indian-missionary encounters must also be seen as interactive and processual – as meetings and negotiations between different systems of meaning, embodied in complex human individuals.

The Moravian mission of John and Edith Kilbuck to the Yup'ik Eskimo, for example, was successful in that, by 1895, it had drawn many converts, implanted many aspects of Western technology (such as sawmills, boats, printed language) and reduced the credibility of shamans. The real basis of success, though, was the integration of native and white ideas. Although the Kilbucks' efforts represented some beneficial aspects of Christianity, the power of these elements was, as Fienup-Riordan explains, traditionally defined. Both Christianity and Yup'ik religion were based on a connection between thought and action. The Christian idea that prayer would evoke a favourable response from God was compatible with traditional Yup'ik ideas of hunting magic. Because the Yup'ik were familiar with the idea that ritual performance would ensure the success of future action, they could make sense of the Kilbucks' message. In addition, the missionaries' use of Indians as preachers and translators provided still more integrative dimensions in their work.[9] The real impact of the Kilbucks' work was that it created a transformed world with a place within it for the Yup'ik.

Preaching the value of time, money, and the written word, their practical mission engendered a novel perception of the world and the Yup'iks' place within it. "Although the [Yup'ik] increasingly spoke English, lived within four walls, worked for wages, and attended church, they remained independent, their lives focused on extended family relations and the pursuit of the fish and game on which they had relied for centuries ... the people ignored ... eminently 'civilized' activities when they conflicted with traditional subsistence and settlement patterns. Though much had changed, much also remained of the Yup'ik Eskimos' traditional view of the world."[10]

James Axtell emphasized some years ago that historians must evaluate mission success by asking the question: Why did Indians convert to Christianity?[11] Similarly, when studying interactions between Methodists, Catholics, and Ojibwa at Berens River, we need to ask why many Berens River Ojibwa converted, what meanings those conversions held for new Christians, and how the Ojibwa and Christian world views interacted in following years.

The work of Methodist missionary Thomas Crosby who worked among the Tsimshians in Port Simpson, British Columbia, between 1874 and 1897 provides another example of Indians assuming "a decisive role in the conversion process and in determining the success of the mission."[12] Prior to Crosby's arrival, these people had rejected the overtures of Anglican missionary William Duncan because at the time, they saw no need to take on Christianity. Their views changed by the 1870s for a number of reasons including: a desire to acquire Western material goods, a love of the music and drama in Methodist worship services (which offered some parallels to their own rich ritual and ceremonial life), a wish to acquire additional power from Christianity that could help ward off disease, and a hope that their Christianity, by serving to show that they had taken on the newcomers' lifestyle, would bring them economic and political power.

The essential point is that the Tsimshians determined their own responses to missions; they themselves sought out the missionary and later rejected Crosby. By 1885, they were disillusioned. Although they had worked hard and spent much money in improving their village and building a school and church, money and work were scarce and the land question had not been settled to their satisfaction. The economic and political power that they sought was, in the end, denied them.

Although their conversion was sincere and the Tsimshians changed their village into an ideal Victorian Canadian town and "offered little resistance to the dismantling of their way of life,"[13] many traditional customs were retained. Christianity, education, and medical aid changed the lives of the community members who got rid of communal longhouses, dancing, gambling, feasting, potlatching, and the idea of communal ownership, and replaced their traditional leadership with a village council led by Crosby. The giving of hereditary names, property rights, rules of exogamy, customs controlling marriage, and laws pertaining to funerals, however, "remained operative beneath the veneer of western mores."[14]

Sergei Kan has studied traditional beliefs and practices that are still flourishing among Alaskan Tlingits who consider themselves to be Christians.[15] The Tlingits incorporated Christian rituals and objects into older ceremonies, while retaining beliefs about reincarnation and practices such as the potlatch as a memorial rite.

There have been exciting developments beyond North America in history, anthropology, religion, and sociology. This study of the Berens River area has also found inspiration in the ways that Aboriginal peoples around the world interpreted the transmission of ideas and generated new belief structures through the strength, flexibility, and influence of their traditional world views. These ongoing processes ensured that Aboriginal peoples reshaped their cultures and dealt with change.[16]

Along the Berens River we see much evidence of many-faceted responses to Christianity. Chief Jacob Berens (ca. 1835–1917), for example, was baptized as a young man by the Methodists in 1861 and the missionaries were thrilled when this convert became the Treaty Chief at Berens River upon the signing of Treaty 5 in 1875. Chief Berens raised his children to be Methodists. Anthropologist A. Irving Hallowell, however, found in the 1930s that some of these children had extensive knowledge of the Ojibwa Midiwiwin or Grand Medicine Ceremony and the Shaking Tent rituals and Jacob's son, William, proved to be the key collaborator in Hallowell's studies of the Ojibwa world view and history. William Berens revealed the essence of syncretism and integration at Berens River when he told Hallowell, "My father used to say to me … you will see lots of new things and you will find a place in your mind for them all."[17]

This book has been given sparkle, vitality, and nuance through the stories of women and men who live in the Berens River community. These people essentially breathed life into the text. Like any other methodology, oral history brings with it its share of problems and requires the historian to apply the same critical questioning of sources as she or he would in the case of any other source. While A. Irving Hallowell was a friend and collaborator of William Berens, the community of Berens River is not generally familiar with Hallowell's writings (although William's sons and daughters remember the anthropologist). Thus, people's memories are not influenced by reading Hallowell; nor is there a sense of animosity, of having to "set the record straight" or a sense of needing to tailor stories to fit a prescribed mould.

It was the Ojibwa people who live in Berens River who injected life-breath into my work and, in so doing, turned my work about the past into living passionate humanity. It was one thing to read and think, for example, about how the Ojibwa incorporated new ideas or rituals into their midst, but a multitude of meanings and a rush of lifeblood were transfused into the study when I sat with the people of Berens River who opened their hearts and minds to me. They blew off academic dust and turned on lights. They were the prisms through which light shone and refracted into nuance and clarity. I realized that their voices were central to this story and that I needed to justice to their passions and convictions.

After examining a plethora of written records, I made arrangements for a research trip to Berens River. A good month before I planned to arrive in the community, I spoke several times on the phone to a pleasant helpful man who worked in the Band Office. He assured me that he would arrange for me to interview some of the elders in the community and that he would meet my plane at the airport. But when my small plane landed in Berens River on a freezing cold, grey December morning, my telephone friend was conspicuously absent.

Through some lucky encounters and the kindness of the owner of the Berens River Hotel I finally made it to the Band Office, feeling vulnerable but hopeful. My stomach literally turned over, however, when my inquiry was answered at the front desk by, "Percy? Percy's in the bush!" Vulnerability shifted to panic. I had limited time to do some interviews and my sole contact was in the bush. Not one person in the office seemed to care a wit about my agenda. Someone told me to sit down on a bench, which I did. I

sat and sat in mute misery and tried to imagine what I would say
to my dissertation advisor when I returned with blank tapes.

But something *was* happening, although I didn't realize it at
the time. I was being carefully observed. After an hour and a half,
I was frantic and becoming quite bitter. Just then, someone came
over and invited me into one of the offices. A group of Ojibwa
men were gathered there and they calmly surveyed me. They
asked what I wanted and what I was doing in Berens River. I,
somewhat less calmly, explained why I wanted to speak to people
in the community. Their expressions were impassive except for
one man who introduced himself as Andrew Bittern and who
smiled once when I explained how much this work meant to me
and how worried I was. They went away for a while and came
back. Within minutes they made a list of some of the oldest,
accessible people in the community. It was Andrew Bittern who
volunteered to drive me everywhere I would need to go during my
stay in Berens River.

I had read a great deal about Ojibwa adaptability and
flexibility. It was amazing to see in action what I had read in
the abstract. Here was a clear example of people choosing to
participate and facilitating events on their own terms. As it
turned out, I would have been lost without their support. Because
he had decided that my work was interesting and worthy of his
effort and attention, Andrew faithfully picked me up, dropped me
off, and picked me up again from many homes within a fairly wide
geographic radius, taking me back to my hotel to eat or to pass the
time between appointments. It was Andrew who went first to the
door of the people's houses and spoke to them in Ojibwa, telling
them what I wanted and asking them if they wanted to see me.
They did. It was Andrew who got people to take their big dogs
away (even though I know for a fact that a couple of times he was
almost as intimidated by them as I was).

Meanwhile, the people in the Band Office spread the word.
Within a short time, one young man approached me, suggesting I
talk to his grand uncle. After breakfast in the hotel, another man
told me I should speak to his mother, whom he drove me to meet.

Somehow, I was becoming as flexible as they all were and this was key to the trip's success. I was open to any and all shifts and encounters. Word spread with remarkable speed, and it was not long before people were saying upon my arrival, "I heard you were around! I'm surprised you took so long to get here!" The people had decided they wanted to talk to me, and they did.

Another important phenomenon occurred in every interview, illustrating how the older people I met decided on courses of action and controlled dynamics. Each person listened politely while I explained what I was doing. Each person spent the first hour answering my questions pleasantly and reservedly, along fairly standard lines. They related the names of their ministers or priests, and told me about attending Sunday School as children. In many cases it appeared that outsiders had talked to them before, and they had some stock responses in hand. The tone was always polite, impersonal, and guarded. In each case, I began to wonder if the person would ever really talk to me and was afraid that I would not be able to make a connection.

And then, a magic moment would arrive when these people suddenly opened up and their souls shone out. I am still not sure what made the grey cloud-covering blow away. Did they become satisfied that I honestly wanted to know what they thought? Did they decide they simply liked me and wanted to help? Did they realize that this was a way for them to make their stories heard? Whatever it was, they became passionate and open and spoke from their hearts. Walter Green, for example, had been used to making public appearances in many schools throughout the province, including Winnipeg. It was remarkable to witness the moment when he stopped relating standard stories of Ojibwa lore and began talking to me about his own visions and his fears and the deep loves of his life—his love for music and the beauty and power of some of his dreams.

Sometimes I had to have the courage to reveal a little of myself before the transformative moment. Fred Baptiste, for example, answered questions for an hour in a chant-like monotone. As I looked around the walls of his tiny house, I was suddenly struck by his many pictures, all of which illustrated Biblical stories and themes. I told him I loved their brilliant, vivid colours. He sat quietly, looking at me for a long time. Then abruptly, he asked me to interpret the meaning behind a picture of Christ knocking at the door of a house. "You know that's a picture of Jesus," he said. "Can you make anything out of that?" I was mindful of creating bias and contaminating the conversation with too many of my own ideas. And so, a bit antiseptically, I answered, "Well, I see Jesus knocking at a door, and it's closed and it's night. What's *your* take on that?" Fred jumped up and leaned over the table, his nose in my face. "He's standing at the door, knocking at the door. He's knocking at the door to your heart. And would you let him in or not? I want you to answer that!" I froze. What if I said the wrong thing and this interview would be held up years later by some academic as proof of my lack of a proper approach? "You want me to answer that?" "Yes! Yes! If Jesus knocks at your door – that's your *heart's* door, eh? – are you going to let him in?" I said faintly that I thought I would.

And with that personal exposure, Fred went on to lay himself bare also. "Sure! Sure! Nobody'd ever turn him down!" Then he told me that for years he had owned a wonderful feather. It was, he explained, the feather of a baby Thunderbird. This new and real Fred shared his response to the recent funeral of his friend, Alec McKay. Inspired by his painting of the Last Supper, Fred put a piece of cake in Alec's coffin. He explained that he was having the Last Supper with Alec and that he would take the food with him on his road to the next life.

On one level, Fred's response represented a wonderful example of his blending of the Christian idea of the Last Supper with the Ojibwa concept of placing articles of food and tobacco with a deceased person to prepare his spirit for the journey to the afterlife. On another level, it was a heart warming shared experience. Fred was talking to me as one human being to another.

In the same way, other concepts, relationships, and beliefs were illuminated by the old peoples' discourse and remembrances.

I had gleaned from the letters of Rev. Niddrie, Brother Leach, and his superior, Father De Grandpré (who was sometimes at Berens River with Leach) that Protestant-Catholic dynamics were sometimes rather strained at Berens River. This tension took on a new dimension, however, when I heard Percy Berens and Fred Baptiste roar with laughter, Percy remembering how "they used to fight just like a cat and a dog! Really! I'm telling you the truth!"[18] The letters of the missionaries told of strong denominational tensions and I had the impression that this was a truly divided community. But sitting around kitchen tables at Berens River, I realized that, despite the enmity between clergy, the Ojibwa members of the churches generally got on very well with one another and many attended services at both Catholic and Protestant churches on Sundays.

The real presence of the Ojibwa belief system in the lives of modern Berens River folk was best conveyed through the stories and thoughts of the people themselves. Walter Green, a dedicated United Church member, told me about an angel who had taught him to play the organ in a dream and of the protective vision he had on a series of evenings as he lay in bed with a severe illness. It is one thing to read of Ojibwa peoples' belief in spirits, and quite another to hear a voice filled with warmth and awe say, "oh they're just so wonderful, they can do anything!"[19] Walter's eyes shone as he said this and I remember, at that moment, contrasting the light of his eyes with the hours I spent in the archives struggling to read microfilm in the darkness.

A. Irving Hallowell wrote about fears around bad conjuring. Intellectually I had what I thought was a grasp of this idea. However, its power and reality were lost on me until I heard the bitterness in Percy Berens's voice when he told me about the price his brother, Jacob, paid for incurring the jealous wrath of a conjuror. "One of my brothers *died* of that kind of thing," he said, "because they were jealous of him. They thought my brother was using medicine for his dog team to be so good."[20]

The esteem for the good that medicine men could do was also conveyed clearly and passionately by the same people who spoke with passion of the contributions of the churches and schools in their community. When I asked Percy Berens about Leach's and Niddrie's abhorrence of medicine men, he vehemently explained, "Because they didn't believe in it. That was what was wrong. That's the trouble. They didn't *really* have it explained to them what it means for an Indian to be a medicine man. They should have known better. That man there, that medicine man, he's going to save lives! For other people! It's a good thing! I very appreciate your bringing this whole thing up, this medicine thing. The old people lived long in my time, no babies died that much as what they do now because the Indians knew the medicine."[21] Other elders explained that it was unfortunate that the missionaries had not realized that the power of medicine men and women had come from God and that older people used to use that medicine to accomplish wonderful things.

The Thunderbirds also came alive for me in these homes. When I asked Percy Berens if he believed in these beings, he was passionate. "Oh yeah! It's a bird! It's a bird. You should go to Poplar River [to see their nest of boulders]. White people don't believe it's a bird, a Thunderbird, they don't believe on that. But we Indians absolutely believe it's a bird." Without the Thunderbirds, he explained, there would never have been rain and everything would have long dried up.[22] Equally impassioned on this subject was John Edward Everett, a practising Roman Catholic. "Today I'm a Catholic," he said, "Cross – water – God, there is only one God. The Holy Water is good. My religion is one religion. When I was born, they baptized me Catholic. I'll stay that way 'til I die."[23] About Thunderbirds, he explained, "We smoke our pipes west – all the directions – north, east – because we see a big cloud and where's it coming up from? This moving cloud! What's going to happen? All of a sudden it's like a *bomb*, eh? If you smoke, the thunder cloud will go past. The Thunderbirds. Many moons. Love your neighbour as you love yourself. Listening to the white people today, you hear Thunderbirds come when there's cold air with hot air. No way.

Young Thunderbirds in the fall, they're just like – oh! they make a really loud noise!"[24]

Oral history vastly enhanced my understandings about the power of belief and Ojibwa flexibility or give-and-take regarding choice of belief. Percy Berens probably summed it up best. "You say you don't believe in spirits at all," I said to him. "No I don't," he replied, "I've got only one belief and only one spirit." I asked him if he was saying that spirits do not exist at all or whether he was simply saying that he did not *choose* to believe in them. He was clear. "I don't *choose* to believe in them spirits.... But they can exist for other people. If you believe strong enough to believe that there's spirits there, then they're there. And that's what those old time Indians had. They strongly *believed* in them spirits of evil and righteousness. That was their belief, see? Evil and righteous spirits." I pressed him a little on how he integrated aspects of two different world views – a practice so foreign to Christian missionaries. "Percy," I asked, "Some white people say you should believe in the Bible but that you shouldn't believe in the ability to conjure or in Thunderbirds. So how come the Indians are different from the white people that way?" I will never forget the laughter that filled the sunny room on that winter afternoon. "That's very easy to answer that question! Because the Indians are smart, clever – but the white man is stupid, ignorant. Isn't that correct enough? Sure! *We* believe."[25]

Finally, my encounters at Berens River had a formative impact on my work. As I suggested earlier, I realized the necessity of stepping out of the structure and order shaped by archival research and into another kind of order. Historically, when I encountered new situations, especially those where I had a limited time to accomplish a great deal of work, I tried to control things by planning ahead. What the people at Berens River taught me is that the real way to ensure quality, of work and of life, is to embrace everything – from chance encounters, to unforeseen bends in the road – to be open, listening and flexible – words truly reminiscent of the Ojibwa world view. It was fascinating, as well, for me to not only read about but to experience Ojibwa people assessing a situation in their midst, deciding whether or not to participate and initiating a gentle control over the events.

The voices of the actors in the dramas that played out between Ojibwa people and missionaries gave a meaning and added a dimension that I never could have experienced through written sources alone. These people did much more than simply fill in gaps; they breathed life into my work and made it sparkle. Indeed, in the end, oral history led me to begin to comprehend the depth of the Saulteaux capacity to integrate aspects of both the Ojibwa and Christian world views. The only way for me to understand the Berens River elders' passion behind their feelings about the power of belief – was to listen to them. I hope this work provides examples of the magic that comes from the life and light that can infuse scholarly work when one makes a connection between written sources and the lived lives of the human beings who try to speak to us through these sources. For historians, these worlds are usually separated by a great chasm. If we do it well, oral history enables us as researchers to step easily across that abyss.

Both oral and written sources rely on conventional, culturally-specific narrative genres that help people construct, maintain, and pass on understanding of how the world works and should work, restricting one's analysis to written sources ensures that interpretations will not always ensure that nuances and dimensions are evoked. While it is true that oral and written sources are very different from one another, it is largely *because* of these differences that historians must take oral evidence into account when it is available.[26]

Cultures based on oral transmission of knowledge privilege oral history as a spoken "archive" to be carefully passed on. Yet the methodology of oral history has drawn criticism from some historians who question the wisdom of reliance on memory, suggesting that memories change with age and that this yields somewhat fickle narrative. While memories can and do change over time, it is interesting that so many of my informants shared both details and interpretations of events – not in so close a fashion that one might suspect teachings had been imposed on

them, but close enough for me to draw some strong parallels
among sources. Interesting, also, is the consistency of findings
from oral testimony and written texts. For example, Maureen
Matthews and Roger Roulette compared the written and oral
sources regarding the origins of Fair Wind's Drum Dance and
were struck by the persistence and accuracy of peoples' memories
and their correspondences with Hallowell's texts. Sixty years
after Hallowell's visits, the oral stories of the Ojibwa people of
Pauingassi, Manitoba, about Fair Wind's dream and the ceremony
itself, compare strikingly with Hallowell's contemporary
observations.[27]

Another criticism of the use of oral evidence comes from
historians who believe that those informants who speak highly of
missionaries and Christianity are glibly uttering dogma. I spoke
with many members of the Berens River community about their
thoughts and feelings about Methodism, Catholicism, and the
missionaries whom they had encountered. Of startling note were
their positive interpretations of Christianity. To what extent were
community elders romanticizing their pasts? Were these people
carefully repeating orthodox positions, uncomfortable about
admitting to holding traditional Ojibwa beliefs as a result of years
of missionary sanction? While one cannot read the minds of the
men and women who told their stories, it is surely not up to an
academic scholar to impose her own sanctions on their words.
Anna Mahase, my East Indian grandmother, whom I described in
the preface of this book, held, within her world view, many Hindu
concepts. She was also the treasurer of the Presbyterian Church
and a staunch Christian. To imply that she had been a victim of
loss or that she had somehow been frightened by missionaries into
espousing the church is to patronize her intelligence and integrity.

It is difficult but crucial for ethnohistorians to avoid laying
prior moral interpretations over their findings. When I was in
the first year of my doctoral work, I decided to write a paper
on the Presbyterian missionaries in Trinidad who worked in
the community where my mother grew up. I was resentful of
what I believed to be the condescension and manipulation of

these missionaries, of the ethnocentric ways they viewed East Indians, and of the pejorative views they held. My mother, two uncles, and four aunts were important as oral history sources. It was devastating for me when only one aunt expressed angry views about missionary interference and patronization. I needed to explain away the views of my mother and her brothers and sisters – to make them change their minds – to say that they were romanticizing their youth – to say that they should know better – to say that they had been bamboozled by missionaries. I see now that, in fact, I was the one who was patronizing; I had no right to expect that their ideas should fit within the context of my academic morality that loathed these Christian "bad guys."

Winona Stevenson, a Cree scholar, writes of the interpretive problems she encountered when writing the history of Charles Pratt, her Cree-Assiniboine grandfather who was an Anglican missionary in present-day Saskatchewan. Dealing with the discrepancies between her family's oral history and Pratt's written accounts was terribly difficult for her.[28] Throughout the writing of this book, I, too, have had to struggle to separate my subjective and emotional self from my objective and analytical self. This separation can never occur completely, however, and I have come to realize that, as with Winona Stevenson, this has produced deeper understanding on my part.

The idea that the stories and experiences of "ordinary people" would actually be put into a book was warmly received. It is my hope that Hallowell's work and this work will find their way into the community where they belong, for they have relied so heavily on the contributions of the people. The people who helped me were conversant in English, a lucky thing for me since I am not fluent in Ojibwa. All the interviews presented in this book are literal transcriptions and have not been reworked in any way.

Acknowledgments

Percy Berens, Walter Green, Ida Green, Betsey Patrick, Fred
Baptiste, John Edward Everett, and Virginia Boulanger, all
residents of Berens River, Manitoba, opened their hearts, minds
and lives to me.

Jennifer S. H. Brown has provided keen insight, immeasurable
support, and constant encouragement both personally and
professionally for over a decade. Her guidance has been invaluable.
Funds from her Canada Research Chair in Aboriginal Peoples in
an Urban and Regional Context enabled me to complete this book
and to include photographs and a map. John Kendle, throughout
my academic career, has inspired and grounded me as has W.
H. Brooks, who has been "a light through the trees and into the
darkness" in both the life and the work. Theresa Schenck provided
me with excellent insights which made this work so much better.
John S. Long was a great support, providing me with helpful
criticism, advice, and encouragement, while sharing his own work.
Maureen Matthews was extremely generous in sharing her sources
and thoughts. I would also like to thank Darlene Rose Overby
for giving me the wonderful family photograph of Jacob and Mary
Berens to use in this book, and Bruce Hanks for his technical
expertise in reproducing it here.

I would like to express my sincere gratitude to many people
who helped me in the preparation of this work. Diane Haglund,
the United Church archivist at the University of Winnipeg, Gilles
Lesage, archivist at the Oblate Archives, Manitoba Province,
and Ruth Dyck Wilson, Reference Coordinator at the United
Church Archives at Victoria University, Toronto, provided great
assistance.

Thanks are also due to the staff at University of Calgary Press (especially Walter Hildebrandt, John King, Peter Enman and Karen Buttner) and to Jean Llewellyn for her thoughtful and meticulous copyediting.

I need to express special gratitude to friends and family: to my dear friend Valerie Regehr for her sense and sensibility and to my parents Elaine and Al Gray for their eternal encouragement. Deepest thanks to David McCrady, for his steadfast support, vision, and for carrying my heart.

Finally, I was humbled and deeply grateful for the generosity and gentleness of the Very Reverend Dr. Stan McKay, who kindly wrote a foreword for this book. He, and the elders of Berens River, have made this all worthwhile.

My thanks and my love to all of you. May you have good dreams.

1   Life along the Berens River from 1875 to 1940

....

Between 1875 and 1940, the Ojibwa
communities along the Berens River experienced some profound
transformations. Social and technological changes came about
in many ways. For example, in 1875, the Canadian government
negotiated Treaty 5 with the Ojibwa people of the region that
includes Berens River. Commercial fisheries were established,
introducing outsiders as well as new fishing technology, fishing
boats and new capital. Steamboats became more common sights
on Lake Winnipeg and the fur traders' large canoes and York boats
disappeared.

Euro-Canadian institutions, including Protestant and Catholic
churches and schools, as represented by various missionaries, and
the Department of Indian Affairs, represented by Indian agents
and inspectors of Indian agencies arrived at the mouth of the
Berens River. The growing roles of these institutions in the lives
of community residents brought profound changes. Throughout
the 1875 to 1940 period, Berens River Ojibwa people negotiated
these changes within the structure of their world view as they
selectively adapted to or rejected features of a new life.

These decisions were always made within the realities of life
in a subarctic climate. The Berens River area with the Poplar,
Berens and Bloodvein Rivers making up its major river systems,
contains a topography which ranges from rolling to hilly to
fairly flat. Although climate and precipitation allow much tree
growth, glacial ravages have exposed and polished the ancient
granitic rocks of the Canadian Shield and soils are thin and
acidic, precluding agriculture on more than a small scale. Average

temperatures in winter are −32 degrees Celsius and summers
do not get much warmer than 22 degrees. Winters are long,
with snow often appearing before November and accumulating
to anywhere between 38 and 254 centimetres by February,
the coldest month of the year. Snow begins to melt in April
and deciduous trees yield leaves in June. Summer in northern
Manitoba extends from June to August. Annual temperature,
wind and daylight changes in this seasonal cycle determine
the arrival and departure of migratory birds and the habits of
fur-bearing animals. The economic activities of Aboriginal
communities were closely regulated by the limitations of climate
and habitat in this subarctic forest.[1]

The economy was based on hunting and trapping performed
by individuals acting within small kin groups. People dispersed
or congregated as game populations fluctuated. Large, permanent
settlements were only possible during summer fishing seasons.
Adaptations to these environmental conditions required a high
degree of independence, self-reliance and individual effort,
combined with a need for self-restraint.[2]

Historical Conditions: The 1870s

By the time Egerton Ryerson Young established the first Methodist
mission at Berens River in 1873, Ojibwa communities along the
river had been interacting with one another and, to some degree,
with Crees and with British, French and Métis fur traders for a
century and a half. There existed, by Young's initial forays into the
area, a dynamic situation which embodied a host of adaptations to
community life. By the 1870s, Berens River was "a crossroads for
Ojibwa fur traders and for missionaries, government administrators
and other outsiders."[3]

By the time Treaty 5 was signed in 1875, a church and
school house had been erected in the community and classes
had begun. Steam navigation was beginning on Lake Winnipeg
and valuable minerals and timber had been found in the Lake's
vicinity (causing a flurry of applications to the government to
buy land). David Laird, Minister of the Interior, wrote of good
land for agriculture on the west shore and added, "with pending
Pacific Railway construction west of the Lake ... the Lake and
the Saskatchewan River are destined to become the principal
thoroughfare of communication between Manitoba and the fertile
prairies in the West."[4]

As a young man, Jacob Berens, in 1860, was probably among
the Ojibwa at Berens River who approached Rev. George
McDougall, then en route to the Rossville Methodist mission at
Norway House, asking for a missionary and expressing an interest
in Christianity. McDougall baptized Jacob at Rossville on 25
February 1861, and it was there that the future chief learned
Cree syllabics and moved on to establish the base for a Methodist
mission in the Berens River community. His conversion and
baptism, and the rumoured conversions of a number of others in
that area led the Methodist Egerton Ryerson Young to found the
1873 mission (although for much of this time, Jacob was away
from home working on the Hudson's Bay Company York boats on
Lake Winnipeg or at White Dog, a Hudson's Bay outpost).[5]

Young left in 1876 and was replaced by Rev. John Semmens.
Of his first arrival at the Berens River mission in July 1876,
Semmens wrote:

A beautiful ... Mission House was erected by Rev. E. R. Young
in the summer of 1874. A school house was erected at the same
time on the lean-to or shanty principle, but no church adorns
the spot.... There are 11 houses – native homes – here and there
among the trees, with little garden plots attached to each....
The fisheries are close and inexhaustible. The forest – varied
and interminable. The Mission House filled twice a week with
respectably dressed and orderly congregations. There is an average

attendance of 25, a resident Church membership of 24, a total population of about 60.[6]

By the signing of the treaty, Jacob had been back at Pigeon Bay – living in one of the area's first log houses and trading furs with the Berens River Hudson's Bay post – for five years.[7] Methodism and log houses notwithstanding, the old ways were a major part of both family and community life for Jacob whose father, Bear, held Shaking Tent and Midewiwin ceremonies until his death in 1873.[8]

With the signing of the treaty, Jacob, a leader in the negotiations, was elected chief of Berens River, Little Grand Rapids, Poplar River and Pikangikum. This moved him onto centre stage in a region facing significant transitions. After 1875, Jacob became an active regional player in the bureaucratic world of Indian Affairs.[9]

Historical Conditions: The 1880s

In 1883, the first commercial fisheries opened on Lake Winnipeg and, with this, came a boom in the fishing industry with its new steam schooners and access to American markets. Young men like William Berens moved seasonally into these new labour activities while continuing to work with their families on winter traplines in the bush. Some, like Berens, also found work as interpreters. Far from being incapable of coping under oppressive changes foisted upon them, these people moved between worlds with a skill that was a source of admiration to some white traders, missionaries and government agents – and a source of frustration to others.

New pressure brought difficulties, however; in 1885 Ebenezer E. McColl, Inspector of Indian Agencies, reported that the Ojibwa were upset over fishing parties from Winnipeg encroaching on their waters, saying, "if allowed to continue the destruction of

whitefish and sturgeon at the present rate [they] will exhaust
the supply and deprive them of their principal source of
subsistence."[10] The next year, Indian Agent Angus MacKay noted
the Ojibwas' displeasure over the encroachment and their anger
over the application of Manitoba game laws to the Indians in that
part of the province.[11]

Generally, however, the 1880s in Berens River, with the
exception of illness from an epidemic in 1887, were a time of
good hunting and plentiful fishing. MacKay, in 1883, reported
excellent fishing with plenty of food over the winter and, in 1885,
wrote that there was no shortage of food in the difficult winter/
spring period due to the prevalence of fish, deer, rabbits and fur-
bearing animals. The year 1887 again yielded a plentiful food
supply and good prices paid for furs by traders, although much
sickness occurred. MacKay reported that many died and many
more were unable to hunt regularly. By 1888, MacKay was still
reporting an abundance of moose and deer as well as good fall
fishing – the slaughter was particularly good that year as unusually
deep snow made it impossible for animals to run far or fast.[12]

Historical Conditions: The 1890s

While hunting, trapping and fishing remained central aspects
of Ojibwa life, many depended increasingly upon commercial
industries such as sawmills, cordwood camps and commercial
fishing companies for employment. They built permanent houses,
owned cattle, grew hay and planted gardens on land that was fairly
hostile to serious agricultural endeavour.

The community experienced hard times between 1889 and
1899. In 1889, a bush fire swept over a large portion of the area
around the reserve, burning the hunting grounds bare.[13] Fishing
(especially for whitefish, pickerel and pike) and the hunting of

moose and caribou were the two staples most depended upon by Indians in northern Manitoba.[14] Drastic depletion of fish and game prompted the Inspector of Indian Agencies to report in 1890 that "now that fishing and hunting grounds are becoming depleted, Indians (who formerly only cultivated potatoes) are looking more to the Department of Indian Affairs for help."[15]

Indian agent reports for the decade reflect the struggle in Berens River. Angus MacKay noted in 1890 that winter was severe, fur-bearing animals were rapidly decreasing, and that many children and elderly people had died from influenza, which had swept the district.[16] In 1892, the community was still self-supporting but the fur hunt turned out poorly again and farming, as MacKay admitted, was very difficult owing to "wooded, rocky land and cold lingering springs." The people, however, were pleased that year that the government had finally excluded portions of the Lake and rivers from licensed fishermen.[17] A severe measles epidemic in April, May and June of 1893 resulted in need for medical aid from the Methodist Missionary Society and the Hudson's Bay Company, and many cattle died of disease and starvation.[18]

Perhaps the most revealing document is the report of Superintendent Inspector Ebenezer McColl who wrote in 1894, "The majority of Indians are beginning to realise the advantages [of] devoting themselves to agriculture ... and less to the wild, nomadic and precarious pursuits of the chase."[19] Government agents almost universally expressed frustration over Indian reluctance to become seriously involved with agriculture. When Angus MacKay, in the same sentence, noted the impossible farming conditions and then remarked that, "even if conditions were excellent, Indians still would not be interested in farming,"[20] he revealed assumptions and stereotypical attitudes that were deeply ingrained in the official thinking of his time. The fact that the Ojibwa of Berens River were facing enough economic hardship to cultivate crops in the poor lands around the community is telling. The fact that agents expected them to do this, even in good times, is also telling.

The year 1894 was a particularly bad year for both fur-bearing animals and gardens; scarlet fever and influenza also hit Berens River. Huge storms ruined the fishermen's nets and fishing was so poor that the community finally had to receive aid from missionaries, government and the Hudson's Bay Company.[21] Correspondence between Agent MacKay and the government reflected the seriousness of the times. In a visit to Berens River on 10 February 1894, the agent noted that fish buyers could no longer be depended upon to buy fish at good prices as traders had stopped purchasing the whitefish which were getting increasingly scarce. The hunt in fur and game, he also noted, was very poor. On 31 March, he alerted McColl to the fact that the "Indians [were] very bad off for fish – they [could not] catch any whitefish or other fish." MacKay wound up buying 1,200 perch from Mr. Disbrowe, the Hudson's Bay post manager, to "relieve them of their suffering." When he returned on 23 April, he was alarmed, saying "The Indians are very badly off for fish. [I] never saw them worse off for fish at this place – their nets are down everywhere possible but this yields nothing. I have given them now over 1,000 whitefish of my own."[22]

Hunting conditions improved slightly over the last half of the decade; the Indian Agent reported that moose, caribou and rabbits were available "in fair amounts," although apparently traders were not "paying so well."[23] Environmental conditions continued to yield sluggish fishing, resulting in more and more Ojibwa working in lumber camps, mills and fisheries. Health was poor and the community battled waves of scrofula and tuberculosis. By 1898, Agent J.W. Short noted that there was significantly more land cultivation due to the fish scarcity on the reserve and the hunting income was well below average.[24]

There is no doubt that commercial fishing seriously disturbed the Native economy. While Ojibwa people living north of the Berens River in 1888 were catching substantial amounts of whitefish, native people south of the river were catching few. Frank Tough explains that overfishing was the culprit behind declining whitefish yields.[25] In 1890, the Norway House band petitioned Lieutenant-Governor George Schultz for the protection of the whitefish. In the summer of that year, chief Jacob Berens at Berens River requested that the fishing company remove its nets and some band members talked of sabotaging the company's sturgeon nets.[26] The depletions caused by the ravages of commercial fishing was a major factor behind Ojibwa demands for exclusive areas for Indian fishing in the late 1890s.[27]

The 1890s also saw the arrival of the first long-term Methodist missionary, James Arthur McLachlan and his wife, Sarah. Before his arrival in 1893, the mission at Berens River had experienced a considerable turn-over of resident preachers. Semmens's departure was followed by a gap of three years before William Hope arrived to live in the community from 1881 to 1883. He was replaced by Rev. Enos Langford who was transferred to Winnipeg in 1885. Rev. J.W. Butler replaced him for a brief year in 1888. It was not until 1893 that these "Supply Missionaries" were replaced by McLachlan as resident missionary.[28]

The Methodist church membership rose steadily and rapidly during McLachlan's tenure (1893–1903). The number of full members increased from fifty-eight in 1893 to ninety-three by 1903. Between 1896 and 1898, membership rose from sixty-two to eighty-seven members – possibly due to a huge revival conducted by MacLachlan in the winter of 1897.[29] Although hard times probably stimulated this growth, causing interest in Christianity as a source of added power and support, people were responding to a missionary whom they liked and who became involved in community life over enough time to establish some trust among residents.[30] His drowning in 1903, along with six children was felt as a terrible tragedy.

Fred Baptiste remembered the trust that the Ojibwas had for the missionary and the impact on the community of the event:

> F.B.   They took a bunch of kids in a sailboat to [the Brandon Industrial] school in the south. And this minister here [James McLachlan] his body's right across here [points out the window]. He drowned with a bunch of kids. He took

a bunch of money to put in the bank for them and he took kids to go to the school – but they all got drowned. And then when they found those bodies there was a parade right across here [points]. The church was way back in there and there was a lot of bush around it. They buried everything in one long grave.

S.G. What did the people think about McLachlan? Did they blame him for the accident?

F.B. No, no. People used to give him money to take to the bank.

S.G. They trusted him with their money and their children. That seems to show that they trusted the man.

F.B. Well he was a minister – they trusted him with everything.[31]

To this milieu was added the first Roman Catholic chapel at Berens River in 1897. Although the Oblate presence in the community would not become substantial until the opening of their day school in 1918, the Protestants would never again enjoy a denominational monopoly.

Historical Conditions:
The Early Twentieth Century

From the mid-1890s on, Indian Agents Angus MacKay and J.W. Short increasingly mentioned with pleasure the marked progress towards civilization being made by the residents of Berens River. Ebenezer McColl wrote (albeit somewhat naively) in 1895 that "In the Berens River Agency, the Indians are under the absolute control of the Agent [MacKay], whose instructions are implicitly carried out ... his influence among them is great on account of his thorough knowledge of their language and character."[32] The fact that the people had just emerged from what may have been the hungriest winter/spring in a long time might have had something to do with their seeming compliance toward the Agent who had given them fish. The Ojibwa of Berens River were indeed changing as the environment and the world changed around them; they were, to the repeated frustration of government workers and missionaries, however, selecting the nature of these changes and controlling the speed of their adaptation to them.

During this period, the community became increasingly involved in commercial industries. In 1900, a government fish hatchery was built on the reserve and two fishing stations opened at Berens River on Sheep Island and Yankee Island. Inspector John Semmens reported in 1901 that the Indians were "in excellent condition due to the good fishing industry and extensive lumber interests of Captain Robinson of Selkirk."[33]

Annie E. McEwen and her husband Doug arrived from Winnipeg in 1906 and spent four years in the community where Doug worked at the fish hatchery.[34] Her memoirs provide some glimpses into community life in the early 1900s. After Rev. McLachlan drowned in 1903, he was replaced by Willis Shoup until Rev. Thomas Neville and his wife arrived in 1904. The Nevilles were just leaving Berens River when the McEwens arrived, as Thomas had been transferred to a Winnipeg church. In September, Rev. Arthur Okes and his wife, Jane were stationed at Berens River. In 1909, after having spent "the required three years" on the Reserve, the Okes were transferred to southwestern Manitoba and Rev. Joseph Henry Lowes arrived with his wife in 1909. That summer a student, Douglas Durkin, arrived as a supply missionary for three months.[35] The Lowes stayed in the community until 1916. Mrs. Lowes took on an active role in teaching the day school.

As the Methodist missionaries came and went, people in the community joined the church or retained their membership during the tenures of missionaries whom they appreciated and who made a connection with them. In turn, they rejected the church when it was led by preachers whom they found wanting. For example, Thomas Neville increased church membership from ninety to ninety-eight, but the mission lost fourteen members during Okes's tenure from 1906 to 1909. In the 1908 *Manitoba Conference Report* of the Methodist Missionary Society, one finds the brief but telling statement that, "At Berens River ... some difficulties have been encountered through the opposition of some new methods introduced by a change of ministers."[36] Lowes would take seven years to build the number of full members back up to ninety-eight.[37] Annie McEwen contrasted the two missionary wives, describing Mrs. Lowes as "a bright, attractive woman," who "was quite popular with the Indians for, though not particularly religious, she treated everyone fairly and did not try to tell them their religious duties as Mrs. Oke had done."[38] Jane Oke, she said, was a generous woman with a nursing background and provided much medical aid. However, "none of this seemed to offset her bossiness ... I think the Indians, women as well as men, prefer women to give their lectures privately."[39]

While the Ojibwa welcomed those missionaries who proved congenial and helpful, their own world view remained central in their lives. John Semmens wrote in 1903 that

> even the medicines supplied are not administered as directed, and in many ways are not given at all, and not infrequently the complications are brought on by the combined use of Indian and white medicines. The morality of the people is not sufficiently developed to merit high praise. This is the outcome of old associations and old methods of living.... It is not easy to correct wrongs which are winked at by the elders of the tribe.... However we hope that society is moving out of darkness into light and knowledge and that the future will bring a purer social condition.[40]

Of note, here, is Semmens's condescension and poorly informed interpretations. Also noteworthy, however, is that the Ojibwa were not casting off traditional lifeways.

Berens River people were, by now, used to missionaries and other resident outsiders and could be amiable and supportive. McEwen wrote favourably about life in Berens River, remembering the friendly rapport between her husband, Doug, and Chief Jacob Berens. Her son Norman's best friend was John James Everett, the chief's grandson. The family received a warm farewell when they left in 1910, wrote McEwen: "What a crowd of Indians came out … to see us leave; either they liked us or they were glad to see us go."[41]

It was not only in their reception of missionaries that historical change can be seen in the Berens River community. William Berens, who became chief in 1916 on his father's death, exemplified the willingness of at least come Ojibwa to embrace agriculture.

Until 1920, the fishing industry paid good prices which helped to offset the instability and poor prices in the fur market caused by World War I. By 1919, the value of fish and fur prices had doubled from what it had been during the five years prior to the War.[42]

The state of health in the community was unremarkable until 1918, when the huge 1918–1919 influenza pandemic hit Berens River. The first burial was held on 7 November 1918 and twenty-wo more died over the next eleven days. Death rates on the eserve clustered around a hundred per thousand, the under-six ge group suffering the most with the high death rate of 250 per thousand.[43] Records show a decrease in the Methodist population. This was likely caused by deaths of Methodist Ojibwa. There was also an increase in Catholic church membership at this time.[44] While this may have been a partial result of conversions resulting from the Spanish Flu, Catholic records do not mention the connection.

On the mission front, Joseph Lowes left Berens River in 1916 and was replaced by Percy Earl Jones and his wife Nellie who remained there until Rev. John Niddrie arrived in 1920. Jones was a good friend of William Berens, who chose the minister's name for one of his sons at baptism. Seven decades later, Percy Earl Berens, son of William and Nancy, has fond memories of the Jones family and the minister, his namesake.

He was a good man. It's not very many ministers that goes into these Indian settlements to go and visit the chief and councillors.

Percy Jones used to be at the house visiting my old man, my dad. That's how I happen to know ... Winnona and Leslie Jones [the Jones children]. He [Leslie] was a little boy like myself; we used to play outside while they were talking inside.[45]

In 1918, Father Joseph De Grandpré and Brother Frederick Leach opened the Roman Catholic day school under the auspices of Brother Leach. Percy Berens also remembers Leach favourably:

P.B.   I'll tell you something, I'd sooner have that Brother Leach on that Berens River Reserve instead of that nursing station. Because if Mr. Leach had to walk to visit around ... the Reserve with the snow up to his knees, he did. And them on that Reserve today, they'll never walk in my house and see if I'm alive or not.

S.G.   So you thought that Brother Leach cared about the people?

P.B.   Yeah, he did – very much he cared for the people.[46]

During the 1920s and 1930s, Ojibwa men of Berens River continued with hunting and fishing as their main line of work.[47] The people in the community had also, by now, clearly chosen to at least partially adapt to many Euro-Canadian institutions. They participated in commercial ventures, attended the day schools, erected permanent buildings and raised stock according to their needs.

Rev. John Niddrie arrived at the Methodist mission in 1920 and remained as minister until his retirement in 1938. For most of that time, his Catholic counterparts were Joseph De Grandpré and Frederick Leach.

In 1927, Annie Niddrie arrived in Berens River to help her brother, John, keep house. She wound up staying for thirty-three years and wrote in her memoirs of life in the community, the beauty of which affected her deeply. "The scenery up the River was beautiful. The green and gold leaves on the trees was a sight to behold.... I never had one lonesome day all those years."[48]

In the 1930s, she remembered, everybody rode in a boat, and
fishing and trapping were the primary ways to make a living.
Older people made fish oil, smoked fish and moose meat, made
pemmican and dried berries for winter. Mail was brought across
the Lake by dog train until the late 1950s. In the 1930s, airplanes
began landing at Berens River, small outboard motors began to
be used on canvas canoes or the new wooden fishing yawls and
tractor trailer "cats" replaced dog teams for winter freighting.[49]

Annie also wrote of the increasingly difficult economic
conditions faced by the people. The Depression hit Berens River
hard and many families were extremely short of food and clothes.
Babies were fed on the water in which whitefish had been boiled,
or on water that had been used to boil the roots of plants found
in the bush (although they thrived on this). The reserve was
full of tuberculosis and other illnesses. By 1940, food shortages
warranted the opening of a home for the poor by the Department
of Indian Affairs and Annie Niddrie was placed in charge, taking
in any people the policeman sent her way.[50]

The sources used here require much critical questioning, and
do not always lead to solid conclusions. Times were indeed hard
at Berens River during the 1930s just as they were hard across
the country. However, Indian-agent and missionary reports of
starving Indians were prepared for superiors from whom the
writers needed attention and financial support. In addition, the
stereotype of the dependent Ojibwa was a deep-running and often
useful one. Communities of helpless and needy native victims
conferred a feeling of power and importance on government
agents which helped to fuel an entire missionary movement.
Frederick Leach's journal for 1930, at face value, seems to provide
evidence for starving and dependent Indians at Berens River. His
own notes on the view that William Berens took of the situation,
however, calls into question the degree of community desperation
and dependence.

The fishing season in the summer of 1929 had been poor
and on 7 January 1930, Leach wrote, "The Indians here are
almost destitute and the situation is getting serious. There is

practically no fur or fish." On 8 January, Leach sent an aerogram
to the Indian Agent, alerting him to the sad state on the reserve,
and began giving out soup to some families. On 10 January, he
recorded that most families were in a state of semi-starvation.
On 18 January 1930, Leach wrote, "saw the chief today re. his
starving Indians. He has some fool idea that many could live on
rabbits. He forgets that rabbits are very scarce."

Emergency meetings were held on 21 January and 11 March.
Missionaries Leach and Niddrie and the Indian Agent were
convinced that the Indians needed rations, the Hudson's Bay
manager was concerned about the unavailability of rations and
William Berens continued to say that his people did not need
rations. At a third meeting on 30 March, Chief Berens suggested
that, instead of receiving rations, the community could perhaps
get an advance on their treaty money. This was the solution finally
agreed upon.[51]

Obviously, William Berens did not wish to accept rations,
a move that would have placed the community in a dependent
position, and he worked to find an alternative solution to a
problem that was probably very serious. Leach's condescending
disregard of the rabbit-hunting idea shows a superior attitude
and clouded judgement – what, after all, would he have known
about hunting rabbits? Berens, who had spent his life hunting,
understood much more about the viability of this solution. The
issue was dependency, with William Berens wanting to affirm
the community's independence and the missionaries and agent
working, intentionally or not, to decrease it.

By 1940, the Ojibwa of Berens River had been "wards" of the
Dominion government for sixty-five years and the community
had, as had the wider world, undergone many changes.
Throughout, they selected their responses to those changes,
took in stride those aspects of Euro-Canadian institutions which
were either unavoidable (such as the need for children to attain
a Euro-Canadian education) and/or which were of use to them
and moved on with life. Throughout, change and growth occurred
within frameworks that remained clearly Ojibwa.

Methodist Missionaries

At Berens River

Year(s)	Name
1874	E. R. Young
1876–1877	John Semmens
1881–1884	William J. Hope
1885–1887	Enos Langford
1888–1892	supply
1893–1903	James Arthur McLachlin
1904	Willis W. Shoup
1905–1906	Thomas Neville
1907–1909	Arthur Oke
1910–1916	Joseph H. Lowes
1917–1919	Percy E. Jones
1920–1937	John W. Niddrie
1938–1940	Luther L. Schuetze

At Little Grand Rapids

Year(s)	Name
1899–1901	visited by J. A. McLachlan
1905–1907	William Ivens
1908	J. Woodsworth
1909	Joseph Jones
1910	Roy Taylor
1911	J. H. Wilding
1914	Alfred G. Johnson
1917–1918	Mary Nanakwap
1923	supply
1927–1937	Luther L. Schuetze
1938	R. Schuetze
1939–1940	Colin Douglas Street

Roman Catholic Missionaries at Berens River

Year(s)	Fathers
1912–1914	Siméon Perreault
1913	Célien Gauthier
1914–1917	Camille Perreault
1915	Gustave Fafard
1916	Eugène Baillargeon
1917	Siméon Perreault
1918–1921	Philippe Valès
1919	Joseph De Grandpré
1921	Edouard Planet
1921	Etienne Bonnald
1921	Claude Kerbrat
1922–1925	Joseph De Grandpré
1925–1927	Alphonse Paradis
1926–1941	Joseph De Grandpré
1927	Léandre Gauthier
1930–1936	Célien Gauthier
1937	Julien Jalbert
1938	Eugène Baillargeon
1939–1948	Gérard Pinette

Year(s)	Brothers
1917–1922; 1923–1926	Jacques Grall
1918	Théodore de Bijl
1918–1921; 1924–1926; 1927–1936	Frederick Leach
1922	Eugène Paquet
1936–1944	Arthur Limoges
1939–1949	Alcide Gagnon

Roman Catholic Missionaries at Little Grand Rapids

Year(s)	Fathers
1925–1926	Joseph De Grandpré
1928–1929	Léandre Gauthier

Year(s)	Brothers
1926–1927	Frederick Leach

2 "Listen to the *Memegwesiwag* Singing"

The Ojibwa World View

....

In his discussion of Ojibwa ontology, world view, and behaviour, A. Irving Hallowell drew upon Robert Redfield's definition of world view as "the picture the members of a society have of the properties and characters upon their stage of action.... [it] refers to the way the world looks to that people looking out." A peoples' world view comprises "that outlook upon the universe that is characteristic of [them], as contrasted to the perspectives of outsiders looking in at them."[1] The world view of the Berens River Ojibwa constantly found expression in actions that revolved around relationships between human persons and other-than-human persons, and particularly around individual quests for spiritual power and survival.

Missionaries, settlers, and many authors, past and present, have represented Aboriginal religions as being static and "traditional" from time immemorial. The Ojibwa world view, however, encompasses a depth and complexity in a dynamic religious life which, like other great religions of the world, was founded on the power and passion of belief and yet which has an enormous capacity for flexibility, adaptation, critical thinking, and empiricism. As Hallowell wrote, the psychological core of the Ojibwa religion involves other-than-human beings: a faith in their power, trust in their vitally needed aid to human beings, and a dependence on them in order to experience a good life. The heart of this religion is "in the interpersonal relationships [Ojibwa people] seek to maintain between themselves and other-than-human beings." Since humans are always working to increase their own powers through the aid of ever-present other-than-humans, religious behaviour is not a compartmentalized aspect of life that is confined to special rites and ceremonies; rather "this religious core manifests itself in widely ramified contexts."[2]

The history of the Ojibwa healer and leader Fair Wind (Naamiwan) provides an example of the dynamism that existed in the Ojibwa world view and in its ongoing creation of tradition.[3] Hallowell was told that the ideas of drum dances came to the upper Berens River from an Aboriginal visitor to Little Grand Rapids around 1912. Recent research has shown that several features of these dances were very similar to the Ojibwa dream drum ceremonies which spread through Minnesota and Wisconsin in the 1870s. The latter were initiated by Tailfeather Woman, a Sioux, who was told in a dream how to make a large drum and of the songs to accompany it. The ensuing ceremony "became the vehicle for making peace between the Sioux and the Ojibwa."[4] Subsequently, Thunderbirds (*pinésiwuk*) gave Maggie Wilson her drum dance through dreams and it was performed at the Manitou Reserve in northwestern Ontario from 1918 to 1929. Clearly, the pivotal ideas involved were moving throughout the Rainy River and the Lake of the Woods area. It is probable that Ojibwa people carried them north to Jackhead and the Bloodvein River via the Winnipeg River and Lake Winnipeg.[5]

By 1932, three or four big drums were used in a number of ceremonies by different families at Little Grand Rapids. They bore a striking resemblance to those used in Minnesota and Wisconsin, yet like Fair Wind's drum, they were each distinctive. Their histories underscore the Ojibwa ability to receive new ideas, examine them, and either reject, recast, or integrate them (in bits or in totality) into a dynamic life.

The power of belief has been a cornerstone of religions throughout the world. Homer's *Odyssey* begins with the line, "Sing to me, O Muse, of man's many wanderings." This invocation of the Muse expressed a conviction held by such writers as Homer and Virgil – it reflected their quest for aid from a higher power, a source outside themselves, which they sought before writing their classic epics.

In John 14:10 and 12, Jesus discussed miracles saying, "The Father that dwelleth in me, he doeth the works.... He that believeth on Me, the works that I do shall he do also, and greater works than these shall he do." The great composers Brahms, Beethoven and Mozart described their entries into dreamlike states that were infused with God, existences of an almost pure belief during which a higher power wrote through them. In Brahms's words,

> It cannot be done merely by will power working through the conscious mind, which is an evolutionary product of the physical realm and perishes with the body. It can only be accomplished by the soul-powers within – the real ego which survives bodily death. Those powers are quiescent to the conscious mind unless illumined by Spirit. To realize that we are one with the Creator, as Beethoven did, is … awe-inspiring. Very few … have come into that realization and that is why there are so few … creative geniuses. [In the dream states] the Spirit [illuminates] the soul-powers within, and … I see clearly what is obscure in my ordinary moods; then I feel capable of drawing inspiration from above … the ideas flow upon me, directly from God, and not only do I see distinct themes … but they are clothed in the right forms, harmonies.[6]

Yellow Legs, a powerful leader of the Midéwiwin and the great-grandfather of Chief William Berens, once walked on the water to an island on Lake Winnipeg in search of a special remedy. On another occasion he sent two men to an island in search of a stone that he described carefully to them. The stone later proved to have magical qualities in the Midéwiwin Lodge.[7] More than sixty years after William Berens described these events to Hallowell, William's son, Percy, discussed them with me. He was clear on the importance of belief.

S.G.   I've heard that your great-great-grandfather Yellow Legs
walked on the water. Have you heard about that?

P.B.   An Indian of that long time ago that was *really really* – that
knew it was a gift given to them – *given* to them – that they
could do them things what you and I couldn't do.

S.G.   Why can't we do them any more? Why can't you walk on
the water?

P.B.   That's a simple word. No belief.

S.G.   What did Yellow Legs believe in so strongly? You say it was
because of his strong belief that he could walk on the water.

P.B.   Because he *had* that belief ... in the spirits. In the spirits,
that's the belief.[8]

Percy Berens explained that he could never walk on the water,
saying, "my belief is not strong enough." Similarly, Walter Green of
Berens River responded to the story of Yellow Legs by emphasizing
the centrality of belief:

I never heard about that [Yellow Legs walking on the water] but
I heard a lot about medicine men. They're so wonderful – they
can do anything. Someone was telling me there was a big rock
in the lake. And someone said, "do you know that the medicine
men in the old days could open that stone in half and put it back
together?" That's how much they believed in what they were
doing. They were blessed.[9]

In the 1930s, Ruth Landes noted that the Ojibwa saw all religion
and magic as medicine or as power.[10] Prior to the 1875 signing
of the treaty at Berens River, leadership was in the hands of
medicine men – those who had gained the most power within
their communities through visitations in their dreams from the
pawáganak (dream visitors conferring blessings and special gifts).
These were the first chiefs and the significance here is in the power
of religion within Ojibwa society.[11]

Certainly religion, and the power and protection that resulted
from relationships with other-than-human beings, were seen

by these people as critical for survival and success. The power
of medicine and magic can perhaps best be seen in one Ojibwa
interpretation of their history: in the nineteenth century, much
animosity existed between the Sucker clan and the clans who
lived in adjacent territory: the Loons to the south, the Moose
and Kingfisher clans on the east shores of Lake Winnipeg and
along the Berens River. It was not military warfare, however, but
shamanistic killings that took lives in the struggle between the
River people versus the Berens River and Little Grand Rapids
folk.[12]

A. Irving Hallowell discussed Ojibwa religion in some depth.[13]
In the Ojibwa world, he explained, humans were extremely
dependent on other-than-human beings that took pity on mortals
and fulfilled their desires.[14] At the core of Ojibwa religion was
faith in the power of these beings, trust in their crucial aid
to survival, and dependence on them for the experience of a
rich life. A good relationship with other-than-human beings
was critical, and this led the Ojibwa of the Berens River area,
especially adolescent and adult males, into a constant quest to
increase their gifts of power. Hallowell, in fact, defined Ojibwa
religious behaviour as any activity by which an individual or
group seeks to "promote a good life for human beings by making
explicit recognition, direct or indirect, of man's faith in and
dependence on other-than-human persons."[15] The issue was not
the accumulation of intrinsic personal power but the blessings
and support given from others. Thus religion was linked closely to
good conduct and respect for the givers of powers.

Since only medicine men had the means to directly invoke the
most powerful other-than-human spirits, average Ojibwa sought
their help; the validity of the conjurors was that they themselves
had been empowered by other-than-human beings.[16] As Ojibwa
theories of causation were more personalized, impersonal causes
did not exist. All phenomena and occurrences resulted from
interactions between human and other-than-human persons
or between humans and other humans.[17] The most vital source
of contact for average humans with their other-than-human

pawáganak or "grandfathers" was through dreams, and the number of guardian spirits whom an individual acquired varied from person to person.[18]

Missionaries usually failed to understand that native peoples possessed a coherent, self-contained system of beliefs that was continually examined and measured against individuals' life experiences. As Hallowell said, it is difficult to present religions of so-called "primitive" (to Westerners) peoples in "rationally convincing" ways. Since these belief systems were buried under the daunting weight of "historic" religions (such as Christianity) not much could be expected of "primitive" religions, just as little could be expected of "primitive man" who "was often conceived as childlike in character, pre-logical in mentality and psychotic in personality."[19] Early in his Berens River work, Hallowell cautioned against assuming that Ojibwa religious beliefs were mechanically passed down with only dogma and mythology to support them. Rather, Ojibwa religious experiences were "a subject of relative thinking and discussion ... [and] inevitably subject to challenge on empirical grounds."[20]

The men of Berens River were primarily hunters and it was critical for them to be intimately engaged with their environments: with the present and with what was actually occurring in their midst. While their traditional world view provided a framework for their outlooks and interpretations, their first-hand perceptions of "celestial, meteorological and biotic phenomena [were] also important."[21] Experience and belief were harmonized in order for beliefs to be genuine and to survive. Western society in the nineteenth century was also in the throes of an empiricism that had been generated in the Enlightenment. The methodology of critical questioning was emerging in science, social science, and religion.

A critical difference between the two societies, however, centred around belief. Although both believed in the power of belief, Ojibwa groups encompassed, within their world view, an enormous capacity for flexibility in defining reality compared with the rather rigid doctrinal structures of the missionaries they encountered. Percy Berens, a Christian, does not believe in spirits but, he explained, this does not mean that they do not exist:

SG   You say you don't believe in spirits at all?

P.B.   No, I don't. I've only got one belief and one spirit.

S.G.   For you, that's the answer?

P.B.   Right. I choose that.

S.G.   But Yellow Legs chose to believe in spirits – was that okay?

P.B.   That's okay too, that's good too.

S.G.   So you're not saying that spirits don't exist? You're saying that *you* don't choose to believe in them?

P.B.   Yes, I don't *choose* to believe in them spirits.

S.G.   But they can exist for other people?

P.B.   Yes, they will exist. If you believe strong enough to believe that there's spirits there then they're there. Now you know what I mean? And that's what those old time Indians had. They strongly *believed* in them spirits of evil and righteousness. That was their belief, see? Evil and righteous spirits.[22]

Empiricism has, for westerners, lent credibility to their institutions and they have often assumed that other societies lacked this tool to apply to their own belief systems.[23] The Ojibwa world view, however, also builds upon the idea that seeing is believing. William Berens grew up in a Methodist home. Yet his parents never allowed their Christianity to separate them from his father's non-Christian family. William participated in a number of Methodist and Ojibwa ceremonies and events, the latter having a lasting impact. After attending the Midéwiwin and seeing his grandfather, Bear, curing with his medicines and conducting the shaking tent ceremony, he decided that Ojibwa rituals had a power that Christian rituals lacked:

[Bear] practised the old Indian religion. He may have died about the time the first missionary came. But if he lived longer he never changed his beliefs. This grandfather had lost all the fingers of his left hand except the thumb, yet he was a conjuror. How could he have shaken the tent himself? I used to see him go into the conjuring tent but the voices I heard coming out of it did not seem like his voice. I saw him cure sick people with his medicine and by nib kiwin. I had reason to believe that my grandfather knew what he was doing and that his beliefs were true. I used to hear my mother talk about God but I did not see anything that my mother did that proved to me that what happened was through the help of God. I saw no power comparable to what I had seen my grandfather use. For I saw my grandfather in the Midéwiwin once. It must have been the last one ever held at the mouth of the river. My grandfather was the headman. That is another thing I can never forget.[24]

Fred Baptiste, an Ojibwa resident of Berens River, is a Christian who also grounds his belief in the Thunderbirds in empirical proof, furnished in one instance by an Ojibwa Methodist preacher. In his words:

When I was up at Pikangikum, Ontario, I used to know guys who came down from Pikangikum and preach here – Fiddler, Adam Fiddler, I think it was. He'd take the service here – old Niddrie let him preach in the afternoon. And then he gave me a feather – a feather that's that wide [measures a two-foot span with his hands] and about that long [measures a four-foot span]. He says, "you know what this is?" And I says, "that's from a big bird." He got that from the high rocks where there's thunder on Percy Island – that's where they [the Thunderbirds] keep their young ones. That's where he got this feather, it's just a young one's feather.[25]

Another Ojibwa member of the Berens River community remembers his doubt, as a young man, in the validity of the shaking tent ritual. John Edward Everett explained:

I didn't believe it myself but I was told then, "okay, you're going to see him." [David Eaglestick, a medicine man at Little Grand Rapids]

S.G.   Then what happened?

J.E.E. I gave him some tobacco first.

S.G.   And then what happened?

J.E.E. Well I wanted to find out about it – it was bolted right to the ground, you know. The thing would shake!!

S.G.   You saw the tent shaking and that's when you believed?

J.E.E. I wanted to find out about it.... it was in that evening – there were five of us. Well, actually, I was just about scared that thing was going to take off – everything was shaking!

S.G.   What did you hear?

J.E.E. Well, one way to find out. You don't have to open that. You talk from the outside. I want to find out how my friends in Berens River were doing. [One of the uses of the shaking tent was to learn of people or events at a distance.]

S.G.   So, John, before you saw the shaking tent, you didn't believe in it?

J.E.E. Well actually I didn't believe. That's the reason I wanted to find out.[26]

Percy Berens told of hearing the drumming and singing of what he called the "mound builders" (*Memegwesiwag*) at three different times in his life. The experiences are what supported his belief in their existence.

P.B.   That's another thing. Mound builders – *Memegwesiwag* – that's an Indian name. I heard them drumming. Maybe it's hard for you to believe. I heard them drumming. Three times in my life I heard that.

S.G.   Why were they drumming?

P.B.   I don't know, I guess they were going to bless me, I guess. It's just as well I heard them drums, see? It was a nice day and I was in the canoe because I was going down on a moose

hunt. And then I was paddling. All of a sudden I heard
drums so I just put my paddle down and I was listening like
that. My cousin on the stern steering the canoe said, "What
do you hear?" I said, "Listen to them drums," I said. "Listen
to the *Memegwesiwag* singing." And he stopped paddling.
The canoe was drifting along the river. "I don't hear
nothing!" he says. "Oh come on!" I said, "you can just hear it
plain." And he stopped again and: "No, I don't hear nothing.
You're all b.s.," he says to me [laughter].[27]

In Percy Berens's words, "But I heard them, three times in my life I
heard that same thing. And that's why I fully believe there's people,
Memegwesiwag, mound builders they are.... I truly believe on that
because three times I heard that drumming and singing."[28] It is
interesting that while, for Percy, the existence of the *Memegwesiwag*
was validated through his own experience, his cousin, who heard
nothing, did not blindly believe Percy at the time.

Percy's brother, Gordon, a United Church minister, explained
the *Memegwesiwag* thus: "There's people living, isolated people
like, that could do a lot of things. They call them *Memegwesiwag*.
They're the people that did a lot of magic things. And they live on
rocks. They had a home on a rock. Their homes were in a rock.
And that's one thing a lot of white people don't believe. They
don't believe their home was in a rock and if they want to bless
you, you'll hear that drum. First you'll hear that drum and then
they'll show in person and give you what you want to know or
what you want to do in a magical way. They come in dreams too.
You could have them in dreams in a dream like. They call them
Memegwesiwag, Small People." Percy was, indeed, blessed by the
Memegwesiwag. Gordon tells of Percy's encounter, remembering
how his brother offered tobacco to the Small People after hearing
them drum. The following day, the tobacco was gone and in its
place lay the rib of an animal not found in those parts. Gordon
says, "Well he kept that thing, you know, and when he was
trapping nobody could beat him. He was always the head trapper.
Nobody could beat him. He was always the highest one."[29]

Gordon Berens's discussions about the *Memegwesiwag* also present interesting glimpses into enduring belief. Gordon remembered another of Percy's experiences with the Mound Builders this way:

My brother Percy heard them beating the drum. Where we have our cabin on the lake, when we were trapping, there's a high rock and there's a river on the east side of the lake and there's a high rock there. And my brother was out, I was out, I was out with him but I turned back … and I came right back to our camp. It was kind of late in the evening. Seen him coming. I had tea all ready, supper all ready, supper waiting for him. So he come in. I look at him and, oh, did he ever look pale. "Oh," I said "what happened? Oh!" I says, "you look so darn pale! Are you sick?" "No," he says "I'm not sick." "What happened?" "Well, boy," he says "I'll just tell you. Boy, I hear them, what you call *Memegwesiwag*. I heard the *Memegwesiwag* singing," he says. "On the last high rock on the lake there," he says, "and I went to the little island there," he says "I went to the little island there. I went to this place where there was open water. I bent down to have a drink and, boy, I could hear that drum, " he says "in the water, like an echo. So I had a drink and, boy, I could hear that drum," he says "in the water like an echo. So I had a drink and I kind of sat, and boy," he says "I sat. Well they start to sing. Beat the drum," he says "and start to sing. Oh, I stay there," he says "I sat there and listened." Well, you know the next thing he had to do. He had to put tobacco where he heard them singing, like, you know. That's a present, like, you know – so he had to go there. He says "Boy, I put that tobacco on the ledge of a rock. Walk away." Next time he went, he went and check if that tobacco was gone. The tobacco was gone and there was a rib, a blade, like, you know – a blade of an animal. So he took that. It was right on top, where he had the tobacco, so he pick it up and he brought it to our camp and he said to my dad…. My dad look at that rib, at that blade…. He couldn't figure out what kind of animal it was. So he told Percy "I don't – this animal," he says "is not from this place. Different place, this animal is from a different place." Well, he kept that thing, you know, when he was trapping nobody could beat him. He was always the head trapper. Nobody could beat him. – 'Cause he used to carry this with him all the time. He used to carry this blade all the time and nobody could beat him. He was always the highest one. Yeah, he was the highest one. So, a lot of them asked him why he was killing so much fur. My, he wouldn't tell them, he wouldn't give away himself, wouldn't give away himself why he was killing so much. He just didn't want to tell them.[30]

When Maureen Matthews asked Gordon if he believed that the *Memegwesiwag* had given powers to Percy, he replied "I believe it. I believe it. Sure there's people living and the only way a person sees them people is when they dream."[31] Of significance here is not just the strength of Gordon Berens's belief, but also his perception and understanding of his brother as a hunter, blessed by the *Memegwesiwag*.

When Gordon discussed his father's belief in the *Memegwesiwag*, he emphasized that seeing was believing: "He believed in them [the *Memegwesiwag*]. He believed on that. He was a strong believer on that because he had seen quite a few things. [That's] why he was such a strong believer."[32]

When asked if William Berens had believed in the Thunderbirds, Percy replied, "he believed on the Thunderbirds because of what happened to him. He seen it with his own eyes.... I believe what I see with my own eyes. And I believe that. Thunder. I believe that. [And earlier] Yes, you can believe in them [Thunderbirds] easily because you can hear them."[33]

Similarly, the Ojibwa of Fond du Lac used empirical observation in drawing their conclusions that cattle possessed magic powers. Traders had introduced these animals to the region by 1806 and, over a period of three decades, the Ojibwa made careful observations, gaining some useful insights. In 1834, they explained to the missionary Edmund Franklin Ely that cattle closely resembled buffalo, a perception that was reinforced by the traders' penchant to allow the beasts to roam freely in the woods.

They noticed that cattle, however, ate many plants that no buffalo or other wild animals ever ate. In her study of Ely and the Ojibwa, Rebecca Kugel explains that this observation led to the Ojibwa conclusion that cattle must possess spiritually derived powers and must have great virtue. Shamans thus worked to harness this power during healing ceremonies, holding up pictures of cows in front of the ill, thus inducing the sick to dream of cattle. "In what was clear proof to the Ojibwa of the spiritual power of cattle [they observed that] after such dreams the sick [recovered]."[34]

The validity given to personal testimony is carefully distinguished from second-hand reports and provides corroborative evidence for Berens River Ojibwa in cases of doubt. When Peter Berens, a young boy of eleven or twelve, told of seeing a strange bird lying on the rocks after a storm, elders were sceptical. In his field notes, Hallowell explained that this was because "it [was] so unusual to have seen pinesi with naked eye." Only when his description was supported by another corroborative source, did people believe that the boy had actually seen a Thunderbird. "An old man had dreamed of this p- [*pinesi*]. By description he said the boy was right – he had seen p- and would live to be an old man."[35]

Multiple testimonies have always been seen as even more difficult to contradict, especially in cases involving the sightings of giant animals. William Berens, together with his two sons, sighted the Great Snake, for example, and this had real validity in their community. Discussing the high ranking given to first-hand testimony as observed fact, Hallowell said, "Oral testimony among the Saulteaux ... parallels the exaggerated emphasis upon the authority of the written word among us as presented, e.g., in the newspaper reports, 'true story' magazines, etc."[36] In Ojibwa history there have been very few reports of sightings of the giant animals and this, too, adds credibility to the stories of those who *have* seen them.

Yet, even personal testimony was seen critically. Not all sightings were considered valid. Someone who described an encounter with a strange creature outside the realm of recognized mythology and tradition would have been, in Hallowell's words, "subject to ridicule."[37] Percy Berens's contempt for charlatan conjuring at Berens River provided an example of critical reflection.

S.G.   Have you ever seen a conjuring tent?
P.B.   I've seen it! *But* it was a mockery. They did that at Berens River. But they didn't really know what to do.
S.G.   Why not?
P.B.   Because it was lost! And that guy that went in that tent didn't have no power at all from the spirits.[38]

Ojibwa beliefs in a flat earth and in the daily journey of the sun across the sky were similarly based on practical daily observation. While it was true that the idea of the earth existing as an island was rooted in dogma, contact with white transoceanic visitors supported the idea that their world was surrounded by water and schoolroom maps reinforced the idea of "flatness."[39]

The Thunderbirds provide an example of Ojibwa empirical measurement. In April, both the Thunderbirds and the ordinary birds arrive in Berens River from the south. In the fall the Thunderbirds and birds move south, following the "summer birds' trail" (the Milky Way). The existence of thunder is linked to the presence of birds and is supported by the Ojibwa conviction that natural phenomena are animate.[40]

Dreams have been an exceedingly important part of the religious culture among Ojibwa who believe that they "obtain direct personal knowledge of the spiritual entities of the cosmos, e.g., the 'bosses' or 'owners' of the phenomenal world, as well as other beings, through dreams."[41] Jack Fiddler, a leader of the Sucker clan from Sandy Lake, once told Edward Paupanakiss, a Cree missionary from Norway House, "I believe in my dreams. Everything we dream is right for us.... Our dreams are our religions."[42]

The puberty fast, undergone by young boys, institutionalized the importance of dreaming; this was the time when the *pawáganak* who would bless and aid the boys throughout their lives were attained. As far as Ojibwa people were concerned, men were rendered practically powerless without these "grandfathers," especially if they aspired to lead religious ceremonies or be especially good hunters.[43] Different people, however, attained varying degrees of power from other-than-humans; one man might have several guardian spirits, another might have only one, while another might not have acquired any at all. Only a few acquired exceptional powers.[44]

For Ojibwa people, dreams have been a source of empirical evidence regarding "the genii of the cosmos."[45] Interestingly, in the case of the boy who saw the Thunderbird lying on a rock, the later source which confirmed the sighting came from a man who *dreamed* of Thunderbirds.[46] Since the *pawáganak* (dream visitors) were normally seen only in dreams, the boy's story of seeing the Thunderbird had to be confirmed by the testimony of the man who *dreamed* of them, rather than the other way around.

Hallowell described the dream of a Christian Ojibwa that showed how dreams were concretely tested by the Saulteaux. The man was having a poor hunt and lay down to sleep, dreaming of a long trail running north. In his dream he walked on this path toward a deadfall until he saw two attractive girls dressed in white. One was setting a table with food and it was she whom he approached. As she told him the food was for him, he awoke and began walking north, despite the fact that the path was dangerous since he had just set many steel traps on this line. "But when I got there [to the deadfall], I found a fisher.... It was female. I knew what my dream meant then."[47] A female creature had provided food for the man both in his dream and in reality. For him, the dream's validity was obvious, Christianity notwithstanding.

The Ojibwa attained empirical proof of the validity of pawáganak by observing relative hunting success. All men in a community had good hunting skills and shared a similar technology. Fur-bearing animals were distributed fairly evenly. How, then, could one explain wide variations in hunting results? Successful men had clearly been blessed with the help of animal "owners." The less successful had either not been helped or, if so, something had gone wrong: either their *pawáganak* were weak, or a man had failed to properly honour an "owner" – or he was simply a poor hunter.[48]

Also central to the Ojibwa world view is the interpretation of dreams. The telling of and learning from dreams played major roles in the Saulteaux sociocultural system in a way that, as Hallowell explained, gave meaning to individuals' lives. The vision quest was, of course, a key element in the process of growing up Ojibwa and dreams in general were often seen as insightful ways to teach lessons to young people. Some dreams offered prophecies or ominous warnings of future events and others authenticated waking incidents (such as in the case of young Peter Berens whose Thunderbird sighting was confirmed through the dream of an old man).[49]

Betsey Patrick, an Ojibwa woman from Berens River, described a dream which changed the course of her life and which illustrates the kind of help offered to humans by other-than-humans through dreams. Although she could have been a very good medicine woman through a dream gift that came to her, she chose, in her youth, not to follow this course. Sarah Jane MacKay, from Split Lake, was an excellent medicine woman, able to cure those whom nobody else could cure. Sarah's granddaughter had died and, missing the company of a little girl, she became fond of Betsey Patrick. When Betsey was twelve years old she went on a canoe trip with Sarah. They camped on an island. Betsey knew that Sarah wanted her to become a medicine woman and to teach her in this art. Although Betsey was frightened on the first night of the trip, she said nothing to Sarah.

That night she dreamed of a river. A log led across the water to a huge rock which sat at the top of a waterfall. Betsey crossed the log, moving towards this rock in which a door appeared and opened. "A tiny little old shrunken man was in that rock. He told me to come in. I went in and he gave me a book made of birchbark and told me to read this book, he said these were the secrets of life." Betsey remembers that the pages, she recognized, described "the joy of the human heart."

When she had finished, the man told her there was something else to see. Another door appeared in a wall of the rock. As she passed through this door she encountered a Thunderbird and as she looked at his eyes, she saw that they were filled with lightning. They dazzled and terrified her. Betsey ran away – away from the little man, away from the rock, across the log and back to the shore.

When she awoke, Sarah was making tea and Betsey said to the older woman, "I cannot do what you want me to do." As Betsey Patrick sees her life, this was her choice and she made a decision not to take on those powers.[50]

A dream that Walter Green had as a child reflected the continuing impact of dreams on the lives of the Saulteaux, the significance of the power of belief in their religious life, and the syncretism that has come from Ojibwa people creatively integrating aspects of both Saulteaux and Christian concepts.

S.G.   Did you learn to play the organ from [Rev. Niddrie]?
W.G.   This is what I call a gift. You know, when I was a little boy
       … a couple of my uncles sent an organ to where my aunt
       and I were living. And they used to ask my uncle to play
       the organ. Boy, I used to wish I could play – many times
       I'd stand there watching him. But one night when I was
       sleeping I had a dream. Somebody came to me – like an
       angel, you know – a lady. So she took me and grabbed my
       hand and said, "Come on over this way." Her face was just
       beautiful and there were flowers all around her. So she
       took me out and we came to a great big building. It was
       a building like marble, you know. And she took me into
       that building. We walked for a long way and, while we
       were walking, she turned to one room and said, "This is
       the place." And I looked around and saw an organ – a pipe
       organ. So she said, "Is this what you want to play?" I said,
       "Yes, very much." And then she sat down and I sat down

beside her and first she played *Jesus Loves Me* – do you know
that song? Then she played it twice. Then she said, "Okay,
you play." So I sat down, and I played for a long time. That's
how I learned. When I was fourteen, I played the organ in
the church, prayer meetings, wakes.

S.G.   What did the angel look like?

W.G.   Well, like what you'd see in a picture. Her dress was white
and she had a glittering crown, a long white gown, a little bit
of something around her waist. What she had on her head
was just glittering, like silver or gold. Some kind of wings, I
couldn't see very good.

S.G.   Can you tell me about how dreams are important?

W.G.   It all depends on who you were. If you don't believe in
dreams, they're useless. You got to believe in them.[51]

Shamans, too, had to be blessed by certain kinds of *pawáganak;*
their powers were not seen as inherited, nor were they formally
taught. Each shaman had to receive his or her powers from
the *pawáganak.* Although medicine men and women imparted
technical skills to proteges, spiritual power could not be taught.
Here too, abuse or false claiming of one's powers could result in
abandonment by the *pawáganak.* It is in the realm of the conjuring
tent that we see one of the strongest modes of empirical testing in
Ojibwa society. Here people could have direct contact with many
pawáganak.

During the ceremony, the tent, which was shaken by the
controllers of the winds, was filled with the voices of the entities.
One could hear rather than see the spiritual entities. Always
present were *Mikinak* (the boss snapping turtle), one or more
winds, and the spiritual "owner" of the conjuring institution,
"the one who takes them out."[52] This ritual was used to obtain
information about people living or events occurring at a distance
in time or space, to recover lost or stolen items and, at one
time, to detect and combat sources of witchcraft. This last was
especially important in curing illness because it was important to
discover whether a person was ill due to sorcery or due to his or

her own moral transgressions. With the help of a good conjuror one could foretell events, kill another person, or bring the dead to life.[53]

Conjuring was empirically tested in Ojibwa society. This was based on auditory perception as well as on direct results. Was the information obtained correct? Was the lost article recovered? If so, there was no room for scepticism. Although many Euro-Canadians have looked at the shaking tent ceremony with condescension, Hallowell makes an interesting point when he remarks that white culture applies the same tests to fortune-telling.[54]

Certainly, the art of conjuring had a dark side. Hallowell noted that even Christianized Indians believed that sorcery by conjuring could come from one's relatives or neighbours: "In the last analysis, almost every Saulteaux believes that it is possible for another person to harm him by covert means."[55]

William Berens's family experienced some bad times at the hands of conjurors and Percy Berens remembered this vividly. In one story, a conjuror sold his muskrat furs after the spring hunt to a trader. The man owed money to the Hudson's Bay Company, for whom William worked at that time.

P.B.   He had that bill in the Hudson's Bay store where my dad was, see? And then he goes and sells his furs to this trader – his spring hunt furs.

S.G.   Instead of paying off his debts to the Hudson's Bay?

P.B.   Yeah…. Then this old man, I guess because he was looking for trouble, this conjuror you know, he walks into the old man's store, the Hudson's Bay store. So he says, as soon as he opens the door, "Tobacco! Tobacco!" My dad told him, "You go and get your tobacco from the trader. You're not getting any tobacco in here."

S.G.   So did the conjuror make life miserable for your dad after that?

P.B.   He tried. After he [the conjuror] moved out to Poplar River, they [William and Nancy] moved out there too and that's the time that thunderstorm came.

S.G.   And the conjuror made that happen?

P.B.   Yeah, yeah. Mom was there, she used to talk about it too. It so upset her, that thunderstorm. You could see the lightning on the rocks.

S.G.   Is that why William always told you boys not to get into conjuring – because you could hurt people with it?

P.B.   Sure! Sure! That's why he told us that. Never have anything to do with it, that conjuring kind of business.[56]

Percy remembered a tragedy that occurred as a result of bad conjuring:

One of my brothers *died* of that kind of thing.

S.G.   Which one?

P.B.   The oldest, Jacob was his name.

S.G.   Jacob died from bad conjuring?

P.B.   Yes, yes. Just because that man – when the Hudson's Bay Company used to have dog trains taking the fur in, dogs from Island Lake and Oxford House, that's called a fur train. And they used to get a train of dogs and a guy from Poplar River, maybe. And that's where my brother – he beat them guys from Island Lake and Oxford House and Nelson House. Because they were jealous of him, they thought that my brother was using a medicine for his dog team to be so good.[57]

On the positive side, however, in the history of the Ojibwa people, shamans with full powers were usually leaders in their communities. This was because of their ability to heal and cure, find animals in hunting seasons, and ward off attacks from other shamans.[58] Gordon Berens, in discussing Fair Wind, revealed the complexity and ambiguous nature of both conjurors and the institution of conjuring:

G.B. He was helping people ... as much as he could. Even when
       some person was sick, he was right there to make that
       person well, give them medicine, you know, out of herbs,
       bark of a tree. He knew what to give a person to make them
       right again.

M.M. Were the people at all afraid of him?

G.B. They were afraid of him because they knew they'd die if
       they didn't. That's right, he used his magic, like see – yeah,
       they were afraid of him. They had to respect him but he
       knew, he knew that he was respected. But if he knew that
       a person didn't respect him, like, try to make a fool of
       him, like, that's the person he was after. And he laid him
       underground. Six feet underground too.[59]

Finally, in establishing a context for the study of syncretism and
Ojibwa encounters with Christianity, a discussion of a Supreme
Being is essential. This Being was the only entity who never entered
the conjuring tent. It was never in any way anthropomorphized
regarding sex or bodily form and there are no iconographic
representations of the Creator and Ruler of all things – the Boss of
Bosses.

  Although scholars are divided on the question of whether
this Being was a pre- or post-contact phenomenon, by the mid-
nineteenth century, Ojibwa people generally believed in some
form of Supreme Being. There are two ways to say God in
Ojibwa: *Gaa-dibenjid* or *Gaa-dibendang* (the all-encompassing
power of life). These words are generally never spoken but may
have been linked to thoughts about the genesis of metaphysical
gifts. The Ojibwa concept of a Manitou or *manidoo* refers to more
accessible spirits such as the Thunderbirds. Likely the concept
of a Supreme Being was not missionary-induced as the idea of
an intimate and personal relationship with God is a Christian
one and the Ojibwa relationship with the Supreme Being was
highly impersonal.[60] Even today, this difference is a real one.
Betsey Patrick, for example, discussed her confusion over the two
concepts saying "I always grew up hearing about God the Father

and praying to God the Father – but now I hear so much talk
about God the Creator. How can people pray to God the Creator?
Because this is Manitou?"[61] The statement shows the personal
relationship involved with one god and a more impersonal one
with another god. The term Manitou is reserved for one being by
the people along the Berens River.

Pre-Christian Algonquian beliefs were not centred around a
dualistic notion of good versus evil; a high god versus the devil.
Seemingly through Christian influence, however, this concept did
gain a firm foothold in Ojibwa religion. By the mid-nineteenth
century, the existence of good and evil forces was a part of the
Saulteaux world view.

Percy Berens had strong words regarding both Ojibwa belief in
a Supreme Being and on the incorrect assumptions made by Euro-
Canadians that they had been the ones to introduce God to native
communities:

> Sure! *We* believe. *We* Indians believe this world was created by
> one person. The Great Spirit. Manitou. You know, when the
> missionaries first came here, they thought that our ancestors that
> were Indians they didn't know God. Yet everything they did, these
> ancestors – way back before they ever seen a missionary – they
> were talking about Manitou. What is Manitou? God.[62]

The Ojibwa along the Berens River, grounded in the knowledge
that power came from the strength of belief, thoughtfully
incorporated new concepts and elements into their own framework
as they saw fit and applied empirical thought to their religious
life. Their mental landscape was wide and inclusive and it is from
the vantage point of *this* truth that we need a new look at their
religious history.

The fact that most missionaries, settlers, and traders suffered a
failure of understanding on all these fronts profoundly influenced
missionary/Indian encounters, sculpted interactions between
the two cultures, and coloured Euro-Canadian interpretations of
present and past. The newcomers' sense of possessing exclusive

truth sustained both their convictions and prejudices. The next chapter looks at these players, exploring their efforts to grapple with the Ojibwa whom they encountered in the field and their efforts to prepare souls for the world to come.

3 "They Fought Just Like a Cat and a Dog!"

Catholic-Protestant Encounters on the Mission Field

....

Roman Catholic and Protestant missionaries often occupied the same mission fields in northern Manitoba, especially after 1900, although the complex dynamics of coexistence varied from territory to territory. In northern Manitoba, competition between the two denominations was usually fierce, but a crisis or hard economic times might require Catholic and Protestant missionaries to pull together in a common quest for survival. Truly fascinating is the hybrid between Christianity and Aboriginal religions that developed out of these positive experiences compared to the ongoing heated and passionate competition to win souls for Christ and save "their" Indians from the folly of membership in the wrong church.

Catholics and Protestants both held that the only road to salvation was a wholehearted acceptance of Christianity. Mathias Kalmes's story of "Kinebikons" made this point blatantly clear. "Kinebikons" was a well-known serial story about the salvation and subsequent leading of a Christian life by a young Ojibwa woman named Kinebikons. Kinebikons and her grandmother, Teweigan, were found by a missionary and taken to a school at the Fort Frances Mission. The two resided there and a baptized Kinebikons was renamed "Lucy." The Sister at the mission worked to make old Teweigan see the errors inherent in Ojibwa religion and spoke fairly brutally:

Open your eyes, Teweigan…. Where are all those Indians who lived around Rainy Lake and Lake of the Woods? At the end of the last century they were four thousand. Why have they nearly all disappeared? And those little wooden huts which you erect on their graves … what happened to them? Were they not supposed to protect [your dead]? They have fallen away and their dust mingled with the dust of the dead has blown all over…. Look at the White people living around you. They do not offer themselves to Manitou and yet they live long and are increasing so rapidly that they are invading all your lands…. And you, followers of sorcerers, your population decreases. If some metis had not come to mix with you your Reserve would be empty.[1]

Like Protestants, Catholics of the time saw Indians almost as a different species of humanity. Adrien-Gabriel Morice, writing in 1910, expressed a typical view:

The [North] American Indian is a being possessed of aspirations, ways of thinking and standards of judgement which are entirely different from ours…. A degraded creature who partakes more of the child than of the adult, without being blessed with the innocence of the former or the control over the passions of the latter, the redskin must be treated with firmness, the prudence and foresight required by the government of youth, to which must be added a little perspicacity, so that the wiles of a naturally shrewd, though naive, nature might not lead to false conclusions. Above all, the missionary must aim higher to hit lower … he should ask for more, because he is sure to get less…. Being a grown-up child, the native must constantly be watched, often reproved, and … at times tested.[2]

As Rosa del C. Bruno-Jofré explains, late-nineteenth and mid-twentieth century Oblate fathers saw the Indian as "an unfortunate natural being," a "sad offspring of an ignored race" who lacked an intellectual culture, a sense of morality, and "a comforting religion."[3] Their useless and barbaric state was capable of redemption only through the Oblate fathers, with intensive follow-up work, if possible, by the work of Sisters from various congregations.

As noted before, however, the clergy actually working with native peoples interpreted events depending on their individual character and background, the group of people with whom they worked, the nature of circumstances occurring during contact, the length of experience, and the degree to which Christian ideas were accepted or rejected in the field. By 1937, Brother Frederick Leach had spent nineteen years among the Ojibwa along the Berens River. His views reflected a tolerance and understanding that came from being there for a long time. On 19 November 1937 he wrote:

> It's quite a problem to know what to do for some of these people; one can see that some are badly in need of extra food but some don't seem to try sufficiently. Then again ... if I were continually living in a half-starved condition would *I* find much energy to do things? ... Only those who are in charge of issuing the destitute rations can know what a problem it is.[4]

While missionaries shared some similar perspectives regarding conversion, however, they competed intensely with one another for converts and were not afraid to criticize or devalue their fellow missionaries. Communities along the Berens River were stages on which were displayed some wonderful examples of auditions to win converts, rivalry for leading roles, and dynamic theatrical productions. They were also the scenes of an interesting mix where rival Oblate and Methodist missions played to their audience to varying degrees on one hand and united to form one voice on the other hand.

To the chagrin of the Methodists, the Roman Catholics built their first chapel at Berens River in 1897. They became a truly active presence in the community in 1918, when Oblates Father Joseph De Grandpré and Brother Frederick Leach opened the Roman Catholic day school under the auspices of Brother Leach.[5]

From the beginning, the Catholic missionaries at Berens River felt the effects of being "on the outs," religiously speaking, with the Berens family. In 1919, the Oblates wished to establish a school at Bloodvein. On 9 April, Frederick Leach wrote from Berens River to his Provincial:

> The people [at Bloodvein] are greatly in favor of a Catholic school and said they would wait until this summer to give us a chance to build one.... The danger is that if we don't build one *this summer* the Methodists certainly will for the chief of this Reserve [William Berens, who succeeded his father Jacob in 1917] has a position with the Hudson's Bay Company and he reports all our doings to the Methodist minister.... Father [De Grandpré] has just interrupted me to tell me to report again that this church must be built this summer ... and he adds "the Indian population there have a better disposition than those here."[6]

Leach's comments imply a good deal about the secondary place of the Catholics in Berens River at that time; his letter suggests the extent of teamwork between the chief and the Methodist missionary.

The Methodists' underlying belief was that individuals could transcend their circumstances through the power of the Gospel. In 1876, Egerton Ryerson Young wrote of unconverted Berens River Ojibwa: "While rejoicing [that many desire to learn the plan of salvation] we have to mourn over the absence of ... the genuine conversion of the inner man by the transforming power of the Holy Ghost." Writing of the conversion of mixed-blood Nelson House postmaster William Isbister in 1875, John Semmens noted, "He became a child of God and utterly changed. The people ... were amazed at the sudden and complete change of character."[7] And, of the Nelson House community, he asserted that the mission was enjoying positive results by 1876: "Those who have not seen such a transformation cannot properly realise what is implied in all this. Our poor imperfect human efforts did not account for this great change ... they who had been born in the shadow of death rejoiced in the dawning of the gospel morning."[8]

This belief was a sustaining force in all mission work, and missionaries rejoiced in the glory of what they perceived as God's work with them in the field. At times, it must have been easy to hang on to this faith. In 1883, for example, Alexander Sutherland, superintendent of Methodist missions, was proud of the field work in British Columbia. "As a direct result of missionary efforts among the Indians ... tribal wars have ceased entirely, heathen villages have been transformed into Christian communities and the gross immoralities ... have given place to assemblies for Christian instruction."[9] Of the Mississaugas, Sutherland wrote in the same year: "These Indians were notoriously the most drunken and filthy in the country, the very lowest of the low, and yet they received the Gospel more readily than any others and its transforming power upon them was wonderful ... now they began to live in a Christian fashion."[10]

At other times, however, it must have seemed that many of their ideals from home were being soaked in rains, frozen in cold, and trampled upon by the heathen. Methodist records were full of disappointments. Yet there was always a strong accompanying current of hope and an expectation that true conversion was just around the corner. As Methodist missionary S. D. Gaudin wrote in 1903: "I do so long for a real deep spiritual work among our people, and yet it seems not to come, or at least permanent results are often so disappointing. And yet, I thoroughly believe ... these poor people are sincerely longing and hungering after God."[11]

Missionaries in the northern Manitoba field believed, as did missionaries around the world who dealt with the conversion of non-Christian peoples, that their duty was to eradicate all aspects of indigenous culture in order for salvation to be achieved. Their perceptions of their native clients ran along a continuum which placed Native peoples as falling anywhere from a degraded species to children of the forest to fairly noble savages. "For years the Indians have been pleading for a missionary," wrote Egerton Ryerson Young from Berens River in 1875. "It is ... cheering to hear voices ... once accustomed to ... unmeaning mutterings of a vile and debasing superstition, lifted up in prayer."[12]

The Berens River missionaries belonged to the Canadian Methodist mainstream. It was thus much more an agency of the modern state than was Catholicism: although ultramontanists cooperated with the government, they represented the forces of reaction against the efficiency of the modern state. For them, perfection was never to be attained on this side of the grave. The Methodist notion of grace was non-Calvinist. John Calvin, in the early seventeenth century, held that grace was irresistible, due to the power of God. In Methodism, however, grace could be resisted in spite of the power of God; unlike the Calvinists, they were not caught up in predestinationism. Methodists, in fact, called themselves Arminians, after the Dutch theologian Arminius who clearly opposed Calvinism. Methodist theology left much room for individual initiative and social action. By the 1850s, Methodism in Canada had joined the Protestant mainstream;[13] it was very much an agency of modernism (the idea that we are constantly in an open-ended state of improvement and that the new is always better than the old), with an increasing stress on organization and lack of mystery.[14] Catholic spirituality, in contrast, contains an elusive and untouchable dimension, conveying a sense of mysteries that cannot be fully comprehended, that are beyond human grasp, and that embody unanswered questions. This was especially pronounced before Vatican II when altars were hidden from view and Latin text abounded.

Catholics and Protestants shared the view that conversion produced a complete transformation in the life of a new Christian, but the two denominations differed in their ideas about how one actually got into heaven. Methodists believed that conversion and faith ensured a safe passage. For Catholics, getting into heaven depended on continual good works and actions, such as mission work or penance. This conviction seems to have bolstered missionaries in the tough conditions they often encountered in the field. In the winter of 1926, for example, Brother Leach frequently wrote in his journal about the great loneliness and feelings of isolation he experienced in the long periods when his partner, Father Joseph De Grandpré, was away at other communities. Just as often, however, he recorded making those sacrifices in order to get into heaven. Even an Oblate brother could not rest on the laurels of his baptism, church membership, and faith in God.

Leach never took for granted that he was assured a place in the hereafter. It seems he continually sought extra support from his community of parishioners to help ensure his ultimate arrival in heaven. On 5 May 1929, one of the Berens River women, Pat McKay, died. Leach wrote, "Pat, pray for me so that when my turn comes I may go and join you in Heaven forever." Writing on 15 May 1929 of Catherine Goosehead, who had died a month earlier, Leach said, "I often think of Catherine and Pat [McKay]. If I have been even a little help to them on earth may they help me with their prayers to gain Heaven."[15]

In order to understand encounters between Ojibwa people and Roman Catholics, it is necessary to examine the Catholic understanding of salvation, conversion, and baptism. Writing a piece for *The Indian Missionary Record* in 1939, Father Guy de Bretagne provided a view of Catholicism that was representative of the position of the church as a whole: "There is no fanaticism in the heart of a true Christian Catholic. Broadmindedness does not mean that he thinks all the religions are good: there is only one God and one Faith and one Church."[16] For Roman Catholics, salvation could only be attained through the church and the sacraments which integrated the newly initiated into the institution and its structure. Clergy and hierarchy thus lay at the heart of mission work. Conversion involved a rejection of customs that ran contrary to church doctrine, and a change of heart and belief. Original sin could be transcended only through the conversion of the individual who, through baptism, joined the Catholic Church, which was sanctioned through the redemptive blood of Christ to provide the mechanism for salvation:

Christ, the sole repairer of heaven and earth, unites Himself
with the Church in the unity of the same body for the work of
Redemption. The Church ... integrates Christ, priest and victim,
the entire world.... Thus the mission of the Church is that of
Christ Himself ... she has the power and the duty of universal
expansion ... the hypothesis and theory of mission rest on the
existence and universality of original sin. All men have sinned in
Adam, thus destroying their supernatural resemblance to God
and becoming ... subject to death and eternal damnation. It is
impossible for man to escape this state through his own strength
and means. But God provides for this powerlessness. In an
excess of love and mercy, He gave him a Redeemer ... the plan of
Redemption is ... the salvation of all men through Christ.[17]

For Catholics as well as Protestants, conversion was expected to
produce complete change. In the words of Father de Bretagne, the
Truth "will bathe their life in a new light, and make them partakers
of the divine gifts, and live a life honest, pure and beautiful."[18]

Roman Catholics believed that inspiration for conversion and
baptism could come from God, from Mary or from the saints.
To this end, the distribution of amulets or medals in the mission
fields was common. Reporting on "The Conversion of an Indian,"
Father François Poulin attributed his success in this case to Mary.
He had been working with an Indian for some time, asking him
to "choose the right path and become baptized" but to no avail.
Then one night, after a powerful dream, the Indian approached
the priest, asking to be baptized. Poulin puzzled for some time
over the change, finally concluding that it "is because the Blessed
Virgin Mary wanted to prove ... even by means of a vision, [that]
any soul trusting in her help will not be forsaken. I had previously
given him a miraculous medal of the Blessed Virgin Mary and
confided him to our Mother's care. She did the rest."[19]

Catholic and Protestant spokesmen often expressed mutual
contempt and distrust. For example, in 1948 Joseph Etienne
Champagne, writing out of the Canadian Catholic mission
experience of the previous half century, listed lack of stability,

lack of unity, and confusion of doctrines as the weaknesses inherent in Protestant theology. As for what he called Protestant psychology, Protestants were fundamentally weakened by their sense of individualism which "rejects 'authority' ... as a 'support' and a 'guide.' Deprived of this ... they find themselves alone."[20] This solitude, he wrote, generated religious anxiety and distress, emptiness of soul, and depression which was aggravated by "the pollution of contradictory religious opinions."[21] It also created "a great danger of becoming immersed in subjectivism ... never forget that [a Protestant] lacks the unfailing magistery and effective *ex opere operato* of the sacraments."[22] Concluded Champagne,

> Protestant theology has no system. The whole "credo" is drawn up on ... intimate, personal intercourse with the Holy Spirit of private inspiration. The foundation of Protestant religiosity ... lives on this non-dogmatic and consequently purely psychological and humanitarian mysticism ... a ... fanatic formalism seeks to make up for the dogmatic void.[23]

Father Guy de Bretagne also wrote critically of Protestantism as a "deliquescent, creedless, codeless modernism [with] no supernatural and unique 'authority.'" It would, thus, never hold up over time.[24]

Writing of denominational rivalry between Protestants and Catholics in the last century, J. R. Miller concludes that Catholics saw Catholicism as embodying the one true church and viewed Protestantism as, at best, a poorly refined religion – and at worst, heresy. Quebec ultramontanism, he says, was the main bastion of this outlook that infiltrated prairie Catholicism during the 1880s and 1890s.[25] As Champagne wrote in his *Manual of Missionary Action*:

> When we speak of Catholic missions and Protestant missions, we speak of two totally different things...

.... Properly speaking, the only Christian missionaries are the
Catholic missionaries, because Christ has given the missionary
mandate only to the Catholic Church.... [Protestant missionaries
are] missionaries of a human society of a church which is not the
Church of Christ.[26]

Protestants chafed against this arrogance and became embroiled
in the "Papal Aggression" controversy which "conditioned them to
regard Rome's representatives with suspicion at the best of times
and active hostility at the worst."[27] All non-Catholic bodies at this
time shared animosity towards Catholicism.

Certainly, Protestants were guilty of the same arrogance
concerning the superiority of their religion. In 1918, Methodist
missionary Percy E. Jones wrote an item for the *Missionary
Bulletin* entitled, "Our Work With the Indians at Berens River." A
Roman Catholic Ojibwa woman told the missionary that Jesus had
visited her at her bedside during the night. According to Jones,
Christ said to her, "You see two churches here at Berens River, the
Catholic and the Methodist; one teaches that which is right, the
other does not ... go to your Catholic friends and tell them that
they must go to the Methodist Church to hear the gospel ... for
there it is preached right."[28] While the truly interesting thing here
is Jesus appearing to this woman in a dream, Jones crowed loudly
about Christ's validation of the truth – that the Methodists were
superior to the Catholics.

Ill-will between Catholics and Protestants had been generated
in the 1880s and 1890s through arguments over separate schools
west of the Ottawa River; the 1888 Jesuits Estates Act; the
founding of the Equal Rights Association and the Protestants
Protection Association; and accusations of clerical interference in
politics. Such animosity embittered relations in the mission field.

Catholics in the dioceses of the northwest, which included
the Berens River area, expressed some of the most negative views
regarding Protestant-Catholic coexistence. Protestant missions
there were well-organized by 1900, and friction between French-
and English-speaking settlers added to the problems. Protestants

received substantial financial backing from bible societies, eastern Canadians, the Methodist Bureau, and the Church Missionary Society, while Catholics did not have this wide range of support. The Oblates were angry with federal and local governments for showing bias towards Protestants in competition for jobs in the Department of Indian Affairs. Protestant employees, they said, purposely worked to spread Protestantism on reserves in their capacities as Indian agents.[29]

In Berens River, Catholic and Protestant missionaries did not get along well on theological matters. Percy Berens, son of Chief William Berens remembered with humour the rocky relationship that existed between Rev. John Niddrie and Father Joseph De Grandpré at Berens River.

P.B.   Father De Grandpré was the priest's name, and Niddrie was the United Church minister – and they used to fight just like a cat and a dog [laughter]! *Really* ... I'm telling you the truth!

S.G.   What would they fight about?

P.B.   Their religion. Niddrie thought his religion was better than Father De Grandpré's religion [laughter]. Sure! They fought just like a cat and a dog.

S.G.   Did the people [in the community] get involved in the fighting?

P.B.   No, just them two, the priest and the missionary.

S.G.   Yelling?

P.B.   No – they'd just send notes, they had messengers [laughter]. Father De Grandpré would send a messenger to go and give that note to Niddrie [more laughter]. Yeah, they never contacted each other to talk business, like, you know – no, they just sent notes – Niddrie would answer the note from Father De Grandpré [laughter].

P.B.   [Niddrie] was too generous, I guess I have to use that word – too generous to the people, to the United Church members. But it was different with the Catholics, he didn't have nothing to do with the Catholics.

> S.G.   What about the Catholics? Did the Catholic [clergy] only
>   give to the Catholics?
> P.B.   No.
> S.G.   They gave to everybody?
> P.B.   Uh-huh [yes].[30]

Fred Baptiste had similar memories.

> S.G.   You know, Percy Berens told me that Father De Grandpré
>   and Niddrie used to get into fights.
> F.B.   They didn't get along so good them two [laughter]! You
>   know, this Father De Grandpré wanted to change some of
>   the people to be a Catholic, like.
> S.G.   He wanted to convert the Methodists?
> F.B.   Yes, yes! And so they didn't get along too good. After
>   they both died, everyone got along fine – every one of
>   them. There's one thing I can say about Mr. Niddrie; when
>   somebody died from the Roman Catholic mission, they'd
>   take the body to the church and he'd ring the bell when he
>   seen this body going by – he was, like, saying goodbye, eh?[31]

Virginia Boulanger also remembered that although Catholic and
Protestant members of the community got along well, Niddrie
and De Grandpré were constantly fighting. Although she never
understood the details of the battles or exactly why the two did
not get along, she recalled the two clergymen being in heated
competition for church members.[32]

Methodist records contain some extremely agitated responses
to proposed Catholic missions encroaching on their territory. On
17 August 1911, for example, Rev. Joseph Lowes wrote to T. E.
Egerton Shore, general secretary of the Foreign Department of the
Methodist Mission Society, about the Catholic mission at Berens
River:

> I am very much afraid that the Roman Catholics are going to best
> us here. They are going to build a new church here this fall, at

least so I am told. Two priests are expected, one to stay right here
[Brother Leach] and the other to visit about [Father De Grandpré]
and both to proselytize as much as possible then press for a
Boarding School of their own at Berens River. They use all sorts of
underhand methods and means. Perhaps I do take this to heart too
much but I do feel very badly about it.[33]

The prospect of a new Catholic boarding school at Cross Lake
prompted a similar letter to Shore from Methodist missionary S. D.
Gaudin.

[Should the Catholics build a boarding school] our church will
have a very poor chance at Cross Lake. With things even as they
are at present, with only one priest on the ground we are having a
hard battle to anything like hold our own but what it will be with
the added prestige which a boarding school will give them with
priests, Brothers and Sisters galore. You can hardly imagine how
the Catholic religion appeals to the Indian nor how the Indians of
that faith are seeking to win over their Protestant friends.[34]

The Catholics were equally negative in their correspondence
and private papers about the Protestants. Sometimes this was
revealed fairly subtly. In March 1927, Brother Leach and Methodist
lay missionary John James Everett were both called to George
Boucher's home to visit George's dying eleven-year-old daughter,
Elizabeth. Leach was critical of his Methodist counterpart. "Saw
the little girl and told them [her parents] the only thing was prayer.
She died within an hour.... Thank God I am a Catholic. A short
few lines of the Bible, a short prayer was all [from Everett]. Not a
word about God to the child. No names of Jesus and Mary on her
lips."[35]

On 23 December 1928, Leach and the Methodists found
themselves together again, this time helping a sick baby at Joe
Boucher's home. The next day, however, Leach wrote critically of
the Methodists' participation in the incident: "Saw Joe Boucher's
baby. Someone [obviously the Methodists] gave it *Aspirin*. Mrs.

Street [the Methodist school teacher's wife] gives some other dope, following my usual rule [I] will not give anything to be taken internal. It is going fast."[36]

Sometimes sharp conflicts flared, especially over children. In January 1919, Leach wrote to his superiors in St. Boniface, saying that he may have "gained a victory over the Protestant minister." Cubby Green was an Ojibwa Methodist man living at Berens River. His wife had died and he apparently relinquished control of his two Protestant daughters, Alma (who was subsequently adopted by a Catholic woman named Sarah Shaw) and Sophia (who was adopted by Margeurite McKay, also a Catholic). The girls were baptized in the Catholic Church in November 1913. In 1918, Rev. Percy E. Jones was apparently working to have the girls taken away from their adoptive Catholic parents and sent to the Protestant school at Norway House. According to Leach: "the minister came while I was away for a few minutes, took the children and hid them until the boat came and placed them in the Captain's charge. I nearly had a fight with the minister for he was most insulting."[37] The girls did go to Norway House, however, and a major battle ensued. Leach wrote to his superiors in St. Boniface that "Mr. Jones thought he had us cornered because he made one of the guardians sign a paper releasing the children ... saying that if she didn't sign he would expose her (she was with child through another man not her husband)." Leach appealed to Indian Agent Carter who, on 28 September, ordered that the girls be returned to their guardians and attend the Catholic school at Berens River. Carter also wrote to Indian Affairs minister D. C. Scott in Ottawa recommending the girls' release from Norway House. Ottawa acquiesced.[38]

Leach's letters recorded other struggles with the Protestants over children. In the summer of 1919, for example, he wrote angrily:

They wish to take another child from us. Name Alfred Berens, protestant Mother, Catholic father dead. Mother has given us a writing request wanting her boy to come over to our school. He has been at this school one year. He refuses to be baptized at present as all his relations threatened him with bodily injury if he became Catholic. His mother wants him to be baptised.[39]

In July 1919:

My attendance [at the day school] is very good. I am not going to say it is easy work to keep the children regular. It is very hard work indeed. The Protestant minister is trying his best to get us out of here, and he is getting very powerful support from the Methodist Society. Children will be children and a few of our members find it hard to understand why the minister feeds and clothes his children and we can't.[40]

He was still writing in this vein a decade later:

The Methodists have concentrated their forces this year [1929].... They cannot get the children by ordinary means so are using rather foul means. Last fall, over 30 bales of used clothing were sent out. Any Indian wishing to get some must attend the Protestant Church or School. We had our school register Catholic children whose parents, practically speaking, had no religion. These parents are offered clothing by the Methodists and in consequence changed their children from our school to the other. I now here [sic] that the children are Protestant.[41]

Catholics, however, were not always the losers. In 1928, Leach wrote to Father Josephat Magnan, his provincial, that "The Methodists have given us very keen competition and are by no means pleased as I have taken away 4 of their best pupils. I have every right to do so as these children are Catholics."[42]

Each side was clearly willing to use almost any means to outdo the other. On 22 August 1919 Leach wrote to the Oblate headquarters in St. Boniface that he had asked the provincial government for an allowance of one hundred dollars a year for teaching non-treaty children, and that Deputy Minister R.

Fletcher had granted the request. Wrote Leach: "By the letter you
will see that he knows nothing about the Methodist school and I
suppose it is not necessary for me to tell him about the other Non-
Treaty children who go there. In fact unless you think necessary
otherwise I am keeping it quiet from all."[43]

If Protestants worried about being bested by the Catholics,
Catholics had the same fears about their Protestant competition.
Wrote a somewhat wistful Leach to St. Boniface on 4 January
1926:

> All kinds of tricks are used [by the Methodists to attract children
> to their school], the chief attraction being quantities of clothing
> given *free* to parents and children ... the children are bought. It
> is the lack of spiritual faith which does so much harm. I often
> wonder how the Protestant minister has such a hold over his
> people. There are several belonging to his church living close to us
> and regularly you will see them passing our gate on Sunday to go
> to church a distance of over three miles. Not only that but I have
> often seen our own Catholics coming out of the Methodist Church
> on a Sunday afternoon and they number not a few. Why? Is it
> because the service is more popular, more attractive?[44]

It is necessary to read these sources critically. Catholic and
Protestant missionaries in the field, when writing letters to
their superiors at home, often emphasized the worst aspects of
a given situation. This may have been a way of soliciting moral
or financial support or of making sure that people at home
grasped some idea of the hardships of living in a remote northern
community. Overstatement and some selection of data served a
tactical purpose. Robert Choquette believes that a real difference
existed between the business writings of field missionaries and
their actual life experiences. He goes so far as to say that the
difference between writings and actual life make missionaries
look "schizophrenic" – a psychologist would have a "field day."
Choquette is speaking with some humour here; nevertheless the
point merits serious consideration.[45]

One must not generalize too much in the interpretation of Catholic-Protestant relations. Unique and complex situations resulted when diverse individuals entered mission fields.[46] As Robert Choquette says, the wide range of theological tenets within Protestantism makes too much generalization about the feelings and reactions of clergy dangerous (although within Methodism this wide range was drastically narrowed, to be sure). Relations between Catholics and Protestants during the latter half of the nineteenth century commonly exhibited mistrust, rivalry, and animosity. Yet not all priests and ministers felt this way – nor did their converts. Some clergy and lay people, in fact, "managed to overcome their prejudices and develop constructive and charitable relationships with people of the other camp."[47] In her study of nineteenth century missions to the Dene, Kerry Abel concluded that, although historians have long given the impression that Catholic and Protestant missionaries were forever at one another's throats in her region of study, there was no evidence of conflict between the two groups. Any contests for influence and power among the Dene had always occurred between shamans.[48] In Choquette's words, "Protestant-Catholic relations could be complex, not easily reduced to simple formulae. The same people who hurled ideological and theological missiles at each other one day could end up embracing each other on the next."[49]

In Berens River, hard times or shared interests could create unions between Catholics and Protestants. In an earlier chapter, the hunger of the Berens River Ojibwa in the winter of 1930 was discussed. Brother Leach, Rev. Niddrie, and the Indian agent united in the face of this crisis to persuade Chief William Berens to take more rations for his band. When need arose, Leach and Niddrie were able to work in concert.[50]

The winter of 1931 in Little Grand Rapids presents another an example of the bitter cold of winter generating warmth among missionaries. Luther Schuetze wrote in his memoirs about the scarcity of food, the prevalence of illness, and the many deaths. He had heard that Boniface Guimond, the Roman Catholic missionary-teacher, was having a particularly hard time making ends meet. One day, Guimond passed by Schuetze's home on his way home from the store. As Schuetze recalled: "His eyes looked very hungry when he said, 'My, you have a lot of nice fish.' [I gave him a stick of ten white fish.] ... he was overcome and finally stuttered 'Mr. Luther I'll pray that you will be a Saint in heaven.' I replied, 'Not yet, I'd like to stick around a little longer.'"[51]

Different missionaries also evoked different responses from communities. In the 1950s, the teacher at Little Grand Rapids wrote to Luther Schuetze asking him about the methods he had used in his work among the people. She was not achieving success at teaching English, and the only Ojibwa on the reserve who could speak this language were the ones Schuetze had taught. Schuetze answered that he had combined a sincere love for the children and community with the fact that he, unlike those who had preceded him, had stayed in the mission long enough to be effective. He and his wife had made their own paddles and snowshoes and so earned the Ojibwas' respect. His words are simple, respectful, and a far cry from the pompous, condescending tone of others: "Somehow they sensed that we knew what we were talking about for these Saulteaux Natives often described by writers as black hearted and stiffnecked people, were not so at all, when you got to know them you found them to be kind hearted and generous, who would do anything for you."[52]

Finally, despite typical Christian dualism and evangelical concerns that saw native religion in the oppositional terms of Satan against Christ, some missionaries in the field actually learned to bend a little sometimes. Luther Schuetze, for example, changed his attitude toward the drum dance, while F. G. Stevens, another Methodist missionary working in the northern Manitoba field, remained hostile toward the practice, which he denounced as evil without so much as making a passing study of its real elements.[53] Schuetze said that when he first arrived at Little Grand Rapids, he felt the same way as the missionary who had preceded him, "who saw in the drum dances something pagan that had to be done away with." He thus took "forcible action

and kicked the drum in and said it was of the devil." But, in
the winter of 1931, there was much illness and many deaths in
the community. Schuetze concluded that much of the problem
stemmed from the "modern dances" that had begun to be held in
peoples' homes. Participants became overheated and then chilled
in the night air. He wrote:

> Later when I became accustomed to it I still more or less talked
> against these seemingly pagan dances.... But now I used all means
> to stop these modern dances in small crowded houses, for I saw the
> evil they caused, and since the Drum Dance was always outside in
> the open, I was all for them, if they were done in a thankful mood
> of happiness and so I encouraged them to go back to their Drum
> Dances.[54]

And so Catholics and Protestants worked on, ever-conscious
of themselves as being parts of a greater whole. Protestants
endeavoured to evangelize and create the Kingdom of God on
earth. Catholics were motivated by their desire for the unity and
universality of the Catholic religion. While the mission field often
existed as a battleground between competing denominations,
underlying kinship within the human race could, under the
right circumstances, prod warring missionaries into truce and
cooperation. Frederick Leach and John Niddrie are remembered in
Berens River with warmth and a gentle humour. Both missionaries
chose to remain among the Ojibwa; Leach retiring to Winnipeg at
the end of his life and Niddrie living out his days at Berens River.
For the people of the community, perhaps theological battles were
not very important to achieving success in the mission field. More
important was the missionaries' willingness to bend to Native ways
(if not to the ways of each other!).

4 "You're Pretty Good; but I'll tell you what Medicine to use"

Encounters, 1875–1916

My religious background really did shape almost everything. It gave me the mythological framework I was brought up inside of, and I know from experience that once you're inside a mythological framework you can't break outside of it. You can alter or adapt it to yourself, but it's always there. (Northrop Frye)[1]

When Ann Fienup-Riordan studied the encounter between the Yup'ik Eskimo of western Alaska and John and Edith Kilbuck, two Moravian missionaries, she traced a long process of negotiation in which the Yup'ik eventually internalized many Christian concepts without, however, surrendering their cultural integrity.[2] Similarly, the history of encounters between the Ojibwa people and Christian missionaries between 1875 and 1916 yields a rich story in which Indians took a leading role in determining their religious courses of action and shaping those ideas that they chose to accept and integrate into their world view.

Methodist missionary Frederick G. Stevens and his wife, Frances, documented encounters that show just such native control over their religious decision-making. In 1901, they encountered the Northern Ojibwa Sucker and Crane Indians while they were travelling from Oxford House to Island Lake. The Cranes, Frances wrote, "were anxious to hear more of the Gospel." The Suckers, however, "were more or less indifferent and clung stubbornly onto old ideas."[3] According to Frances, both bands were practising polygamy and the Stevenses used "wisdom and diplomacy" to deal with the situation.

> The Cranes felt that they should take on a new way of life and readily began to make the drastic change. The youngest wife was invariably chosen and that meant that many former wives had to be looked after. This was agreed to. The Sucker band was indifferent and clung stubbornly to their life as it was. Our efforts met with some success but enthusiasm for the new life was conspicuous by its absence.[4]

F. G. Stevens continued the story. In 1907, the chief of the Sucker clan, Jack Fiddler, and his brother were charged with the murder of a woman who had become a "windigo" or, in Ojibwa thinking, a cannibal monster.[5] Jack Fiddler hanged himself while on trial at Norway House and his brother died in Stony Mountain Penitentiary. According to Stevens, "when this happened, the Suckers realized what paganism had done to them and decided to become Christians."[6] Adam Fiddler, already a Christian, offered to teach his people what he could, and the community sent word to Norway House and Berens River, asking for an annual visit from an ordained missionary and offering to convey him from and to Berens River free of charge. Unfortunately, no missionary took on the job.

In 1910, some of the Sandy Lakers who had come under treaty moved to Deer Lake. It was not until 1913, however, that Stevens ventured to these people and, on his arrival, found a warmly welcoming but frustrated group. "Their church was there but, tired of the long waiting, those inclined to paganism had put up the 'long tent' and ... said, 'If the missionary does not come soon, we will begin drumming again.'"[7] When Stevens left, the chief told him "My experience has taught me that all men are liars, especially missionaries. We see you now. You say you will come again next year – we are not sure. If you come again next year, we will accept the Sacraments of the Church."[8]

Along the Berens River, Ojibwa likewise maintained control over their religious life. In 1854, Rev. John Ryerson stopped at

Berens River on his way to Norway House. At that time, although the Hudson's Bay Company factor told him that the Indians there wanted a missionary, his interaction with them was not so encouraging.[9] The Ojibwa likely resisted Ryerson because they had no interest in either the man or his ideas. It was Jacob Berens who, in 1861, became the first Berens River Saulteaux to convert.

In speculating on the possible reasons for Berens's conversion, Jennifer S. H. Brown surmises that the experience could well have been a quest for new powers. As well, Jacob wanted to wed Mary McKay, a Christian woman. His religious status may well have been a prerequisite as far as Mary's parents were concerned.[10]

His baptism and ensuing conversion made the Methodists optimistic. Then, in 1871, Rev. Egerton Ryerson Young was approached at his Norway House mission by a group of Saulteaux from up the Berens River. These men asked Young to visit and, in 1874, after some preliminary groundwork was laid by his assistant, Timothy Bear, Young opened a mission at the mouth of the river. From there he also made trips to the Little Grand Rapids area. As Brown explains, Young's visits "and those of upriver people to his mission were the first in a long chain of encounters between missionaries and the upper river Ojibwa, with results that ran the gamut from confrontation and avoidance to dialogue and conversion or creative syncretism."[11]

Jacob Berens and his wife, Mary, an educated mixed-blood woman, encouraged their children to welcome technological and social change.[12] This flexible attitude enabled his son, William, to choose his own ideas and pathways throughout his lifetime. As a young man from a Methodist family, William chose not to seek out and take traditional Ojibwa sacred power; he did not embark on a vision quest that would have enabled him to connect with his *pawáganak*. However, such knowledge was a part of his world view and William always believed that he could have access to that route of power if ever he chose to seek it out. Brown wrote that William Berens was not a pristine aboriginal Ojibwa from a static, unchanged Saulteaux community. He was the product of several centuries of cultural change and adaptation ... despite his life-long involvement with things and ways Anglo-Canadian, he lived largely with an inner Ojibwa world view, sensitized to Ojibwa views of sacred power and well-being, committed to fundamental Ojibwa norms and styles in personal relations and interaction.[13]

With the signing of Treaty 5 in 1875, Jacob Berens entered into an era of intimate interactions with government and missionaries. Just as the chief welcomed Euro-Canadian change, however, his Methodism did not cause him to dissociate himself or his family in any way from his fellow Ojibwa who practised traditional religion. His children participated in "both Methodist observances and in Ojibwa religious events that left lasting impressions."[14]

An example of his ability to bridge Ojibwa and Canadian worlds occurred in November 1876. Three Berens River men killed their mother in their winter camp because they were afraid she was becoming a windigo. At the hearing conducted by Roderick Ross, the Hudson's Bay Company factor and justice of the peace for the Kewatin District, Jacob pleaded for the sons. He explained the boys believed that, by killing the windigo, they would actually be saving lives in the long run and that those Ojibwa did not yet understand Christian ways. In a letter to Alexander Morris, Ross wrote that "There is a good deal of excitement here among the Indians at Berens River ... about the probable punishment of the parties implicated in the murder.... [They] are opposed to any further actions in the case."[15] The charges were ultimately dropped.

The Ojibwa at Berens River have a long history of participating actively in mission and government life in their community. Their reactions to the Methodist day school in the 1880s provide examples. In 1880, the Methodists sent William Hope to teach at Berens River; the young man had received a liberal education at St. John's College in Winnipeg but held no provincial teaching certificate. Ebenezer E. McColl, inspector of Indian agencies,

wrote a scathing report to the Department of Indian Affairs for
the year ending 31 December 1881. "The whole band complains
of the inefficiency of the Mission school and ask for a Government
school. The chief [Jacob Berens] stated that he valued his religion
and loved his minister, but that he never knew of an instance
where any of his people were educated at the Mission schools,
as only the most inferior teachers were invariably employed."[16]
McColl's report for the next year showed that the situation was
no better and community members were taking matters into their
own hands. Mr. Hope's school was not progressing well and the
attendance was very poor. The Ojibwa at Berens River placed
enough value on providing education for their children to become
actively involved; in this case the value of a good education
won out over loyalty to the Methodist missionary. The people,
explained McColl, "started to build a school house of their
own last winter, but were prevented by an epidemic breaking
out among them ... but they intend on finishing it as soon as
possible."[17]

It seems that a major disagreement occurred in the community
in 1884 over the whole day school issue: should the new
building be a government or a Methodist school? Initially both
a government and a Methodist school began operations in 1885.
Agent Angus MacKay reported to the department that Miss
Jane Flett had been recently appointed by the government to
teach in the newly appointed government Indian School; she
had forty-four names on her roll. Wrote MacKay: "now that the
band have got what they long asked for – a teacher appointed
by the government, who can speak Indian as well as the English
language, and the school is solely under the supervision and
control of the Department ... there will be a change for the
better."[18] Of the Methodist school, however, he wrote:

The band disagreed and divided in opinion and a bitter feeling
arose amongst them on the question of giving consent to grant
a piece of land in the centre of the reserve to the Methodist
Missionary Society, and one of the reasons ... was on account

of the school. They said they did not want it to be under the management of the mission, and they feared that an effort would be made to get control of the school if they ... established themselves on the school site ... they [objected to] the school being under the management of any society ... other than the Department.[19]

Ebenezer McColl's 1884 report to the department as inspector of the Manitoba superintendency shed more light on the dynamics of the meeting. He wrote:

In accordance with the instructions received from the Department, I summoned a meeting of the Indians to ascertain if the majority of them are favorable to surrendering to the Methodist Mission the ground within the Reserve whereon their present buildings are situated. Mr. Agent MacKay and the Reverends Messers. Ross and Parkinson together with the Chief and Councillors and all the resident members were present. After an exhaustive discussion ... a decision ... in favor of granting the request of the Mission [was made] by a two third vote.[20]

A year later, Angus MacKay told McColl in a letter dated 25 March 1885 that the mission school, taught by Miss Gussie Parkinson, was "poorly attended because parents want a government school instead." Seven treaty children (three being the chief's children) and two non-treaty children were in attendance. William and his brother Jacob, aged about fifteen and seventeen, were among the students and MacKay remarked that the two wrote and spelled very badly.[21] The government school had obviously closed with the continuation of the Methodist school and parents were still not only dissatisfied but were looking for other options. On 25 April 1885, MacKay wrote to McColl, saying:

After the closing of the Government School in Berens River, Miss Flett opened a private school at the request of the people of the Hudson's Bay Company Post, for the benefit of some White and

Treaty children of men belonging to the establishment. Many of the Indians asked for permission to send their children there also but Miss Flett refused them admittance lest it might be said that she was hindering them from attending the Mission school.[22]

On the Methodist side, the annual report of Rev. Enos Langford for the year 1884–85 is interesting. He explained that there had been no missionary at Berens River for the past four years with the exception of occasional visits from Rev. Andrew W. Ross from Fisher River. The Indians, he said, had been upset over the loss of their missionary.

> Last June [I] was appointed to take charge of the field. We were welcomed by the Indians, who said their prayers had been answered. They appeared ready to cooperate with us.... We had great hopes of a successful year. But through counter-influences the poor Indians were sadly perplexed and unnecessarily disturbed. We ... had fully expected the aid ... of all, Indians and whites.[23]

Langford's phrase that the Indians had "appeared ready to cooperate" is revealing. It seems that not *all* the Indians had been ready to cooperate! Were community members taking a vocal, active role in a situation that meant much to them? Had the Methodists simply assumed that these people would welcome a Protestant school wholeheartedly or taken for granted that any recalcitrant parents could be easily won over?

The interplay between missionaries and Ojibwa communities along the Berens River and native responses to aspects of Christianity may be traced in records of conversions and baptisms as well as in evidence of survivals of Ojibwa ideas and customs. Some interesting dynamics appear in the fluctuations in Methodist church membership at Berens River and Little Grand Rapids.

For Berens River, the first extant statistics begin in 1889 during the tenure of Rev. James Arthur McLachlan. His church membership increased steadily and rapidly from fifty-eight in 1893 to ninety-three by 1903. McLachlan was respected in the community and lived at Berens River long enough to win the support and confidence of the people. His large, sizzling 1897 revival especially spiked enrolment by twenty-five. McLachlan's tragic drowning along with six Berens River children rocked the community in 1903.

By 1909, membership had dropped from ninety-eight to eighty-six.[24] This was during the tenure of Rev. Arthur E. Okes (1907–1909) and his wife Jane. As noted earlier, they were not popular in Berens River.

Membership rose steadily during the ministries of Rev. Joseph Henry Lowes (1909–1916) and Rev. Percy Earl Jones (1916–1921), however. Jones's tenure saw a particularly abrupt jump of thirteen members in 1918.[25] This was the year of the influenza epidemic that killed many people in the community; it is possible that the crisis spurred some people towards conversion and baptism.

Membership continued to gradually increase between 1921 and 1928, moving from eighty-five to 117 members under Rev. John Niddrie's ministry (1921–1938). A particularly large increase occurred in 1923 with a leap of twenty-five converts.[26] The same year, the number of Methodist families in Berens River increased from fifty-one to fifty-seven. It is possible that new people moved into the community and were converted by Niddrie, or that existing Roman Catholic families changed denominations, but the records reveal no explanation of the rise. Between 1928 and 1934, Niddrie, it seems, did not preserve detailed records. His submission for 1936, however, shows that the membership in his mission had risen from 117 to 158.[27] Membership would only increase by two by 1940.

Although Methodist statistics for Little Grand Rapids do not begin until 1909, we know that Rev. McLachlan occasionally visited that community from Berens River until his death. William Ivens arrived to teach there in 1904.[28] Evidence suggests that the Ojibwa here were receptive to Ivens and interested in education. In 1904, S. J. Jackson, inspector of Indian agencies, reported from Little Grand Rapids, "The acting councillor and the band are very much pleased at the school opening and would like … to have a school house built."[29]

Joseph F. Woodsworth replaced Ivens in 1908; Joseph Jones took over in 1909 and was replaced by Rev. Roy Taylor who stayed for 1910. Statistics for 1909 submitted by Jones reflect a sudden drop in church membership which fell from fifty-four to zero.[30] Some major event must have caused fifty-four Ojibwa to leave the Methodist church and possibly made Jones leave that community almost immediately thereafter. Jones's biographies make no mention of his tenure at Little Grand Rapids and Methodist records are mute. In 1905, Rev. Thomas Neville had reported that William Ivens was working "among a really pagan people."[31] While Ojibwa resistance clearly prevailed here, the people seem to have also been open to Christian ideas since there was a significant enrolment in the church prior to the Jones year.

We know that McLachlan's 1897 winter revival had affected Little Grand Rapids. In his annual report that year, the missionary wrote:

Last winter this mission [Berens River] enjoyed a gracious revival, during which most of our young people professed conversion and united with the Church. As a consequence our work has been largely along the line of education and consolidation.... I visited the [Little Grand Rapids] Indians. A volunteer band [group] from Berens River accompanied me and did splendid work.... [now there is] a class of 20 members where none existed before.[32]

One possible explanation for the drop in church membership at Little Grand Rapids during Jones's tenure lies in the memoirs of Luther Schuetze. Discussing his own growing understanding and tolerance of the drum dancing at Little Grand Rapids, Schuetze mentioned that initially he, like a missionary before him (possibly Jones), had originally been very uncomfortable with the practice. This former missionary "saw in the drum dances something pagan, that had to be done away with, he took forcible action and kicked the drum in and said it was of the devil." It is likely that this kind of "forcible action" offended the entire community and resulted in the Ojibwa rejecting the mission.

In 1911, J. H. Wilding was in charge of the mission. Alfred G. Johnson replaced him in 1914. For the years between 1917 and 1923, Methodist records generally stated "native assistance" in their reports for Little Grand Rapids; in 1919, however, Mrs. Mary J. Nanakwap was named as teaching at the day school. It is possible that she was the native assistant referred to by the Methodists. No statistics are listed from 1909 to 1916 when we learn that apparently eight infant baptisms occurred and five marriages were solemnized that year.[33] It is not until 1919 that we see an increase from zero to twelve, bringing the total church membership to twelve.[34] Was Mary Nanakwap, an Ojibwa woman, responsible for the sudden 1919 success?[35] Did the threat of the 1918 influenza epidemic spur some Christian conversions in this community?

Significantly, Methodist church membership at Little Grand Rapids rose after the arrival of Luther Schuetze. Between 1931 and 1934, enrolment soared from twelve to 135.[36] By 1937, 148 Ojibwa belonged to the church, and forty-one children were enrolled in the Sunday school.[37] Schuetze was a dedicated and sincere man who spent many years among the Ojibwa in this community. Yet it is interesting that even *he* made no increase in church membership for five years; it likely took him this amount of time to establish trust and acceptance.

Along the Berens River between 1875 and 1916, we see a complex dialogue between missionaries and Ojibwa. It is important, however, to distinguish between syncretism and situations where Indians carried out both Christian and non-Christian activities in their daily lives. As Antonio Gualtieri explains, syncretism is "a ... radical form of culture encounter in which the traditions entailed are fused – either deliberately or, more usually unconsciously, over a period of time – into a novel emergent whose meanings and symbolic expressions are in some respects different from either of the original singular traditions."[38]

That native people accepted missionaries and aspects of Christianity on their own terms and at their own speed reverberates through the history of these encounters. At Berens River and Little Grand Rapids we see a growing involvement in Christianity among the people in the communities. On the surface, missionaries' reports seem confusing; in one paragraph they lament the persistence of pagan practices among native peoples and in another, often within the same document, they rejoice in the triumph of Christianity over heathenism. The heart of the issue was that missionaries expected conversion to automatically reorient native people to a Euro-Canadian agrarian and social life. Since this model contained no frames of reference for the social phenomena they witnessed along the Berens River, they could only interpret such phenomena as a failure of conversion and mission work.

The essential point here is that the Ojibwa had different responses at different times to different missionaries. Reasons for their acceptance of Christian ideas were many, and often depended on local circumstances or environmental factors. It was possible for a group or community to reject a missionary at one point and accept parts of his message on another occasion depending on local changes or events or the extent of the rapport with an individual missionary.

F. G. Stevens, for example, wrote of an 1898 encounter with the Sandy Lake Indians who "asked me to come the next year ... to teach them the Gospel." These people expressed genuine interest, telling him: "Once we men listened to the missionary [Edward Paupanikiss] at Island Lake and we allowed ourselves to be baptized and returning home we found we could not stand against the old people. So now we do not want to hear the Gospel unless all ... hear it with us."[39]

Sometimes, native people had other material reasons for being receptive to missionaries. Stevens wrote of an 1899 encounter with a group of Indians at Kiche Mut-ta-kwum (Big Teepee) who were starving. "They were heathen but longing to hear more of religion."[40] Rev. and Mrs. Stevens fed the people, talked with them and went on their way. Shortly, however, the missionaries were the ones to get into trouble; a shortage of food caused them to return to Big Teepee where they were grateful to get a bit of dried deer blood. "Next morning," wrote Stevens, "we tried to give them some religious instruction but it seemed almost hopeless."[41] When the Stevenses next met these Indians in 1900 they pressed in around them, hungry and asking for food and tobacco. Once again, they were interested in communication and trade.

Sucker clansman Robert Fiddler probably converted in the early 1900s because of treaty interests. The Island Lake Indians had been experiencing poverty from the late 1880s onward, and by 1891 were asking the government for a treaty, writing to Angus MacKay at Berens River. By 1909, the opportunity for negotiations was nigh and Robert Fiddler, leader of the Pelican, Sucker, and Crane clans at Island Lake, was thinking seriously about terms of a possible treaty.

Fiddler had a near brush with conversion while attending a prayer meeting led by Methodist missionary, A. H. Cunningham. His descendant Thomas Fiddler says that Robert had been very upset over Bible verses discussing punishment for sinners. "Robert amongst others," he explained, "were greatly shaken up, came near a crash but got away."[42] After what Thomas Fiddler described as "more Bible onslaught," Robert finally converted. His conversion led to the subsequent conversion of his "warriors" and Cunningham reported that "everything went from there in a flood time, they flocked in and around until I could not get away at night."[43]

It is interesting that, while Thomas Fiddler described Robert as "[breaking] ... under this onslaught against boreal belief," and sobbing, he also made it clear that the Suckers adopted Christianity in order to help them "gain sympathy with westerners in their [the Suckers'] quest for survival."[44] At least part of the reasons for conversion may have stemmed from these people's wish for a treaty. This is not to say that Robert Fiddler was insincere in his taking on of Methodism. It suggests, however, that reasons for conversion among northern Manitoba Indians could be multi-dimensional and complex.

Another story beautifully illustrates different responses made by different groups of Indians. In 1901, Stevens and his wife were en route to Island Lake from Oxford House when they met the Little Crane group who were in bad shape; four had recently starved to death and in a seeming response to trauma, "they all became Christians."[45] Also present were men from the Sucker Clan who, Stevens said, deceived them, saying to the missionaries, "We are sorry we did not know you would be here or we would have brought our women and children just like the Cranes." After the Stevenses left, they found that the Suckers had hidden their women and children across the portage; in his words, "They did not want to become Christians."[46]

Epidemics could also spur a leaning toward Christianity by groups who believed during a time of crisis that they needed all the spiritual power they could get. In his 1874–75 annual report for Berens River, E. R. Young wrote:

> An epidemic that raged during the winter months has been made a blessing to some of the people. The Missionary, while acting the part of a doctor, was able to recommend the Great Physician ... at a time when hearts, even of the obstinate ... were susceptible to religious truth. Some, alas, ... with returning health went back to their old ways, but others have remained true to their vows.[47]

And in 1894, James McLachlan wrote:

> Our people have passed through fiery trials this year in connection with the measles epidemic; but God has brought them out with a deepened Christian experience, that will be helpful in our future work. It has not all been sunshine, however: There have been many difficulties.... Evil influences from without [medicine men?] have been hard to meet and have greatly hindered the work.[48]

Conversion stories of individuals also show that some genuinely seemed to have been affected by the Christian message. Sandy Hartie, son of Nelson House chief John Hartie, was converted by Egerton Ryerson Young in 1871. According to Young and to John Semmens who later encountered Hartie, the young man was truly excited by the Gospel. In this case also, however, he had a need to take on the new religion. Accidentally shot in the leg while hunting, Hartie was carried to his father's camp where, "his homecoming was ... an unwelcome one."[49] His illness was, "a keenly felt burden to his family" who, to Rev. E. R. Young's surprise, brought the boy to Young's Rossville mission at Norway House. There, the boy received nursing, schooling and Christian education. Hartie was converted at an evangelical meeting and became an enthusiastic Methodist.[50]

At this time, Semmens passed through on his way to Nelson House to begin the first mission there; he remembered Sandy Hartie's invaluable help in teaching him Cree and Cree syllabics. The two went together to Nelson House where Hartie worked hard to round up the summer hunters, telling them that, "a teacher had arrived who would preach to them the truthfulness of the Great Spirit."[51] Many responded by bringing their canoes and going to hear Semmens preach thanks, in large part, to the efforts of Hartie.

Conversion to Christianity did not necessarily generate a loss of faith in Ojibwa religion and medicine. While Jacob Berens did, on his conversion, cast away his medicines sometime during his mid-twenties, he did not cast away his faith or belief. This became apparent years later when his son, William, had a severely injured knee. A medical doctor in Winnipeg extracted two grains of shot and two pieces of metal from the wound, but the knee refused to heal. The mystery was that the young man had never been shot in his life. Jacob could not explain this to the Winnipeg doctor and therefore lost no time in taking William to a medicine man – in this case his brother Albert. Although Jacob would not perform the cure himself, he gave Albert tobacco for his services, saying, "I know you are pretty good ... but I'll tell you what medicine to use."[52] Jacob, however, was able to clearly explain the cause to his minister, telling James McLachlan, "You white people don't believe it. But I've told you about such things. This is through an Indian's magic power."[53]

Percy Berens talked about Jacob's conversion and subsequent casting off of his conjuring practises:

S.G. Do you know people who weren't Christians and then decided to become Christians?

P.B. Yeah. My grandfather, Jacob, he wasn't a religious fellow.... He was a man who believed on nature. Conjuring is the right word – conjuring. He was a conjuring man, my grandfather. When the religion came to Berens River, the missionaries, you know, want him to quit. So he packed up parcels of tobacco and he got two men to take this to Jackhead. He sent it out to the Jackhead conjuror, you know? It was given out. He was letting all this thing go, conjuring. He sent it to Bloodvein, Jackhead, Little Grand Rapids, even Deer Lake – that's 300 miles from Berens River to go to Deer Lake. He sent guys there to take that tobacco, he's finished with it.

S.G. So he converted?

P.B. So he was converted.

S.G. What did that mean for him?

P.B. It changed his life altogether. He didn't believe none of that stuff that he had believed.... He's getting over with that.

S.G. Why did he want to convert?

P.B. Because I guess the missionary was preaching the *gospel* and he believed what he heard so he thought he had to let it go, his conjuring. That's why he quit.[54]

Clearly, Jacob let his conjuring go out of a conscious choice that he was required to make upon his baptism; however, he and his children never lost their faith in the reality and validity of this magic and its power. At no time did they decide that their beliefs constituted shallow superstitions. The rejection of conjuring was likely done out of a respect for Christianity and perhaps some fear of the repercussions of the "dark side" of this kind of magic.

In the same vein, William Berens, out of respect to his Christian faith, chose not to go on a vision quest; this did not mean, however, that he did not believe that it would be entirely possible for him at any time to do this and acquire a *pawágan*. Percy discussed the family dynamics that centred around this issue.

> S.G.   I know that William told Hallowell that *he* could have gone on a vision quest but, because he was a Methodist, he chose not to. *But* he always felt that any time he wanted, he could have met up with his *pawáganak*. Did he really believe that?
>
> P.B.   Oh yeah – oh yeah! He talked to us family about it. He could have been like that because his dad used to ask him to believe the same as this conjuring business. He wanted to hand it over to him, but dad said that "I wouldn't want it."
>
> S.G.   Jacob asked William to take that on?
>
> P.B.   Yeah.
>
> S.G.   Because he was in line for it?
>
> P.B.   Sure – it was Jacob's son. But my dad said "no."
>
> S.G.   Did that upset Jacob?
>
> P.B.   No. It's okay. He never used to say his dad got mad at him because he turned that down. He [Jacob] said "that's yours, that's your choice – so do what you like."[55]

Discussing his own decision to follow Christianity, William was clear, telling Hallowell "When the missionary Egerton Young came and preached to us about the love of God and his Son, I wanted to understand what this man was talking about. Finally I got enough sense to believe in Christianity. A lot of others had the same experience."[56] Methodism played an important role throughout his lifetime and he raised his children within the church. At no time, however, did he cease to believe in the existence of spirits or lose respect for or deny the power of Ojibwa religion.

The conversion and baptism of the medicine man Sowanas (South Wind) during the tenure of John Semmens is another interesting example of retention of belief in things Ojibwa. Sowanas's words reveal a quest for knowledge and an idea that the Gospel could provide an extra safeguard for the afterlife:

> I have lived many years in sin. I have served the Devil.... In witchcraft I was chief of all the people here. In medicine work I have long led the van [been in the forefront]. My pagan countrymen look up to me as the priest of my tribe.... Now I wish to put all evil from me and learn wisdom before I die. My children and my wife are baptized. They have gone their way and I have gone mine, but my heart tells me ... I ... am wrong. I have listened to scriptural teaching and ... I feel most anxious to be saved after the Gospel fashion. It seems to be my only hope.... Perhaps the Indians will follow me in right paths after they have gone in wrong directions. At any rate, I will try by divine help to set them a good example.... I am [hoping] ... I may at least attain to everlasting life.[57]

Semmens may, of course, have added to or embellished the speech either for dramatic appeal or because memories can change over time. It is likely that Sowanas wanted to be baptized, but it is difficult to know how many things were phrased in a way that would be acceptable to Semmens; after all, if the missionary were not convinced of the Ojibwa's motivation, he could refuse baptism. Sowanas had been observing "conversion-style" rhetoric for many years and would have known the right things to say. The old man could well have been concerned about the afterlife and believed that Christianity would indeed provide an additional safeguard in eternity. It is also likely that he was under some pressure to convert because his family had become Christians; conversions sometimes followed along kinship lines with converted family urging their "pagan" relatives to convert.

We *do* know, however, that this medicine man was an influential and respected leader in his community, living at a time when Christianity was becoming a force to be reckoned with at Berens River. It is entirely possible that his union with this religion would keep Sowanas on the van. We also know, if Semmens can be believed, that after 4 February 1877, Sowanas buried his medicine in the swamp. According to the missionary, "his deportment wholly changed … his heathen practices were abolished forever."[58] Did this casting off of his medicines, however, show that he no longer believed in Ojibwa medicine? Not likely.

Government and missionary records are full of stories showing that Christianity and Ojibwa beliefs coexisted along the Berens River. The Ojibwa ability to integrate these seemingly disparate concepts confused, angered, and upset many a missionary who expected a shedding of the old and a wholehearted acceptance of the new. Jacob and William Berens, and doubtless other Ojibwa, made a critical distinction, however, that the missionaries would not have appreciated. For converted Ojibwas, *practising* traditional medicine was incompatible with Christianity; *believing* in the powers of traditional medicine was not. This distinction was one of the essential ways in which Saulteaux people harmonized their world view with Christianity.

Varying degrees of acceptance of Christianity between communities, and even among different individuals within those communities, present challenges for observers who wish to make generalizations about Christian conversions on the basis of historical records. While one report may complain of members of a community pursuing a nomadic lifestyle or engaging in "pagan practices," another contemporary document may detail these same Indians congregating at the mission on special days, attending church, or baptizing their children with consistency.

If Berens River people looked positively on some aspects of some missionaries' messages, that did not mean that they were willing to abandon their beliefs wholesale at the behest of preachers. For example, in 1876, E. R. Young reported that, while Christianity was positively received by the Berens River community, it had not been deeply internalized. In 1875, he had written happily that at Berens River "every conjuring drum has ceased to beat and every outward pagan rite has been given up."[59] His report for the next year, however, showed that Ojibwa identity was alive and well; these people were hardly becoming lost in their Christianity. Said Young:

> Not only has the outward appearance of degrading paganism disappeared, but there is now an almost universal belief in our holy religion and, on the part of many, an earnest desire to ... understand the plan of salvation.... While rejoicing, we have to mourn over the absence of that thorough heart-work, the genuine conversion of the inner man by the transforming power of the Holy Ghost.[60]

Two years later, John Semmens reported in the same vein:

> From many a wigwam where, but a few short months ago, idols were worshipped and demons invoked, ascend with ... regularity, the songs and petitions of awakened men. Childish lips have learned to lisp, "Our Father which art in Heaven".... The change has not been so deep as I could wish ... but ... ground has been broken. The soil of their hearts is now ready for the good seed.[61]

Generally, the Berens River community seems to have responded positively to mission efforts with the people partaking in church life to varying degrees. Especially by 1899, numerous favourable reports indicated that the Ojibwa there were pleased with James McLachlan. J. W. Short, Indian agent, wrote in 1898 that Methodist services were well attended.[62] The next year, Ebenezer McColl commented that McLachlan "having contended ... against immorality [has] raised the standard of virtue on the reserve."[63]

John Semmens's 1901 report indicated an interest in Christianity but shows that it did not abound to the exclusion of all else: "I found in every place much regard for the knowledge and worship of God. In two or three places vestiges of an hereditary paganism were found, places where bigamy was tolerated and idol-worship was practised. Yet even there might be discovered a hunger for better things."[64]

Following the McLachlan tragedy, observers found that the Christianity of many people at Berens River was genuine and integrated into their lives. S. J. Jackson, Inspector of Indian agencies, noted that "The Indians of this band ... show the effects of their early religious training and put to shame many of our so-called Christian people. Every night before going to their beds they hold a short service of prayer.... They felt very bad over the loss [of Rev. McLachlan and the children]."[65] By 1908, Semmens could report that "The natives are more or less favourably disposed toward Christianity, and not a few are devout members of ... the missionary enterprise."[66]

The Ojibwa continued to adhere to native medicinal practices and the beliefs surrounding them, however. For example, in 1877–78, fear spread among the Berens River Indians of poisonings by medicine men. On 9 November 1877, Alexander Morris, Lieutenant-Governor of Manitoba, sent a dispatch to the deputy minister of justice about the alleged poisonings, or fear of poisonings at Berens River, perpetuated by a Mrs. Bains. This sparked a major investigation and nothing could be proven despite her reputation for "dealing extensively in what the Indians call 'bad medicine.'" In March 1878, Roderick Ross asked F. Graham, acting Indian superintendent for Manitoba, to initiate legislation "for the speedy suppression of a custom that is constantly being presented to the attention of traders and missionaries who live among Indians." Ross wrote that the whole "bad medicine" issue could be divided into two areas; the "higher branch ... professes to give ... them ... the power of taking human life ... or incapacitating an enemy from killing game, catching fish, or running or walking.... This superstition [is] firmly believed in by all Indians ... and causes a state of terrorism ... that generally impedes the advancement of natives in ... civilized habits of life."[67] The second branch involved a bona fide poisoning through the use of a powder that "only the Indians of southern Saulteaux tribes know how to make ... they sell it for a lot of money to the

northern Indians."[68] The continuance of the manufacture and sales
of native medicines shows the continuing vitality of Ojibwa belief
in the power of traditional cures and the validity of medicine
men.

Certainly, a strong Ojibwa world view prevailed between 1875
and 1916. Records show that Ojibwa people were still practising
polygamy in the 1890s. A report by Ebenezer McColl in 1893
bitterly railed against this. McColl complained that "the law
is impotent to inflict punishment upon ... transgressors for ...
unfaithfulness; consequently this loathsome and infectious moral
leprosy is contaminating Indian communities, destroying the
chastity of the virtuous."[69]

In her reminiscences of Berens River, Julia Asher (neé Short)
wrote of living with her Indian agent father in the community
between 1898 and 1900. Julia remembered the Methodist church
being full on Sundays and the friendly relations between her
family and the Berenses. One evening, Jacob told her a legend
of the windigo, adding that most of the older Indians believed in
windigos despite the church's teaching against their existence.
"Christianized as they were," she wrote, "this belief ... lingered
on, even in our time.... We had two indications of it on our
Reserve while I was there."[70]

At Little Grand Rapids, the Ojibwa world view still prevailed
widely. Belief in medicine men, polygamy, and Saulteaux
ceremonies abounded. Writing about both Berens River and
Little Grand in 1880, Rev. A. W. Ross lamented, "We ... cannot
speak encouragingly of these polygamous bands and yet there is a
longing to hear the Word."[71]

W. M. Chapman, the Hudson's Bay Company trader at Little
Grand Rapids, observed numerous continuing Ojibwa practices
there. In October 1912, for example, he wrote "Many Indians
are attending a dog-feast," and the next month mentioned "The
people are very noisy at L. G. Rapids. They beat their drum
all night."[72] On 2 August 1913, Chapman wrote: "John Duck
conjuring during the night and early hours of the morning.... He
had some very vigorous wrestling inside the tent and the birch

bark 'temple' nearly pulled down on several occasions."[73] Again in 1915: "the dog-feast takes place tonight, incessant drumming until early Sunday morning."[74]

Integrations of Christianity with the Ojibwa religion sometimes produced vivid instances of syncretism. William Berens related an experience to A. Irving Hallowell that represents one of the most fascinating examples of this blending. William saw and interpreted the event within a distinctly Ojibwa context. At the same time, he found the solution to the crisis in Christianity. William and Nancy Berens were fishing at the mouth of Poplar River when one evening, around six o'clock, William felt as if he was going crazy.

> I could hardly see the lamp. When it got later, I was worse and worse. Finally I had to tell my [hired] man to tie me up and throw me in the cellar – to nail it up and take my wife to the mission house.... Both of them were scared. They did not know what to do, did not wish to do as I said.... All of a sudden I thought of something – we had the Bible in the house. I took it and opened it and tried to read it. I could make out nothing. The first word I made out was God; as soon as I did, things got brighter it seemed.[75]

Even in everyday life we have evidence of integrations between the Ojibwa and Christian world views. Typical was the 1903 report of John Semmens who wrote, "not infrequently [medical complications] are brought on by the combined use of Indian and white medicines.... The morality of these people is not sufficiently developed to merit high praise. This is the outcome of old associations and old methods of living.... It is not easy to correct wrongs which are winked at by the elders of the tribe."[76]

Along with integrations, syncretic blends also occurred along the Berens River yielding creative and novel results.[77]

A striking example of syncretism can be found in the life of Adam Fiddler. In 1901, as a young man, Christ appeared to him in a dream while he was on a trip with F. G. Stevens and from then on, according to Thomas Fiddler, "Christ became an other-than-human guide."[78] Thomas describes Adam as

> cautious in his acceptance of Christianity. He did not discard what he found good and necessary in his forest beliefs and he is not described as being a Holy Man among the clansmen rather than a Methodist Christian. Adam Fiddler was a Sucker clansman who could confront windigo, utilize the shaking tent, issue prophecies, and sing over the drum. Adam Fiddler was more than a Christian. Adam's adoption of some Christian beliefs, though, did start a process of change away from some of the ancient ways.[79]

More syncretism can be seen in the life of Fair Wind (Naamiwan), a medicine man at Pauingassi, Manitoba. After 1914, he became a noted religious innovator.[80] His close connections with other-than-humans and a deep kinship with the Thunderbirds made him an exceptional hunter. Interestingly, as his religious influence grew, Fair Wind drew increasingly on a broad range of concepts that were "both Ojibwa and non-Ojibwa, Christian and non-Christian, whose roots lay a long way from Berens River."[81] Fair Wind's drum dance, the inspiration of which came to him in a dream, represented this kind of merging of ideas. The ceremony appalled missionary F. G. Stevens who saw it as threatening and pagan; viewing religion in black and white, Stevens saw those around him as either with the devil or with Christ. However, when Hallowell observed this dance of consolation in the 1930s, he recorded Fair Wind's words: "When a person has lost a brother, child, or some other relative, we call upon them to look down upon us. They have been on this earth once, and before that they were sent from above to come on this earth. Jesus, too, came from above to be the boss of the earth."[82] Hallowell saw that, at the conclusion of the dancing, the group sang a Christian hymn, Fair Wind lifted his hand in Christian benediction style and mentioned Jesus once again. The anthropologist was curious about which spirit had given Fair Wind his dance and asked if it had come to him from the *djibaiyak* (spirits of the dead) or from a *pawágan* (dream helper).

Neither, replied the medicine man: it had come to him from God. To Hallowell, "this dance ... illustrates extremely well how diverse strands of belief and practice can be wielded together under the influence of a strong personality, and yet still be kept within the framework of the Saulteaux interpretation of the universe."[83]

An interesting alternative interpretation of the origin of the drum dance is pursued by Maureen Matthews and Roger Roulette. They suggest that Hallowell's use of the word "God" may have been a translation problem. They suggest, on the basis of linguistic evidence, that a Thunderbird gave the gift to Naamiwan.[84]

William Berens embodied an excellent example of syncretism; throughout his life he felt a profound regard for the power of Ojibwa religion while, at the same time, maintaining respect for Methodism and ministers. Even as a young man this was present. Before he became chief, William visited a missionary he knew at Emerson, Manitoba, Rev. McHaffie, who had been at Fisher River and travelled with him in North Dakota. William told Hallowell that he went into the Pembina Hotel "for dinner and some drinks besides.... I was very careful not to overload myself because I was travelling with a minister and was staying with him."[85] Noteworthy here is that, years later, in reminiscing with the anthropologist, Berens remembered the sensitivity he had felt towards a man of the cloth.

Another brief clue is found later in William's "Reminiscences" to Hallowell. He had just returned to Berens River after a trip. "When we got to Mr. Short's place ... I asked him if the celebration was over at the church, so he told me, 'I just came from there – it's just over.' I was disappointed that I was not there."[86] This is one small statement in a substantial manuscript, yet its very inclusion and simple sincerity have real impact.

In discussing missions to native peoples in colonial North America, James Axtell points out that Christianity added to the cosmology of many groups, giving them an explanation of the new and larger world.[87] The Ojibwa along the Berens River, while experiencing changes and adaptations in their religious life, also guided these changes and influenced the speed at which they occurred between 1875 and 1916. At the same time, offering a parallel to what Northrop Frye said of his Methodism, the world view at their core remained essentially Ojibwa.

Jacob and Mary (nee McKay) Berens, Berens River, c. 1915 (personal collection of Darlene Rose Overby. Used by permission).

Treaty payments, Berens River, c. 1925 (PAM, Berens River 3, N3581).

Shaking tent, Little Grand Rapids, c. 1933 (PAM, Indians 81, N10757).

John Duck and his Wabano pavilion, at or near Little Grand Rapids, c. 1933 (PAM, Indians 83, N22310).

*Wabeno pavilion at or near Little Grand Rapids,
c. 1933 (PAM, Indians 82, N18635).*

*Boys at desk, Pikangikum (United Church Archives, Conference
of Manitoba and Northwestern Ontario, Album No. 4).*

Ojibwa camp at Pikangikum (United Church Archives, Conference of Manitoba and Northwestern Ontario, Album No. 1).

Luther Schuetze's congregation, Little Grand Rapids (United Church Archives, Conference of Manitoba and Northwestern Ontario, Album No. 1).

Mission house and interpreter, Pikangikum (United Church Archives, Conference of Manitoba and Northwestern Ontario, Album No. 4).

Little girls with mother, Pikangikum (United Church Archives, Conference of Manitoba and Northwestern Ontario, Album No. 1).

Luther Schuetze and his wife, Augusta, Little Grand Rapids (United Church Archives, Conference of Manitoba and Northwestern Ontario, Album No. 4).

Pikangikum congregation (many members were absent due to sturgeon fishing). (United Church Archives, Conference of Manitoba and Northwestern Ontario, Album No. 1).

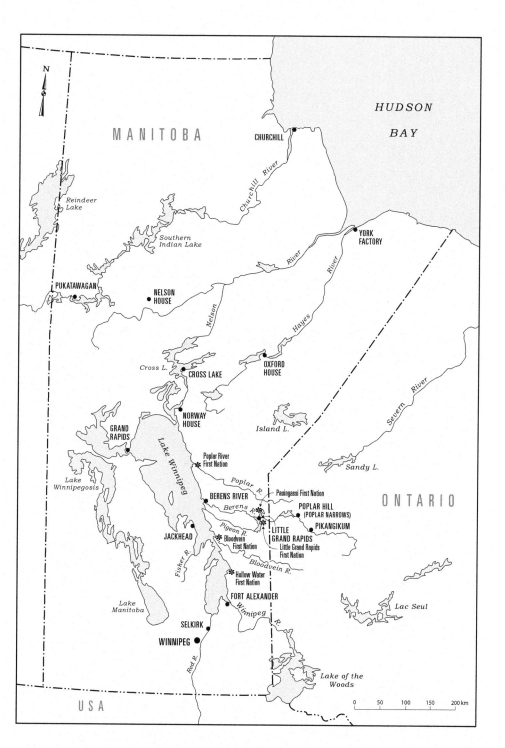

Berens family chart

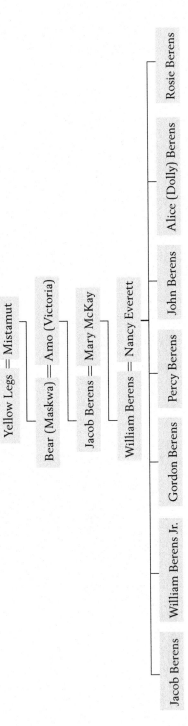

5   "I Got Pretty Close to the Flames that Time; Then I Woke Up"

Acceptances and Rejections, 1917–1940

....

We smoke our pipes west – all the directions – north, east
– because we see a big cloud and where's it coming up from?
This moving cloud! What's going to happen? All of a sudden
it's like a *bomb*, eh? If you smoke, the thunder cloud will go
past. The Thunderbirds. Many moons. Love your neighbour as
you love yourself. Listening to the white people today, you hear
Thunderbirds come when there's cold air with hot air. No way.
Young Thunderbirds in the fall, they're just like – oh! they make a
really loud noise![1]

James Axtell observes that colonial North American native people
converted to Christianity because it provided a solution to urgent
social and religious questions. In the praying towns that sprang up
across New England, Indians used Christianity in the same ways
they would have used a native revitalization led by a prophet – as a
means of surviving their present and by which they could secure a
new lease on the future. Did this represent a tragic loss for native
peoples? A loss, yes, explains Axtell, a tragic loss, no. Tragedy
would only be apparent were we to view pre-contact Indians as
the only *real* Indians (a view which comes dangerously close to
embodying the noble savage stereotype).[2]

    Between 1917 and 1940, many Ojibwa people living in reserve
communities along the Berens River accepted Christianity and

subsequently converted to this religion. There were also instances in which Christianity was rejected.

In 1917, William Berens succeeded his father, Jacob, as chief of Berens River. The community had been under treaty for forty-two years, the Methodists had been established among the people for forty-three years and the Catholic mission would be in full swing the following year. A. Irving Hallowell considered these river-mouth folk to be heavily acculturated due to prolonged and sustained contact with Euro-Canadian culture. A closer look suggests, however, that there was not a simple "one-way progression involving cultural loss and replacement," but rather the story of "a far more complex complementarity or fusion."[3]

By 1917, the Methodist day school had become a fixture on the Berens River Reserve. The people in the community, and particularly the Berens family, had taken an active role in this institution from the beginning. Near the end of Jacob Berens's life and tenure as chief, Berens, through Inspector Bunn, requested that the Department of Indian Affairs hire a competent, preferably older teacher to replace the missionary. Although this may have reflected an effort on his part to aid the Methodists in their selection of a teacher, the partnership itself is of significance.[4]

It is, of course, important not to generalize too much about the feelings and opinions of the entire community based on the actions of the Berens family. Jacob Berens had always been in the vanguard when it came to matters of conversion, education, and the integration of aspects of Ojibwa and Euro-Canadian lifestyles. Even amid the ado over the Methodist versus government school issue in the 1880s, Jacob, although displeased with the situation, continued to send his sons to the Methodist day school. His boys made up two of its only seven students. This attitude had an impact on William; he and his wife, Nancy, valued education encouraging their children to attend school and learn as much as they could. Education, they realized, was the way of the future and learning was a thing to be valued.

Percy Berens remembered this clearly. William and Nancy sent him on to the Brandon Industrial School after his years at the Berens River Methodist day school had come to an end. Decades later, his enthusiasm for this learning experience was still obvious.

S.G.   What was the Brandon Industrial School like?
P.B.   Oh, they taught us everything!
S.G.   Did you enjoy it?
P.B.   I *really* enjoyed it. I learned a lot of things. You know why Indian Affairs shut that place down? Because the Indians were getting too smart.
S.G.   Why did your parents send you to the Industrial school?
P.B.   So that I could have an education.[5]

Although attendance was irregular at the Methodist and Catholic schools, it is important not to infer Ojibwa attitudes simply from statistics and the laments of teachers and agents.[6] Jacob and William Berens valued education, yet their children did not attend school on a regular basis throughout the year. William, and later, his children were present at school when their lifestyle made this possible and convenient; for outsiders to decide that these people did not value education because they attended school irregularly is shortsighted. Rather, this is another example of the Ojibwa at Berens River selecting and adopting aspects of Euro-Canadian life that they found necessary and important within their own frameworks. The continual balancing of many different priorities was an ongoing fact of life for Berens River people.

Statistics show that average attendance remained fairly stable. Families followed a pattern alternating between time spent in the bush and time spent in the community. When they were on the reserve, children, for the most part, attended school quite regularly (with average attendance remaining fairly consistent). The tables located at the end of this chapter, created from data in the reports for Indian Affairs in the Canadian *Sessional Papers*, reveal a fairly steady pattern of attendance.

Interestingly, while the Berens River Catholic school was in a minority position compared to the Methodist school, the Catholic school upriver at Little Grand Rapids seems to have run neck and neck with its Protestant competition. At Berens River, the Protestants had gained a firm foothold and ensconced themselves three decades before the Catholics made overtures. The fact that Chiefs Jacob and William Berens were staunch supporters of the Methodist church may have slowed Catholic advances at Berens River to some degree. Perhaps also, William, as chief, had some problems with a religion that was in rivalry with his own denomination of Christianity and which could undermine his authority. Whatever the reasons, there was always a coolness, still evident today, towards Catholicism on the part of the Berens family.

An example of this attitude can be seen in a dream that William Berens related to A. Irving Hallowell in the 1930s. The dream (c. 1917) predicted the coming of the Roman Catholics to Berens River just before their arrival. It is clear that William, whose Methodist loyalties certainly showed themselves here, was operating within an entirely Ojibwa context in his faith in dreams as accurate vehicles of foreshadowing and prediction. Finally, William's interpretive comments to Hallowell revealed an attitude that seemed to be typical among the Indians along the Berens River – a sense of thinking about and listening to different religious messages, selecting those elements that were sensible, necessary, or desirable and disregarding the rest.

I had this dream before the Catholics started their mission here. I had 4 or 5 children at the time. I dreamed that I was close to the place where the wood pile of the Hudson's Bay Co. now stands. Two Catholic priests were holding me, one on each side. Another Indian was there too (named). One of the priests took his head off. There he stood without any head. I was fighting them but they dragged me off towards where the Catholic mission now stands. We came to a big furnace and these priests tried to push me into it. At the same time there was an old man who stuck his head out of the flames and tried to pull me in. But they were not able to get me in. I kept on fighting them and they dragged me to another place where there was another furnace. There the same thing happened. An old man stuck his head out and tried to pull me in while the priests tried to push me in. This old man had a spear. I got pretty close to the flames that time: then I woke up.[7]

Hallowell noted that "The dreamer commented that he now knew the meaning of the dream. It gave him foreknowledge of the struggle with the Catholics in which he is engaged. The first incident shows that the priests can do what they want with Indians who do not think for themselves. They can put any ideas in your head they want to."[8]

Ida Green, William and Nancy's niece, grew up with the Berens family after they adopted her in 1918 (her mother, Sarah Everett, Nancy's sister, died in the 1918 influenza epidemic). She shed some revealing light on William and Nancy's attitude to the Oblate mission at Berens River.

I.G. I was baptized when I was a baby – Catholic. I didn't know that 'till my Auntie Margaret told me that. She said "You should go to church over there." That's where I belongs to. I said "No, I don't like that." Because I don't like that, to go to church there.

S.G. Why not?

I.G. Well, I don't know – I don't like it. One reason that I don't like it – you know when you take the Sacrament? You have to tell everything to that minister. That's why I don't like it.

S.G. Confession?

I.G. Yeah. Because God sees me what I'm doing – God – don't let anybody else know.

S.G. What would William and Nancy have done if you had decided to go to the Catholic Church?

I.G. They wouldn't have let me go over there. They didn't like that church.

S.G. Why? How do you know they didn't like it?

I.G.   Because they didn't let me go to church [there] – just in
       here – the United Church.
S.G.   Did you ever ask them if you could go to the Catholic
       Church?
I.G.   No, because they didn't like that kind of a church. If they
       would like it, they would have let me go to church over
       there....
S.G.   Did your father ever have Brother Leach or Father De
       Grandpré visit him in his home?
I.G.   Well, Father De Grandpré came and saw me here – after
       I was married. And so he said "Why don't you come to
       church?" I said – I made an excuse [Ida, in typical Ojibwa
       fashion, refused to confront De Grandpré directly], you
       know – I said I got nothing to take me over there and it's a
       long walk because, you know, I couldn't leave my kids alone,
       because Gordon [Ida's husband] was playing the organ in
       the United Church every Sunday so I was alone in here.[9]

Percy Berens also subtly expressed some disdain, despite his
positive memories of Frederick Leach. He explained why Catholic
Ojibwa people in the community ventured to Rev. Niddrie's
afternoon services at the United Church.

P.B.   the service in the afternoon was altogether different from
       the kind of service they had. The United Church preached
       from the Bible and they knew that, see?
S.G.   So they wanted to hear the Bible?
P.B.   Sure!
S.G.   Would you say they wanted both churches?
P.B.   No. They wanted to learn what *really* comes out of the
       Bible, see? That's what they wanted to know. And they
       wanted to *hear* Niddrie preaching – what kind of a sermon
       he preaches about.[10]

Berens River elders who were children in the 1920s and 1930s
emphasize that the community valued its schools and missionaries.

Just as William and Nancy Berens were good friends with Percy Jones, older residents of the community remember Rev. John Niddrie, teacher Colin Street, and Brother Frederick Leach with warmth. Percy Berens says that Colin Street "was the best teacher that ever taught school in Berens River. He was the longest teacher that ever been in that schoolhouse. Because some teachers just came in for a year and said 'oh, to heck with the Indians.' Not like Street."[11]

Some of the stories take on a humorous vein. Fred Baptiste remembered being a pupil of Colin Street.

> S.G. Did you know Colin Street?
>
> F.B. Yeah, I knew him! He was the teacher right here – he was a good teacher! He strapped me once [laughter]. He caught me smoking [laughter]! He strapped me right on my hand I guess and – well, he didn't like tobacco. *But,* later on, I was working on this old boat – this old Keenora – and then I seen him [Street] in Winnipeg and Walter Green said "Freddie, come here!" We were loading freight – we were right in the Redwood dock. He seen somebody coming down the hill there, coming to see us – and he was smoking a pipe! "*Boy,* Mr Street," I said, "you strapped me once at school for smoking tobacco and now here you are out of school and you're smoking tobacco!" Well, what happened to him, he told me, the doctor told him to use that tobacco for his own good.[12]

Walter Green also had poignant and revealing memories about the place of the church and school in the lives of himself and his family.

> S.G. What do you remember about school?
>
> W.G. Well, the school was very good – I liked it. C. D. Street was such a good teacher. He was kind. He really didn't push the kids to learn, he helped them. Because it doesn't help to push. I've been in the United Church all my life.

S.G.   What do you remember about church and the ministers?

W.G.   Well, the church – I must have been about five or six years
old – I went to church with my aunt. The church was one
special day for the people. Everybody would go to church.
Saturday, they would cut all the wood, take it inside and get
ready everything so they wouldn't have anything to do on
Sunday. They would put their axes away, they would put
their guns away, they would put their hunting knives away.
All they thought about on Sunday was going to church.

S.G.   Why was church so important?

W.G.   Well that's what they believed, you know – that's one day
they have to respect and honour because it's Sunday – rest
day. The minister that baptized me was Jones. I remember
Niddrie really well. He was the best minister we ever had.
He used to invite me or some of the boys to supper or to
work for him, like cutting wood, hauling wood, and all that
in the winter. And in the summer I would go there and hoe
his garden and get all the weeds out.

S.G.   When he invited you for supper, what were those evenings
like?

W.G.   Oh, we used to sit and talk. That's how I learned a little bit
of English.[13]

The church was also an important part of life for Percy Berens as
he was growing up. Like Walter, Percy spoke with respect for the
church and Christianity.

S.G.   Percy, your Dad and Mom were in church most times?

P.B.   Oh yeah!

S.G.   And did you like that? Did you like going to church?

P.B.   Oh yeah! I'll explain this. At funerals and weddings,
the church was full because people respected that, they
respected that. Not like today, no respect at all for anything.

S.G.   Why did they respect things like that back then?

P.B.   Because they go to church – and the missionary would
explain what a married life means, the promises you're

making when you're taking the vows on the wedding, see? They wanted to explain.[14]

Responding to the idea that many Ojibwa people believe in both the Thunderbirds and the Bible, he spoke with respect for Christianity and placed a high value on understanding the Bible. "Yeah, but the Bible is best. If you *really* explain it to an Indian what that Bible really means and what's in the Bible, the Scriptures, like – then they'll be able to believe it, see? That's the trouble, nobody ever comes along to explain it properly."[15] A strong and prevalent theme that arises in many discussions with Ojibwa people occurs in the reminiscences of William Berens. This is the great emphasis placed on understanding; without proper understanding there can be no real belief. When asked why William spent so much time reading his Bible, Percy explained that "He wanted to learn! I know many a time I read it for him when he was getting short-sighted."[16]

Fred Baptiste's family always went to church because, as he put it simply, "They believed in God."[17]

S.G.   I have the impression that when you were young a lot of people went to church. Why did they do this?

F.B.   Well, they all wanted to listen to the preaching – the stories about Jesus, all that stuff that's in the Bible. That's why we used to have a Sunday school, the teacher's going to tell those kids about the Bible. In church on Sundays up at the front in the first two rows there was the school kids, they sat up there listening on Sundays. When somebody died, Mr. Street would let us come to the church if it was a school day.

S.G.   Street would close the school if there was a burial?

F.B.   Yes. We would all go to the church and sit at the front.[18]

To Fred's mind, people he knew who had made decisions to become Christians and join the church did so because "They wanted to bring up their children proper like, you know?"[19]

By the 1920s and 1930s, Christianity seems to have been integrated into the community enough for it to serve as a standard for what was proper, acceptable, and right. In the case of Berens River, this grew from the strong relationships forged between missionaries and a good many of the people as well as the degree to which committed missionaries were able to work consistently and over a long period with the Ojibwa.

Betsey Patrick discussed this integration and teamwork between missionary and community.

S.G.   What did the people think of Niddrie?

B.P.   They all liked that old missionary.

S.G.   Why do you think that was?

B.P.   I couldn't tell you exactly why they liked him so much. He used to keep boys there – he used to keep boys in that house, you know. And those boys, they were all good organ players, they all played at church. One was my cousin and another was a Green boy and there was an Everett boy. So they used to take turns in church, you know?

S.G.   Who taught them to play the organ?

B.P.   Well, that was him, that old man. And of course that Annie, that niece of his was really good.... What I really think ... the kids in those days really weren't that bad, they weren't bad when they were with the religious institutions. Like this Mr. Street, you know, we went to school for awhile when we were here. And in the morning when he used to go into the class, he used to say the prayers and we'd read one chapter [of the Bible], you know, St. John or – not a lot, just a little one, you know, each child. And then, after that, we used to sing *Oh Canada* and then we'd start to work. Nowadays they don't teach them no prayers at all – they get into mischief, this sniffing business [glue sniffing] and everything, they steal, break in. And before, we used to pray. The nuns used to teach them what's not good, what's bad and what's good. What they should do at the school, they should get the missionaries to go at least on Fridays and teach the kids.

S.G. So it was the ministers themselves who gave the stability? Or do you think it was the prayer that gave the stability?

B.P. Well, I think it was just that they gave them good discipline. They'd take all the kids and talk to them good and all that and tell them good. Of course some nowadays say they're so bad, but for me I couldn't say nothing [bad]. They taught me good, they taught me everything – how to knit, how to sew and everything. And if you listen to your supervisors and listen to them carefully, they'll teach you, and do that. Teach you not to be ignorant.[20]

Betsey's parents sent their children to church regularly because "They told us that's good for you to go and listen to the preaching."[21] She also, however, suggested another reason for a high degree of church attendance at Berens River. Her mother grew up with Jacob Berens, her grand uncle, and in his household everyone went to church regularly.

B.P. In the olden days, the old people used to go to church all the time. [Looks at a Berens family picture.] You know, I used to visit these old people long ago. You know they used to have church in the morning, church in the afternoon – so those old people used to go twice a day to church.

S.G. Why did they do that?

B.P. I don't know! They had nothing to do on Sundays – might as well go to church. Even on New Year's Eve, you know, they used to get up at eleven o'clock and go to church and they'd have night watch, you know?[22]

Catholic Ojibwa people living in the Berens River community also experienced their church as a substantial part of their lives as they grew up. Virginia Boulanger remembered that there were always many people in church on Sundays. Her father, James MacKay (Indian Agent Angus MacKay's son) and mother,

Catherine Goosehead (an Ojibwa woman) owned a store where, Virginia says, they worked very hard. She explains that it was especially important to Catherine, who had attended the Brandon Industrial School, that her children went to school "Because they *had* to learn."[23] Like Betsey, Virginia is adamant about the positive contribution of the missionaries to the community.

> V.B.   One thing I want to tell you. When I was young, a young girl, I never see kids hang themselves like they do today. [Virginia is referring to the high suicide rate among adolescents on Northern Manitoba reserves.] That's something I always tell white people.
>
> S.G.   Why is it different now?
>
> V.B.   Because back then they used to tell them everything – they would tell kids "Don't do that."
>
> S.G.   Who told the kids what to do and taught them everything?
>
> V.B.   Their families. They taught their kids, and I teach my grandkids, to go to church and listen to what they say and learn things to do and not to do.
>
> S.G.   When you were growing up, do you think both parents and church helped with this?
>
> V.B.   Yes! Yes! Yes!
>
> S.G.   Do you think they acted as a team?
>
> V.B.   Oh yes, yes. They all had the kids listen.[24]

Percy, Betsey, and Virginia all refer with conviction and consistency to the idea of doing right and being good. This idea, so strong in Christianity, also has Ojibwa roots and is, possibly, one reason people felt so passionately about the idea of being taught and helped in this regard. For Ojibwas, bad behaviour which offends a conjuror or other-than-human being can result in severe consequences and bitter regret. As A. Irving Hallowell explained, in Ojibwa culture it is wise to avoid offending others; therefore, putting on a friendly front, suppressing one's own opinions and being helpful are beneficial. The foundation here is one of caution and anxiety.[25] As Ida Green put it when asked why she always tried to listen to what she was told by her parents and minister, "I have to listen because if I don't behave myself, God doesn't like me if I don't behave myself."[26]

John Edward Everett remembers Patricia Fuller, his teacher in the Catholic day school.

> J.E.E. All those days – one open classroom – I can remember her name, Miss Fuller. We had school – Catholics – we had to go to the Catholic school.
> S.G. So what about Miss Fuller? What was she like?
> J.E.E. Miss Fuller. She was a kind teacher. Made sure I say at home "In the name of the Father, the Son, and the Holy Ghost."
> S.G. She taught you that?
> J.E.E. Yes.[27]

John also expresses the place of Christianity in his life when he was growing up.

> Well, when I was a small kid even I couldn't even go to sleep. My aunt used to come and say "Are you going to sleep? Do this." [He folds his hands in prayer.] Thank the Lord. Next morning she asked "Did you say your Lord's Prayer?" Well, in a person's life you just have to continue on – it's a habit. You cannot even eat at the table without prayer. I was brought up like this and what am I going to do? Who am I going to listen to? Auntie. My uncle.[28]

These Berens River people spoke with passionate intensity about Christianity and the gifts brought to the community by missionaries. Does the taking on of Christianity go hand in hand with cultural loss? Recent scholarship suggests that, in fact, they do not. The conclusions about the Yup'ik Eskimo drawn by Ann Fienup-Riordan, for example, support the idea that cultural change as experienced by a group in encounter with Christianity can involve a creative exchange and is not merely a destructive imposition.[29]

Ojibwa religion has always been a dynamic force, moving and changing in response to the importation of new ideas. This was true in the evolution of the dream drum dance as it is true of Christianity. It is not up to outside academics to determine what is a loss and what is a gain. Certainly Percy Berens, Fred Baptiste, or John Edward Everett do not see themselves as victims of loss, and to superimpose a text over their assertions is to demonstrate pompous condescension. What is truly significant is that the same women and men who spoke so positively about Mary, Jesus, or the missionaries in one breath all, within the next breath, describe with equal excitement something inherently Ojibwa. An assertion of Christian faith is followed immediately by an awe-filled statement about the power of medicine men or a passionate declaration about gifts from the Thunderbirds or the *Memegwesiwag* or grief-filled utterances about the havoc wreaked by conjurors. These people are not afraid to assert their faith in things Ojibwa and have no problem with the two beliefs coexisting. It is important that scholars accept that beliefs can coexist; too often, scholars are as apt as missionaries to reject what they do not like.

By 1935, like its Methodist counterpart, the Catholic mission seems to have gained a solid place in the community at Berens River. Leach wrote with satisfaction to his provincial on 24 November:

> The work at the school is most encouraging this year. There are 27 on the register. All agree together as one happy family. Their conduct is excellent and their attendance at mass, in spite of handicaps, is very good.... As you are aware the opposition we have here is most fanatical. For a very long time now I have had a daily souvenir in my prayers for the conversion of both Catholics and Protestants. It seems that God, in His mercy is beginning to hear our petitions. Today, for instance, practically every Catholic who was able to attend Mass did so.[30]

By the 1920s, Christianity had also gained a place within the
Little Grand Rapids community. The year was 1919 when Mary
Nanakwap taught in the Methodist day school and in that year
church membership for this denomination rose from zero to
twelve members on probation.[31] The next year, those probationary
members became full members and although statistics show no
increases until 1934, neither do they show any decreases.

By this year, Luther Schuetze had been working at Little
Grand Rapids for seven years with membership clinging
tenaciously, if not stubbornly, to twelve. No statistics are available
for 1932 and 1933; however, in 1934, membership shot up to
135.[32] By 1936, the Methodist mission had 140 full members and
by 1940 there were 149.[33] Schuetze wrote that "Spiritually we
found our natives much more receptive than our white Brethren
to the Christian Gospel."[34]

The conversion of Machkajence (John Duck) at Little Grand
Rapids is a particularly interesting story. Luther Schuetze
described this charismatic and powerful head medicine man
as being "a striking figure with coal black eyes that seemed
to spew fire."[35] According to Schuetze, Machkajence and his
wife appeared, carrying a drum, at the Methodist mission one
morning. The Indian said "I have come to give you this drum." He
had sold one like it the previous year to a Poplar Hill drummer
for five hundred dollars and A. Irving Hallowell had tried without
success to buy this particular drum. (It was Machkajence who
conjured for the anthropologist so that the latter could find out
how his ill father in Philadelphia was faring.[36]) Schuetze was
adamant that he wanted nothing to do with it because, to him, it
was evil. For years, Machkajence had been the Methodist's great
foe and the source of much frustration. In the missionary's words:

I saw in John Duck my greatest opponent in our Work, he used
to drum and chant in the evening and everyone heard him, and
when a man had done something to displease John Duck he would
make medicine against him, for instance he would [ask] that that
... person would not catch any furs that winter, and it happened

often that it was so. If it was a deadly insult he would sing for their death, and often that person laid down and died. Now here stood this man, no cringing and stuttering, but straight and erect, he had come to a decision to accept Christ as his Savior and Master.[37]

In the end, Schuetze, who saw this apparent transformation as a miracle, told the Ojibwa that he would take the drum and write on it "This drum has been given to me this date for the Glory of God by John Duck."[38] The medicine man and his wife were both subsequently baptized.

Unfortunately, Machkajence left no record regarding his conversion decision and Schuetze's manuscript offers no clues. The missionary was making a serious impact on the community by this time as we can see from rising church membership. Perhaps the Ojibwa was tired of the ongoing rivalry and felt some pressure from the community which was moving towards general acceptance of Christianity as Scheutze became more trusted. In order for Machkajence to retain his power, it may have been necessary for him to keep in touch with his fellow Ojibwa on a political level. The giving up of the drum was a tangible and serious sign that there was sincerity behind Machkajence's motives.

The Roman Catholics made their initial foray into Little Grand Rapids in 1924. On their first visit to the community in the autumn of that year, De Grandpré and Leach baptized twenty-three children. On 4 February 1925, Father De Grandpré wrote to St. Boniface requesting that a day school be erected. Thirteen of the newly baptized children were of school age, twelve more had recently been baptized and this group would be of school age in one to two years. All should have had instruction in Catholicism, he maintained; hence parents and councillors were asking for a school to be established.[39] The community support seems to have been real because parents like John Duck, Charles Dunsford (senior), John Leveque, Hugh Albert Owen, and Charles Dunsford (junior) would be mentioned over the decades by Brother Leach as being supportive to the mission work. Of interest here is the inclusion of the name John Duck, doubtless the same person of whose conversion Luther Scheutze wrote. John Duck, in a not uncommon Ojibwa style, may have been moving between two separate missions depending upon who offered what.

Leach enjoyed his time in this community, writing that life there was good; there was no alcohol on the reserve, the children were pleasant and made fair progress at school.[40] The Oblate arrived in the community to begin his work in the new school at precisely 1:00 P.M. on Monday, 25 October 1926. The Catholic Indians had been persuaded to "build a few shacks and leave their wives and kiddies" (while they went into the bush). Leach was genuinely shocked to see so many children at school as he expected all the Ojibwa to be away. On his first day of teaching, eleven children appeared and he wrote in his journal that night "Hope they continue. Seem to be a bright bunch. Their names are certainly hopeless. Kakijep, Mijiok etc."[41]

The people in the community seemed interested and curious. Leach wrote that their house was "full of visitors all day we are on inspection." That house, he commented, was in "awful condition," but, "Still we're happy. This is *the* missionary life and may God help us to persevere and give us courage and health to carry on."[42] His entries often mentioned that his parishioners attended mass, listened attentively to the sermons, showed interest and filled the Oblates' house on Sunday afternoons. Children continued to attend school regularly and in November of 1926, Leach wrote "All the kiddies and even babies came to school today. Sent a few home."[43]

Another way the Catholics secured a foothold at Little Grand Rapids was through their medical aid. The turning point seems to have come in 1926. The wife of a man called Omimi developed an abscess on her knee. Leach wrote: "At first she had an Indian doctor and would not accept my help, but after a number of days when the Indian remedies proved to be of no avail, she called for me.... After ... successful treatment sick calls [to others in the community] were more frequent."[44]

Knowledge in education and the Scriptures as well as medical help seem to have been actively sought by the Indians at Little Grand Rapids. It is unlikely that Leach was misrepresenting these situations in his journal and memoirs, especially when he clearly expressed dissatisfaction and demoralization over work situations in other communities.

The story of Charley Dunsford (junior) is interesting. Charley and his father were among the first Catholic parishioners on the reserve and supported the mission from its beginning. During the first mass, Charley Dunsford (senior), "a fine old man," was so moved to extend glad welcome that, in the midst of Father De Grandpré's sermon, he had jumped from his seat and approached the priest, shaking his hand and repeating, "Bonjour, bonjour!"[45]

On 26 April 1927, Leach was called out to see Charley (junior) who had been ill for two months. Writing with the usual sarcasm reserved for these matters, the Oblate recorded that "Doctors (?) Baptiste and Duck present with Drums."[46] Six days later, Leach noted that Charley, more ill by the day, had consented to be baptized. Still, however, he "[got] Dr. (?) Duck to doctor him. Dr. (?) Duck plays his drums in Charley's tent during the night." On Good Friday, 15 April, Charley "received Extreme Unction and sent his pagan doctors away. Quite a few came [to Mass]. Charley's conversion had done good to all."[47]

Significantly, until the end of his life, Charley was incorporating both Christian and Ojibwa aid. It is difficult to know whether his final decision to send the medicine men away was because Charley knew that Leach would not baptize him otherwise, or whether he simply made a choice of one over the other in his dying moments. Ojibwa medicine did not require exclusivity of devotion whereas Catholicism certainly does. Possibly, in order to truly acquire the power from the latter, the Indian had to send away the drummers although their absence from his sick bed need not have meant that they were absent from his heart. On 24 April, Charley died and Leach noted in his journal: "May God grant that I die as resigned to His Holy Will as Charley. Since he renounced paganism he has done his utmost to influence all to accept God's Word. His last words to his old Father were, 'Help these White people all you can and take their Belief.' His little son, 'Little Dogskin' was baptized and given the name Joseph Tache."[48] Near the end, Charley was totally alone in his house. "His relatives and friends were following an old old custom.... They were leaving him to die in peace."[49] After Charley's death, Charley (senior) exchanged pipes with Leach, telling the Oblate that since he had taken care of his son, Charley would now take care of Leach.[50] In forming this bond and creating an obligation to take care of the Christian Leach, Charley made his overture within a purely Ojibwa context. He gave his pipe – which he continued to see as powerful and spiritually charged – to the Oblate in exchange for the latter's European-manufactured tobacco pipe.

In 1938, the Oblates continued to report to St. Boniface with pleasure and optimism about their work at Little Grand Rapids. On 17 January of that year, Father De Grandpré wrote that church attendance was thriving thanks to the work of Boniface Guimond. As in the case of Luther Schuetze, Guimond had, by this time, been working in the community for a number of years (since 1927) and had earned some respect and trust.[51]

Methodist missionaries Roscoe Tranner Chapin and F. G. Stevens wrote some similar reports from farther north about the vigour with which their native clientele took on Christianity. Chapin began work at the Island Lake Mission in 1922. Discussing the warmth, sincerity, and goodwill of the Island Lake Cree, he wrote:

During the summer and fall, before they left for their winter camps, Sunday was a gala day. From the more distant points on the lake many would start the night before, camp on the way, and be at the Mission point for breakfast and a visit before the morning service. I have ... counted about 50 canoes heading for morning worship together. Thrilling? It did something to you.[52]

The Sandy Lake Ojibwa embody another good example of native acceptance of Christianity. Rev. Niddrie visited them annually between 1920 and 1930 until he got too old to make the trips. F. G. Stevens explained that, by this time, the popularity of Indian mission work had so declined and the Board of Home Mission had become so incompetent in its planning and training policy that Sandy Lake was neglected and finally dropped from the Methodist field. Only Adam Fiddler remained at work among these people. The group, however, never gave up their quest for a missionary and sent petition after petition to the Home Mission Board asking for aid. In 1937, the Catholics started a mission at Deer Lake, but most remained loyal to Methodism.[53]

In Berens River today, the lives of many older people have long been affected by their Christian faith. The concept of the shedding of Christ's blood for the sins of humankind seems to have had particular impact. In the Ojibwa world view, angry conjurors and injured other-than-human beings can wreak enormous havoc in one's life. It follows, then, that the concept of Jesus Christ shedding blood so that a person's sins or mistakes can be forgiven and so that people can enter heaven is powerful for many Ojibwa.

The connection between death and appeasing "bosses" or "owners" was potent in Ojibwa beliefs about hunting and disease. All species of flora and fauna were believed to be controlled by these "owners" or "bosses" (not discernable by proper names of their own) and animals could only be hunted with their permission. Part of paying some of these other-than-human beings their due respect entailed treating material remains in prescribed ways. Muskrat and beaver bones were returned to the water, bear noses were cut off and hung, festooned with ribbons, from trees.[54] Jesus's death on the cross would have been easily interpreted from this Ojibwa perspective. As well, contemporary Christian Ojibwa with whom I spoke were profoundly moved by the idea of Jesus giving up his life for them. While the Ojibwa world view does not preclude anyone from entry into the afterlife, the idea of added protection from a benevolent other-than-human person – Jesus Christ – is beneficial.

A few years ago, Walter Green had a serious operation in a Winnipeg hospital. Despite his traditional beliefs, the presence of a minister was crucial for him during this time of distress. His telling of the event emphasized his sense of relationship with Christian clergy; he was not comfortable in accepting spiritual support from a rabbi.

> W.G. A minister came in to pray for me because that morning I was to go on the operating table. And I asked that minister which church does he belong to.... He was a rabbi. He wanted to pray for me but I said to him "I belong to the United Church. I don't think I want you." Because he was going to do this thing – they sprinkle something on your forehead and it means you belong to their church. So I didn't want anybody else to come and pray for me, just a minister from the United Church.
>
> S.G. I notice, though, that the time you had [a] vision when you were sick at home with a cold, you talked about that vision to a Pentecostal minister. But you're not a Pentecostal. Was it that the rabbi was more threatening – that you felt he would take you?
>
> W.G. That's what I felt, you know. He, might want me to sign the paper and belong to *his* church. This Pentecostal minister, he's a good friend of mine. There's some kind of relationship between me and him. So I just wanted to know how he felt about my dream.... I want to stick to the United Church where I was baptized.[55]

Fred Baptiste's house was full of pictures depicting Christian themes such as Jesus, the Last Supper and the Crucifixion. A particularly large, coloured painting dominated one wall.

> F.B. You know this picture of Jesus. Can you make anything out of that?

S.G.   Well, I see Jesus knocking at a door, and it's closed and it's night. What's your take on that?

F.B.   He's standing at the door, knocking at the door.... He's knocking at your heart – and would you let him in or not? I want you to answer that!

S.G.   You want me to answer that?

F.B.   Yes, yes. If Jesus knocks at your door – that's your heart's door, eh? – would you let him in?

S.G.   I think I would.

F.B.   Sure! Sure! Nobody'd ever turn him down.

[Then in reference to the Crucifixion:]

F.B.   I like both those pictures. Jesus carried that cross – for our sins – and when he got there to the end, He was stripped and he was crucified. His hands here [points to his palms] – he got five bleeding wounds: His hands, his feet, his side – that's where the blood came out, through here. Your sins should be washed by the blood of Jesus Christ.

S.G.   Does that have a lot of meaning for you?

F.B.   Oh yes! Oh yes![56]

John Edward Everett spoke with similar passion and loyalty: "Today I'm a Catholic – cross, water – God, there is only one God. The holy water is good. My religion is one religion. When I was born, they baptized me as a Catholic. I'll stay that way 'til I die."[57] About Christ, John said: "There's only one. He died for us on the cross. What happened? There was two more on the cross – sinners. What did one say to Jesus? 'Release us from this trouble.' The other one said 'Remember me when you enter paradise.' Many times I take the Sacraments at Bloodvein. Remember. I remember. That he died for you – that's why that blood was shed – for me. My sins he will forgive."[58]

Virginia Boulanger also had religious pictures and Bible verse plaques on her walls. For her, the Virgin Mary had special meaning and significance. She had many pictures, paintings, drawings, and tapestries of Mary and when I asked why she was so important to Virginia, she responded: "[because] she had to suffer when her son was crucified. Only a mother could feel that, you know. And you have to remember – when you pray, you have to sign with the cross and remember that he was dying for you – for our sins. God is helping us every day."[59]

Just as Christianity had personal meanings to the individuals described above, most converts to Christianity had their own definite reasons for conversion. Their reasons varied, even among the members of one family, and were not necessarily about religious belief. My grandfather, Mahase, converted from Hinduism to Christianity in order to go to university. My great-grandmother, Rookabi, converted in order to survive, upon finding herself suddenly immersed among strangers in a new world. Raymond DeMallie concludes that the conversion of the Lakota holy man Black Elk to Roman Catholicism was rooted in the Sioux leader's unwillingness to bear the burden of the destructive power bestowed on him through a vision. Accordingly, he decided to become a Christian and never practise Lakota religious ceremonies again.

Black Elk was probably attracted to the social and material benefits of church life. Although the United States government was hostile to any expressions of tribal solidarity and subsequently sought to systematically destroy all Lakota social institutions, it viewed Christian churches as an acceptable means of congregation. Annual religious conventions united large groups of Indians from several states. By using the Catholic church's access to resources, the Lakota leader could continue to be a source of spiritual and material support while, at the same time, achieving prestige and respect. Thus, Lakota leadership shifted from the political to the religious.[60] However, just as individuals could decide to embrace Christianity, they could also decide to reject Christianity.

Christianity certainly did not thrive and grow at all times in all places. The 1918 influenza epidemic, combined with Methodist neglect of the field, caused trouble for F. G. Stevens at Sandy

Lake. He wrote: "Now, in August, 1918, under a great fear, they had made a relapse into pagan practices. Adam [Fiddler] had become discouraged and had given his work. Vexed and disappointed, he had practically backslidden.... Then they turned against me. Threats had been made on my life if I came. There was no welcome for me ... but I stood firmly."[61] Stevens found, that same year, that the Indians at Deer Lake also possessed a mind of their own and clearly rejected the mission school there. Upon visiting these people, he found that the Little Crane children were not attending the day school that had been opened in 1917. The parents complained that the teacher had taken the names of their children away and firmly told the missionary that this was not acceptable. Also "[he] told our children not to kill little birds. We do not want our children taught that."[62]

Not all Ojibwa people sought baptism for themselves or their families. For example, on 20 April 1927, George Boucher, a Little Grand Rapids man, asked Frederick Leach to come and see his daughter, sixteen-year-old Mary, who was dying of consumption. Five days later, the Oblate wrote in his journal that she was "very weak. I wish I could get her baptised Catholic."[63] On 30 April there was no improvement and Leach asked the father to allow Mary to be instructed in Catholicism. George "deferred his answer." Although (or perhaps, because) the Little Grand Rapids Ojibwa had lost two children that year to consumption, he was certainly in no hurry to join the church or allow Mary to be converted. On 8 May, a frustrated Leach noted that "George is as obstinate as a mule and will not let her be baptised." On 11 May "Mary Boucher had a very bad spell towards evening. Poor little kid it made my heart ache to see her.... Geo. Boucher refuses religious consolation to Mary."[64]

That Christian Ojibwa people have freely selected aspects of Christianity that appeal to them and have rejected aspects that are meaningless to them was made clear in John Edward Everett's theological discussions.

S.G.   I want to ask you about the Virgin Mary.

J.E.E. I can say this: in the name of the Father, the Son, and the
Holy Ghost, amen. Why? Because she's a statue, eh? Virgin
Mary – she's a statue. I don't want to kneel down there and
ask Virgin Mary to forgive my sins. Well, I used to do it, you
know – just because I was taught to be that way. But now
who am I asking today?

S.G.   Who are you asking today?

J.E.E. *Lord*, I say, forgive me my sins.

S.G.   So you go straight to God?

J.E.E. Yeah.

S.G.   You don't go through the Virgin Mary?

J.E.E. No! No! I got a cross – beads – rosary beads for saying that
prayer. But not now. There's many many moons, yes. [He
had been communicating directly with God for a long time.]

S.G.   So you don't feel like you have to go through Mary any
more?

J.E.E. No. There's only one. He died for us. Okay, he died for us
on the cross.[65]

Possibly there was a gender issue here for John. As Hallowell's
informants explained to him "women, because of menstruation,
were, relative to men, *wiinzi*, in a state of impurity, which put
at risk the cleanness or religious purity (*bekize*) required when
interacting with *bawaaganak* [*pawaganak*]."[66] John Edward Everett
probably understood the concept of the Virgin Mary through this
Ojibwa lens. Also noteworthy is the evolution that had taken place
in John's perspective over six decades. His thinking and practice
were not static and, rather than living according to rote belief in
dogma, he rejected ideas that did not have real meaning and appeal
for him. As a child, he had been taught to confess his sins to Mary;
now he had concluded that this was unnecessary – and possibly
risky.

Catholic day school statistics indicate that this mission
occupied a definite minority position on the Reserve, owing in
part to the chief's family's resistance as noted earlier. Catholic
mission records also indicate a fairly lukewarm community

response to their overtures (although this mission's adherents seem to have been as loyal as the Methodist parishioners). The priests' journals and letters are full of references to boredom and loneliness, a problem that does not seem to have been shared by Methodist counterparts at Berens River. Wrote Father De Grandpré to St. Boniface on 5 January 1920: "a little too quiet. We would be bored if we didn't have manual work to occupy us. The work of the clergy is very little – it would not be sufficient to occupy a Father and we are two. Since four months I that have been here, I haven't heard fifteen confessions except at Christmas or where there is a big gathering. In that case, I had seven confessions."[67] "In our poor mission, the days pass by monotonously and tranquilly," wrote E. Planet to his provincial, Rev. Father Jean Baptiste Beys on 22 November 1921.[68] Perhaps one of the most revealing documents is a letter from Father Leándre Gauthier to the Reverand Father Josephat Magnan on 4 October 1927. The passage, besides revealing much about Gauthier's personal biases, reflects a coolness towards the mission on the part of many Ojibwa at Berens River.

> I don't believe the acquisition of language will be the biggest difficulty that I will encounter in mission work – this will be, I believe, to succeed in liking Indians because I find them to be very full of pride, concealment and hypocrisy, not to mention untidy. This causes that ... I haven't a lot of sympathy for them. I believe that the proximity of the Methodists makes them worse than elsewhere. But I hope that, with time, I will succeed in finding some quality in these beings who are, after all of the world. I finish ... with the hope that in my next letter I will be able to write to you in total truth: I like my Indians and am beginning to speak with them in their language.[69]

The most tangible evidence of native rejection of Christian mission work at Berens River is in the story of the Roman Catholic boarding school. In 1936, a residential school was built in the community and the Oblate Sisters agreed to assume administrative responsibilities. However, "In spite of efforts and pains taken by the good teachers, the residential school was not a success due to the lack of co-operation from the parents of the children."[70] When the Oblates decided to use the new building as a nursing station instead, the Ojibwa welcomed the idea. Since the Oblate Sisters did not do this kind of work, the Grey Nuns accepted the job of running the facility and provided day school teaching as well.

While missionaries expected conversion to entail a wholesale reorientation of world view, it is clear that, in most cases, after conversion, indigenous and Christian elements coexisted in the lives of aboriginal peoples worldwide. As Jean and John Comaroff put it, "profession of a new belief belied the fact that other modes of thought and action were never fully laid aside."[71] "Conversion has often meant recasting the message of the missionaries into one's own language and world view."[72]

This duality extends beyond the realm of religion to embrace concepts of Western modernity in general. For example, looking at South Africa, the Comaroffs concluded that, whatever Marxist or modernization theories may contend, global forces "played into local [South African] ... conditions in unexpected ways, changing known structures into strange hybrids.... [P]recisely because the cross, the book and the coin were such saturated signs, they were variously and ingeniously redeployed to bear a host of new meanings as non-Western peoples ... fashioned their own visions of modernity."[73]

Similarly, Robert Hefner observes that conversion is not always "an exclusivistic change of religious affiliation requiring the repudiation of previously held beliefs, [but, rather, it] assumes a variety of forms because it is influenced by a larger interplay of identity, politics, and morality."[74] This idea is supported by scholarship around the world. For example, the Dene Tha' of northwestern Alberta demonstrated to anthropologist Jean-Guy Goulet that while they are nearly all Christians, missionaries did not succeed in abolishing Dene spiritual values. Although the Dene Tha' seminomadic life has gone, the crucifix and rosary are prominent features in the community, and the dreamers (or prophets) pray to *Ndawatá* (the Christian God), the same people still feed tea, tobacco, and animal fat to a fire in the hopes of better health and more successful hunts. To achieve these ends, they still perform tea dances at which the dreamer, "the one with a strong mind able to see into the future," still officiates.[75] For dreamer Alexis Seniantha, the drum and crucifix "have become personal symbols of his role as a dreamer who travels from our land to the other land to help his people. He has become a Christian Dene Tha' shaman who, in the process of his vision, transformed Christian symbols and incorporated them into a distinct Dene world view."[76] Dene dreamers achieve their knowledge from *yak' e wodené* (the spirits of the deceased), *Ndawotá* (the Christian God) and *Ndawotá chuen* (God's son, Jesus).[77] Even the Christian rosary has distinctive meaning to the Dene Tha' who see the individual beads as symbols of places where the Son of God landed when walking between heaven and earth.[78]

Sometimes, integrations were conscious efforts of a group to cope with a new world and, at the same time, maintain identity. An excellent example can be found in nineteenth-century New Zealand. As Christianity became intertwined with the Maori meaning system, long wars were fought in the major Christian churches over giving this hybrid credence through separate Maori services.[79] The leaders of the nineteenth-century Maori charismatic religious movements, which blended Christianity with traditional Maori spiritual ideas, played key roles in the formation of a new identity. All had millennial dreams and all built bridges between Maori and European worlds. At the same time, however, they all advocated Maori independence and sought to preserve the Maori world view.[80]

For many Aboriginal peoples, conversion represented the acquiring of new power that could supplement or enhance the power they already had from their own spirit helpers. In southeastern Alaska, most Tlingit converts to Christianity in the mid-1800s saw conversion "as an additional source of power and material benefit."[81] The Dene Tha' decided that they would have a better chance of success in fishing, hunting and trade if traditional magic formulas were supplemented by prayer to the Christian God. For these people, Roman Catholic symbols and practices served to complement, not supplant, their own belief.[82]

By 1936, the Berens River Ojibwa retained some control over their religious lives. Like the Little Cranes at Deer Lake who had withdrawn their children from school because they did not like the messages that were being imparted, the Ojibwa at Berens River did not support that which was forced on them against their will. That the Oblates would construct an entire building and secure staff before really exploring the wishes of parents says much about their attitude towards that which *they* decided was good, proper, and beneficial for "their" Indians.

It is important to note, however, that Berens River was a visible crossroads. Unlike the residents of Little Grand Rapids and Pikangikum who existed, geographically speaking, beyond the reach of the law, there is no doubt that Ojibwa participation in Mide, drum dances, or other ceremonies would have brought agents and police to the scene. The provision of the *Indian Act* which banned "objectionable features" of native religions in Canada impacted Ojibwa people living in large northern Manitoba communities such as Berens River, Bloodvein, and Jackhead. The Department of Indian Affairs was committed to repress Aboriginal political organization through the supression of ceremonies. For example, at Bloodvein, a giveaway dance was interrupted in 1916. In 1921, the police destroyed a giveaway drum while informing Chief Councillor James Travers that the *Indian Act* prohibited giveaway ceremonies. Indian Agent Carter recommended that Travers subsequently be removed from office.[83] While their northerly setting gave them some distance from the Prairie conflicts of 1885, thus protecting them in some measure from Euro-Canadian pressures, their religious life was profoundly affected by restrictions.

What is clear, however, is that between 1917 and 1940, the Ojibwa along the Berens River did actively shape their own religious ideas and, when necessary, found ways to reject undesirable situations. In many ways, they not only actively decided whether to let themselves be led to water, but they clearly decided where, when, and how much they would drink.

Berens River Methodist Day School

Year	Teacher	Total Enrolment	Average Attendance
1885	Gussie Parkinson	35	16
1886	G. Parkinson	38	18
1887	G. Parkinson	39	17
1888	J. W. Butler	32	14
1889	E. H. West	25	9
1890	E. H. West	36	7
1891	Charles French	39	11
1892	S. E. Batty	59	30
1893	S. E. Batty	22	7
1894	S. E. Batty	33	16
1896	Minnie Wilson	40	10
1897	B. Alexander	48	9
1900	Miss Lawford		
1904	Eliza Postill		
1905	E. Postill		
1906	Louie A. Showler	28	8
1907	L. A. Showler		
1908	L. A. Showler	38	11
1910	Bessie Hayter	24	10
1914	Mrs. Lowes	33	10
1915	Mrs. Lowes	33	10
1919	A. A. Smith	36	17
1920	Ida Fairservice	36	17
1921	Zella Richardson	37	23
1922	A. Wilkie Lonsley	28	16
1923	Colin Douglas Street	29	15
1925	C. D. Street	37	22
1926	C. D. Street	38	23
1927	C. D. Street	41	28
1928	C. D. Street	38	27
1929	C. D. Street	38	23

Berens River Roman Catholic Day School

Year	Teacher	Total Enrolment	Average Attendance
1919	Frederick Leach	25	17
1920	F. Leach	29	20
1921	Josephine St. Denis	29	15
1922	A. Langlais	23	12
1923	Patricia Fuller	25	13
1925	P. Fuller	22	11
1926	F. Leach	22	16
1927	Boniface Guimond	23	15
1928	F. Leach	25	15
1929	F. Leach	25	18

Little Grand Rapids Methodist Day School

Year	Teacher	Total Enrolment	Average Attendance
1906	William Ivens	46	19
1907	W. Ivens	38	14
1908	Joseph F. Woodsworth	43	20
1910	Roy L. Taylor	50	15
1914	Alfred G. Johnson	45	18
1925	Mina Moar	17	8
1926	John James Everett	19	10
1927	J. J. Everett	23	8
1928	Luther L. Schuetze	25	11
1929	L. L. Schuetze	30	12

Little Grand Rapids Roman
Catholic Day School

Year	Teacher	Total Enrolment	Average Attendance
1928	Boniface Guimond	27	15
1929	B. Guimond		
1930	B. Guimond	15	11

6   "I've Had My Dreams
all These Years"

*Survivals and Integrations,
1917–1940*

Is it possible that beneath the Christianity of the native peoples
of the Arctic and sub-Arctic there still flourishes in the psychic
life of emotional orientation and fundamental attitudes, the pre-
Christian aboriginal religion?[1]

So writes anthropologist Antonio R. Gualtieri in a recent book,
citing examples of religious persistence, not only among northern
peoples, but around the world. In New Guinea, for example,
among tribes of Markham Valley, vital native animism and
medicinal ritual were, in 1941, coexisting with the German
Lutheranism brought by missionaries.
     Another example occurs in a rather bitter letter written on
27 November 1883 from Oblate missionary Bishop Paul Durieu
to Father Jean Marie LeJacq in the Cariboo country of British
Columbia. The bishop was upset about native religious ideas
existing beneath the overlay of Roman Catholicism among the
Chilcotin Indians:

It is a truism that the Indian quickly brings his religion in
accord with actions that flatter his self-interest and passion....
The Indians, although baptised, saying their prayers and even
confessing very often, retain within their hearts pagan ideas and
maxims which will often be the norm of their daily actions.[2]

In *The Role of Conjuring in Saulteaux Society*, A. Irving Hallowell
noted that the shaking tent ceremony reinforced Saulteaux values
and beliefs by tangibly validating ideas relating to the dynamic
entities of the cosmos (thereby humanizing spirits and increasing
intimacy between humans and other-than-humans), supporting
the Ojibwa social structure by exposing the dangers of violating
social mores, generating confidence in dealing with life's pitfalls,
and providing entertainment for participating audiences. Thus, he
explained, it was understandable that conjuring had "persisted up
until the present day even in communities where Indians have been
Christianized ... the occurrence of conjuring in such cases is an
index of the validity of native beliefs, attitudes and values despite
the veneer of acculturation."[3]

Even near the end of his career, Brother Frederick Leach was
protesting the ongoing power and influence held by medicine men
in northern Manitoba. In 1952, for example, an upset Ojibwa
friend warned him that he had offended a medicine man who was
consequently preparing to do him harm. Although Leach said he
felt like smiling over a harmless threat, he gave his friend credit
for showing enough courage to actually deliver a warning.[4] That
Leach felt compelled to publish an article about the problems of
Indian people relying on medicine men shows their firm place in
Ojibwa society.[5]

Speaking to Hallowell in the 1930s, William Berens recalled
an incident where he believed, as a young man, he had actually
been bewitched. A number of instances when William had used
Christianity to overcome potential harm from conjurors have
been noted, reflecting his strongly Ojibwa approach to the new
religion. In this case, however, he was actually taken over by a
spell and fell in love with a young woman. While working on
a surveying job up the Berens River, he was smitten with this
beautiful young woman who had "light skin and flashing black
eyes." Too shy to pursue her, William left the next morning;
however, as he passed her, she reached out and touched him.
That night, in another camp with six men, William dreamed of

this woman who was walking on the water, straight towards him. "Come across to me," she said.

The next thing William knew, he was out of the tent and calling for a boat. How he got out over the other men he never knew. They shook him and asked him if he were crazy. The next day after they had started, William asked the boss whether he could pay him off and let him go. Request refused. Still later he noticed that his vest was gone. Where it got to he never knew. Was sure he had it on when he started. Whole thing was the result of a love charm as he could not stop thinking of the girl for several days. Put into effect when she touched him. Must have had medicine in her hand.[6]

William's sons Percy and Gordon Berens, and Fred Baptiste all expressed a real respect for the power of conjurors. As Walter Green put it, "They're so wonderful – they can do anything.... They were blessed!"[7]

Percy Berens provided an explanation for the missionaries' ongoing battles against Ojibwa healers:

S.G.   It seems to me that many missionaries, like Brother Leach and Rev. Niddrie, and even Percy Jones, were pretty down on medicine men.

P.B.   Oh yeah! One reason why. They didn't want this new generation to live that kind of life.

S.G.   What was wrong with that kind of life?

P.B.   Because they didn't believe in it, that was what was wrong. That's the trouble. They didn't *really* have it explained to them what it means for an Indian to be a medicine man.

S.G.   What does it mean for an Indian to be a medicine man? What should the missionaries have understood?

P.B.   They should have known better. That man there, that medicine man, he's going to save lives! For other people! It's a *good* thing! I very appreciate your bringing this whole thing up, this medicine thing. The old people lived long in

my time – no babies died that much as what they do now
because the Indians knew the medicine … the medicine
men had the knowledge and the medicine.[8]

Percy articulated the problem that lay at the heart of missionary
interpretations and expectations. These agents of the Gospel
steadfastly refused even to examine what they deemed to be pagan
practices, so sure were they of encountering the Devil in the midst
of the proceedings. Had they made a point of learning about these
concepts and ceremonies, they would likely have been affected
by the elements of Christianity that had, by this time, become
integrated within them. Once again, however, missionaries had
a rigid, narrow, preconceived template in their minds regarding
the ways true converts ought to act, and medicine men practising
traditional healing were not a part of this model.

While Virginia Boulanger says that she does not believe in,
nor does she trust, the power of medicine, she concedes that for
awhile, the medicine men *did* have real powers.[9] Virginia's Cree
husband was a converted Methodist. Tom Boulanger certainly
experienced first-hand the healing powers of a medicine man
during the 1920s. By that time, Fair Wind (Naamiwan) had
become a powerful healer at Pauingassi. Tom became stricken
with pneumonia while trapping at Charron Lake, about forty
miles north of Pauingassi, Manitoba. A Little Grand Rapids man
took him by sleigh to see Fair Wind whom Boulanger presented
with tobacco, matches, a new pipe, and new store-bought clothes.
The following day, Fair Wind's sons brought roots from the
shore which Fair Wind boiled, adding "a power medicine, about
half a teaspoon." It is interesting that Fair Wind prayed before
administering the dose – a fact that certainly impressed his
Christian patient.[10]

Clearly, the belief in Ojibwa medicine was surviving. Yet, Fair
Wind's prayer before he administered Tom Boulanger's dose of
power medicine is also an excellent example of the integration of
Christian beliefs with the Ojibwa world view.

Had the missionaries allowed themselves to observe this kind of phenomenon, would it have made them breathe a little easier? Percy Berens, with his faith in the ability of human beings to be reasonable once an idea is fully explained to them, would say "yes." Perhaps so; but the rigid world view of most only allowed them one lens through which they expected to be able to view and interpret the extremely complex and nuanced phenomena which took place in their fields; and, sadly, that lens often produced distorted images.

The many instances where Indians called both medicine men and Christian missionaries to the bedsides of the sick and dying are on record. Fred Baptiste's interpretation of medicine men was typical and revealed a highly integrative way of thinking. He discussed this after I asked him about his view of Yellow Legs walking on the water:

F.B.   *Unless* he believed, unless he fully believed in Jesus Christ – maybe he helped him walk on the water. Jesus walked on the water.

S.G.   But Yellow Legs won't have known about Jesus.

F.B.   Well, I've seen a lot of people who believed all the other stuff from before. They used to heal people who were sick. [Tells the story of a Berens River man who was told by his doctor that he had six months to live but who was cured by a medicine woman.] How come he got better? You know, God plans everything in this world. The medicine woman used that plant that God planted in this world – roots, like, you know – because it's medicine.

S.G.   So the power of that medicine came from God?

F.B.   Yes. Everything you see here. The older people used to use that medicine.

S.G.   You said that Christ walked on the water. And Christ says in the Bible that if you believe enough, *you* can walk on the water. But when Yellow Legs walked on the water he had never heard about Christ because that was long before

the missionaries came. So where would he have gotten the
power to walk on the water?

F.B. Well, they had their own power, I guess.

S.G. Where would they have gotten their power from if they
didn't know about Christ? Is it possible that Yellow Legs got
his power from spirits?

F.B. They had their own spirits.

S.G. Well what happened to those spirits?

F.B. I don't know, they're gone, I guess – when they [the old
people] died. Them older people died and now the spirits
are gone. Now there's nothing left.[11]

For Percy Berens, too, medicine men are not separate from
Christianity.

S.G. What do you think about medicine men?

P.B. Well, I'll tell you one thing that's my belief. It's a gift. And
the person knows that – that's a gift.

S.G. A gift from whom?

P.B. Manitou. As I told you, the Indians – before they ever seen a
white man – they already talked about Manitou.

S.G. The Christian God and Manitou – are they the same?

P.B. They're the same. That's the same God.[12]

The theme of missionary against shaman is clearly seen in the
history of the Tlingit of southeastern Alaska. Beginning in the
1830s, shamanism (a key element of Tlingit culture) was isolated
by American Protestant missionaries as the worst example of
paganism. With the help of civil authorities, they embarked
upon a huge war with the result that, by the 1930s, there were
very few shamans left among the Tlingit, most of whom had
converted by the late nineteenth century. Interestingly, however,
in their ongoing efforts to reconcile their traditional culture
with Christianity, Tlingit elders forge various interpretations of
shamanism – generating historical accounts which challenge the
idea of the inferiority of Aboriginal Tlingit religion to Christianity.

The stories, which they continually reshape in the face of current events, vehemently oppose European accounts of their history. Although the Tlingit accepted many Western ideas, they have incorporated within their vision of the past.[13]

Along with abiding faith in the powers and benefits of medicine men, the belief in the power of Thunderbirds (*pinesi*) is prevalent among people in the Berens River community. Fred Baptiste, passionate in his expressions of Christian faith, was also passionate about the Thunderbird feather he once owned. Percy Berens was equally vocal about his belief in these *pawáganak*. "Thunderbirds? Oh, yeah. I believe that. I fully believe. It's a bird! It's a bird. You should go to Poplar River [to see their nest of boulders]. White people don't believe it's a bird, a Thunderbird, they don't believe on that. But we Indians absolutely believe that's a bird."[14] Percy was comfortable with believing in something in which "white people" express disbelief and, in the case of the missionaries, even contempt and repulsion. He and the other Ojibwa with whom I spoke were not simply spouting pro-missionary rhetoric, fearful of confessing belief in anything that was not on the Christian path.

Percy explained that to Jennifer Brown and Maureen Matthews.

J.B.   So the Thunderbirds moved away?

P.B.   They moved, I guess. Too much travelling on that lake.... If you're on the north end of that lake, I was, and you look through on a clear day, look towards the west end there, it's just like that place above all the rest. The main shore is here, like – and that thunder where the Thunderbirds used to nest is way up higher than that.

J.B.   Did they go away partly because of airplanes and things like that?

P.B.   I guess so. And the bush fires used to be on that lake all the time and forest planes would be there all the time. Maybe that's why they're gone.

Thunderbirds are important spirit beings in the world views of most Canadian Native peoples. The gigantic birds migrate during the spring and fall, enshrouded in mist. Appearing as birds or as human beings, the Thunderbirds are spiritual guardians with whom human beings can communicate. They can give blessings and they can kill. Typically, there exists, within Aboriginal world views, enormous flexibility regarding the physical appearance of these other-than-human beings. This is also, in part, because Thunderbirds usually appear only in dreams – in personal and secret exchanges.[15]

Roger Roulette is an Ojibwa from southern Manitoba. His father was a medicine man. He explained the enormous power of Thunderbirds to Maureen Matthews, saying, "They have almost absolute rule. They can take your life, too. I don't know of any other spiritual entity that is capable of doing that. If a person chooses not to understand, that's too bad for them. Because we do.... They are foremost and most fierce guardians. Those are the ones who give gifts to humanity. The most gifted have connections with the Thunderbirds."[16] "They're there," explained Margaret Simmons, William Berens's granddaughter, "Go; look at the clouds. You hear them; you see the lightning; you see the dark, black, ominous clouds and they're there. They just exist."[17]

It is paramount to treat Thunderbirds with utmost respect. They like to smoke tobacco, which is offered to them by human beings who light a pipe for them. Margaret Simmons remembered that as a child, when the family heard Thunderbirds coming, everyone went inside to sit quietly. Harriet Bear, an Ojibwa woman, lives at Brokenhead, a reserve just north of Winnipeg. She too remembered: "We were not allowed to play outside ... Reverence ... is given to the passing of the Thunderers. You must cover everything, so you don't act as an imposter of the power of the Thuderbirds, the Thuderers. That's why things are covered, like glass and metal. That's one of the main Ojibwa rules."[18]

When asked if he fears Thunderbirds, Percy responded:

No. No, I don't. I know lots of people do. Even they just put blinds on their windows when there's a thunderstorm. Old-timers used to be really really afraid of – my mom, myself, my mom used to cover up all the windows and all the mirrors in the house, used to cover them all up when there's a thunderstorm.[19]

As Roger Roulette said, it is only the most gifted people who can hear Thunderbirds. The great medicine man, Fair Wind, had a special bond with Thunderbirds. John James Everett, one of A. Irving Hallowell's Ojibwa assistants, told the anthropologist about an event that occurred during a storm at Pauingassi around 1912. Fair Wind and his wife, Koowin, were in a tent when a great peal of thunder sounded. He explained to Koowin that a Thunderbird had just asked him "whether he had a pipe and why don't I give him a smoke." Koowin fetched Fair Wind's pipe which an *oskabewis* (servant) lit. After a few puffs, the medicine man lifted the pipe above his head and swung it in a clockwise direction. He prayed and "asked pardon from the thunder – pleading for himself." Everett realized that "*pinesi* must have been his *pawágan*." Hallowell, too, concluded that this must have been so, since thunder would not otherwise have communicated with Fair Wind.[20]

Gordon Berens, Percy's brother, who became a United Church minister late in life, was another of those gifted people who can communicate directly with Thunderbirds. This seems to have been linked, in part, with the special ties he shared with his grandfather, Jacob.

I was a baby for him, my grandfather. That old fellow saw a lot of me. I know a lot of white people don't believe the old Indian ways. The old – my grandpa – blessed me with Thunders, Thunderbirds. Yeah, he blessed me with a Thunderbird and there was one time, I was out at a sandbar picking strawberries – so that time, there was a big thunderstorm. Rain poured down. I was out picking strawberries. While I stood out, like, we had a talk – while I stood out – and I hold up my hand like that. "That's enough! That's enough! Let it stop," I said, "let it stop because," I said, "you're going to wet everybody except me." That rain just stopped like that. And none of my hair was wet.... The Thunderbirds blessed me.

And:

> [When my mother went into labour] Thunder!
> Thunderstorm came so heavy and my dad put down two
> tents on top of the other. And when I was born, the water
> poured down them two tents just like as if they was no
> cover at all, except the place where my Mom was lying, not
> a drop. Not a drop of rain. But the rest of it was just pouring
> down between them two tents by pailfuls you see, but
> where my mom was lying, no rain at all. Oh yes, my mom
> often used to tell me about it. My dad did too, so I guess
> that's why I'm still alive today.

M.M. When there was thunder, could you hear the Thunderbirds
talking?

G.B. Well, of course I do.... You know, a lot of people don't
believe me. When a thunderstorm comes, I know what it
is, but try to tell them, they won't believe it. So I just keep
it to myself. I tried it once and they wouldn't believe me. I
said "That's all. You're finished. I won't interpret no more. I
won't interpret no more if you don't believe what I interpret
this time," I says.... But I understand them. I can talk to
them in my own language and they understand me. If I say
[to] a big thunderstorm "That's enough! You scare the kids.
You scare the children. That's enough [softly]!" Thunder
just talk like that, yeah.

J.B. Did you learn a lot from your grandfather, from Jacob?

G.B. Oh, I did – I did. Oh, I wasn't too old, but I learned a lot.
He used to tell me "That's going to happen." He predict
things ahead of time. And that always came true. He says
"Remember, that's going to happen. What I'm telling you,
I'm predicting now," he says "you'll remember as soon
as you, as soon as you hear the thunder," he says "you'll
understand." Yeah, that happened. Still happens to me like
that. Still happens.[21]

After fifty years of missionary encounters, Ojibwa beliefs remained strong at Little Grand Rapids in the 1930s. Just as Luther Schuetze and Frederick Leach recalled drumming going on at the bedsides of sick people, so John Niddrie remembered the community as "a stronghold of paganism, and at eventide, the sound of the conjurors' drums could be heard in all directions."[22] Leach remembered much illness there during the 1920s and 1930s and commented, "on occasions there was little cooperation from the parents or patient; ... many preferred Indian remedies to the white man's."[23] And:

When we were stationed at Little Grand Rapids we heard the beating of drums quite often. At times, it would be the "medicine-man" drumming after he had been called out to give herbs to a patient. This ... was supposed to increase the efficacy of his medicine.[24]

The fear of windigos was still tangible among Christian as well as non-Christian Ojibwa at Little Grand Rapids in the late 1920s. In 1929, the members of the United Church saw their first Christmas tree, in Luther Schuetze's church. They also got their first exposure to the idea of Santa Claus. When the missionary explained that Santa is a stranger who arrives with presents, the reaction was strong. To Shuetze's surprise, everyone "panicked as they were deathly afraid of strangers and had the most weird stories about strangers often being windigoe ... who often killed and ate up some of the native peoples, it seemed a yearly occurrence with them that someone saw a stranger somewhere and it most likely would be a windigoe, they would all pack up and move."[25] Schuetze, at this point, had no idea how strong their fears were. He explained that Santa would arrive at the church and would be accompanied by the sound of bells. On Christmas Eve, he dressed up the ranger from Eagle Lake as Santa Claus. "I have never seen anything like what happened when those bells jingled and the door opened. The whole Congregation all sitting on those log benches disappeared under them, how they did it, I don't know ... there were some real stout women."[26] Schuetze's attempt at light humour notwithstanding, it is clear that his parishioners were not giving up their beliefs while they were taking on Methodism.

Schuetze also told another story which was meant to gently scoff at the phenomenon of windigos and show that the Indians at Little Grand Rapids were "Gradually ... emerging from the yoke of superstition and fear."[27] It seems to suggest more, however, about the prevalence of the Ojibwa world view in this community. The chief of Little Grand Rapids and his brother were paddling a canoe on Pauingassi Lake. Suddenly, the brother thought he saw a windigo, and said they should leave immediately and go home to warn others: "the chief was following suit, and then said he remembered what I had said in one of my sermons, that they should always make certain of anything before they spread a false rumour, so under his brother's protest, he steered the canoe closer, and found it was a tree stump."[28] In this instance, the availability of two alternative frames of reference gave an added scope for Ojibwa empiricism.

Christianity and native world views sometimes melded powerfully when Cree and Ojibwa found themselves under severe stress. Writing from Fisher River, F. G. Stevens complained to Methodist missionary J. A. C. Kell, who was stationed at Oxford House, in 1927, "Nowhere do I find much stability. The Hart-Muskego people were pagans in the bush and Christians at the mission. The others, on the other side, were not much for pagan customs but I always find that when the situation becomes desperate that most find down deep in their heart some paganism. This I found out at Oxford House as I do here and everywhere."[29]

An example of such a desperate situation occurred among the Indians at Deer Lake in 1918. F. G. Stevens had just left that community to return to Oxford House when a man became very ill and could not be cured. Stevens wrote in his memoirs:

All the time, some of the older men were just over the border between paganism and Christianity. Other means failing them, they brought out their drums. The man died. Then they were very much afraid of what they'd done. That was the year of the "flu" and although ... none of them took it, they were excited all winter. More or less conjuring went on all the next spring. Not all of them turned back to paganism. Adam Fiddler remained faithful.[30]

The Deer Lake Indians were in a frightening situation. Aware that people in many communities were dying of the epidemic, they were probably using all possible means available to see themselves through a crisis, rather than simply abandoning Christianity. Although the people were angry over having been without a missionary during this time (Stevens wrote that he had been warned that if he returned to Deer Lake he would be shot), they all appeared at church in the summer of 1919 – presumably with Adam Fiddler presiding. When Stevens arrived he found a mixture of responses that ranged from furious ("I had a desperate time with these") to "Steadfast and faithful." Stevens reported, however, that he "mastered them all"; he left Deer Lake safely and did not return for twenty-one years.

A 1928 article entitled "Wetigoes – Or What?", written by Kell, provides an excellent example.[31] A group of Indians came to call on Kell at Oxford House.

"Donald Wood has been brought in from his camp to the Chief's house. He is afraid that he is going crazy and wants you to give him the Sacrament." That ... sounded simple ... but was it? It was more than half a century since Oxford House Indians finally renounced their pagan beliefs and practices of their ancestors and, as a community, accepted Christianity. For awhile their enthusiasm and the novelty of this new way of living [uplifted them]. But it is not reasonable to expect that a primitive people can in two generations cast off the instincts, superstitions and prejudices inherited from many generations of pagan ancestors. At present ... some ... are leading good Christian lives, but many are semi-pagan and semi-Christian. They realise the power of God but cannot lose their fear of evil spirits and medicine men.[32]

Kell explained that Donald Wood was an excellent bushman, adding that this was an inherited trait as was his vulnerability to superstition. Wood and his son had experienced problems with their health. "Consequently, being naturally of a superstitious nature ... [Wood] firmly believes that his misfortunes are due to evil spirits. He has now got it into his head that the only remedy is the Sacrament, which he regards as superior medicine, able to counteract evil influences."[33] This passage tells of a comfortable and meaningful integration of Cree and Christian religious ideas on the part of Donald Wood.

In another piece entitled "The Social Organization of the Northern Cree," Kell wrote:

> The effect of Christianity on these people is difficult to gauge ... as only very few have understood the meaning of Christianity ... unfortunately [except for a few cases] the great majority of Indians are only half Christian and half pagan. They still believe in bad medicine and wetigoes but have their children baptized, attend church and pray, presumably to the Christian God. Along with their fears of their own old superstitions they add fears of the devil and of hell. They ... alternate between periods of great carelessness and moral recklessness and periods of penitence and self-nourished sanctity.[34]

For Aboriginal peoples worldwide, complex integrations and nuanced syncretic phenomena emerge from the union of traditional world views with Christianity. As Jean and John Comaroff explain, "lived realities defy easy dualisms ... worlds everywhere are complex fusions of what *we* like to call modernity with magicality, rationality and ritual.... In fact, our studies of the Southern Tswana have ... proved ... that none of these were opposed in the first place – except, perhaps, in the colonizing imagination ..."[35]

Poignant examples of this phenomena are found across North America. The Reverand Peter Jones, Mississauga Methodist leader of New Credit mission, southern Ontario, in the first half of the nineteenth century, married a British woman and

moved completely in European society; yet, as was true for the
Lakota leader, Black Elk, his traditional lifeways were ongoing
points of reference. He kept the eagle feather from his naming
ceremony, was proud of his eagle totem, fasted before performing
important Gospel sermons, continually lent money to destitute
Indians, made business agreements orally, gave his sons enormous
freedom during their childhoods, and believed to his death in
the superiority of Native medicines. Those Mississauga to whom
he ministered also blended old and new beliefs. At Peter Jones's
deathbed, they prayed to the Christian God – but made sure to
have an Indian doctor in attendance.[36]

Raymond DeMallie and Douglas Parks found, in the 1980s,
great diversity of religious practices on Sioux reservations,
reflecting a variety of interactions between Christianity and
indigenous religion. Some Sioux groups have amalgamated
the two and other groups keep them separate. But traditional
religious beliefs and practices endure to some extent in every
Sioux community. These include: the pipe, the sweatlodge, the
individual sacrifice of the vision quests, the collective sacrifice of
the sun dance, and the healing and conjuring rites of the *yuwipi*.
In modern times, Sioux people are experiencing a reawakening
of their traditional religious roots. At the same time, many
Sioux, while recovering their heritage, retain their membership
and belief in some Christian denomination. They see no conflict
between Christianity and traditional religious rites.[37]

In his article on the Reverend George Barnley and the
James Bay Cree, John S. Long shows that while the Indians
demonstrated a sincere interest in Christianity and incorporated
Christian rites and European names these were "essentially
additions to Cree culture which need not have replaced or
threatened tradition. . ." Until the twentieth-century economy
impacted their society, the James Bay Cree "could choose to
behave as church-going Christians while at the post for a few
weeks, and do as they pleased while dispersed in their hunting
and fishing camps."[38]

On the international front, some amazing examples of integrations and syncretism can be found. A landmark study by Terrence Ranger looked at groups in late-nineteenth-century Central Africa. He found evidence of general openness to new myths, rites, symbols, and techniques although this openness did not necessarily imply that there was always harmony between African groups. Rather, these bands were generally ready to take on new ideas and respect shown for the spiritual power of outsiders. It was the English Protestant and Catholic missionaries who looked for hostility because they had an exclusive view of the encounters, expecting one religion or the other to win out. Very few African religious spokesmen had such an attitude. They were not only borrowing from Christianity in order to develop and cope with changing situations – when the missionaries arrived, African religions were developing concepts of the high god and seeking from within their own resources to meet an ever-changing world.

Indeed, on some fronts, Christianity was too limited to offer effective solutions to the kinds of problems with which African groups were trying to cope. For example, African religious leaders were searching for new ways – or seeking to strengthen current ways – of dealing with witchcraft and evil. Sometimes, they looked to missionaries and Christianity as effective cleansers; for example, Ufipa charms were piled for destruction at the feet of Roman Catholic priests; the Lala had hopes of a cleansing millennium; in northern Nyasaland, movements of revival in Scottish missions aroused hopes for the eradication of witchcraft; and in Newala (southern Tanzania), the chief sought missionary help for witchcraft problems. Over the course of the nineteenth century, however, African's decided that the missionaries were not prepared to exercise spiritual power in ways that would truly disempower witchcraft. Although different missions dealt with witchcraft in different ways, Christians generally tackled the problem by emphasizing confidence in the power of God. By that time, Christian churches no longer saw themselves as operating in a world of cause and effect – the age of miracles and exorcism had ended. Central African religions were, thus, left on their own to work out solutions to witchcraft and cleansing.[39]

At Berens River, we find a rich history involving the integrations of two world views. Gordon Berens was clear that his brother, Percy, acquired his special hunting powers from the *Memegwesiwag* and that Fair Wind derived his amazing gifts from the Thunderbirds. His discussion of how he and his father combined Christian with Ojibwa concepts is enlightening.

> Well, it combines together. That's the real way to say. The real true word to use, combine together. Church and the other belief combines together like one. So the church believes the people and the people believes the church, both ways, like. So there's no problem. There's a connection, like, that couldn't break off between the old Indian ways and the present belief. The two beliefs are connected together, just like one.... Both are true. Both ways are true. The Indian ways are true and the white man belief is true, so it's hard to break the two links.[40]

While Ojibwa people had no problem integrating ideas in an effort to expand their knowledge and power, Gordon Berens knew that the same was not true of Euro-Canadians.

> They tried to throw it away, they tried to destroy the Indian way.... A lot of white people don't believe an Indian belief and a white man belief are just like one. They can't break the Indian way from the white man, the white people's way.[41]

For Gordon Berens, the Ojibwa and Christian world views are inextricably linked within his being. This integration was the basis of the structure of meaning and belief for him.

> "You'll never be a white man," I says [to his nephew]. "I respect the white man's way, " I said, "but I still hold on [to] my Indian ways," I said. "Just like one, my way and the white man's way. I believe his ways and I believe my ways".... And I says, "There's a

link that'll never be broken apart. The white man's way and an Indian way.... I've had my dreams all these years and I've been with the white people more than I do with my own people and that's what I say. Both ways are linked together."[42]

Gordon's reference to the ongoing importance of his dreams was equally significant. Dreams and visions as vehicles of prediction, and bringers of clarity are such important parts of the Ojibwa world view that they carry over strongly into Ojibwa Christianity.

In the 1930s, William Berens described a vision to A. Irving Hallowell that presents another striking example of Christianity wedded to Saulteaux belief. The apparition in this mystical foreshadowing was clearly an angel:

My wife and I went to bed about the same time as usual one night but I did not fall asleep at once. My head was turned towards the door leading to the kitchen and all of a sudden I saw a woman standing there. She was slender, dressed in white and had golden hair that fell to her shoulders. I caught a glimpse of wings springing from her back. I trembled all over, I was so scared. But I managed to nudge my wife with my elbow. She had gone to sleep but turned over at this. When I looked again I could not see the angel, for that is what the figure seemed to be. All I could see was something misty like a cloud. My wife saw nothing but I told her what I had seen. I wondered what was going to happen. The next day, which was Sunday, my boss drove up with his dog team. He said that he was on his way to Berens River and asked me to go along with him. I told him that I was not prepared to go and that I had no grub. But he insisted. So I got ready and went with him. When we arrived at Berens River I met my brother-in-law. He told me my sister was very ill. She had been continually asking for me. They were even thinking of sending a dog train for me but they could not get one. I stayed at Berens River for ten days. My sister grew worse and worse. Then she died. I was getting worried but my boss, who had returned from a trip up the river by this time, set my mind at rest. He told me that he was glad he had brought me along so that

I was able to be with my sister the last days of her life. It was very strange that he asked me because he did not seem to have any good reason, except that he wanted company. Yet I got there in time although I did not even know my sister was sick when I started.[43]

Similarly, Walter Green, as noted earlier, had a dream in which a Christian angel appeared to him and taught him how to play the organ.[44] Like Gordon, Walter found it perfectly natural to link Christian and Ojibwa beliefs. I asked him about his thoughts regarding the expectations of missionaries that converts should lay aside Ojibwa beliefs. He laughed, saying, "I think they had the wrong feeling. The ministers should have gone first and seen if whether there was anything bad there. This is just what the people believe – that's their belief – either they're going out or somebody's leaving – so they'll come back to the same way they lived."[45]

> S.G.   Is it true that you can believe in Christ and be a member of
>   a Christian church like the United Church and still believe
>   in doing the drum dances and doing the shaking tent?
> W.G.   Oh yes! And when Sunday comes, it's a special day.[46]

Dreams and visions have played integral roles in Walter's life. He described another vision he had had during the previous summer:

I was alone here in June and then I got a very bad cold. I couldn't sleep at nights, I couldn't lay down.... And then I had a dream – it wasn't a dream, it was a vision. There was somebody sitting by the doorway – on a chair by the doorway – looking at me; and I was turning over and over, trying to sleep. And that was the first night. Then, when the morning came, before sunrise, it was gone. Then the next night I was feeling a little better, I could sleep for awhile, then get up and go back to bed for a little while. And the same person came back – and they were sitting closer to my bed than on the first night. Then before sunrise he was gone. It was a man. That night, I was a lot better, I wasn't coughing at night time, I could sleep good. And that third night he came back – he was sitting at the end of my bed. And before sunrise he was gone. So I told this to a Pentecostal minister. Do you know what he told me? He said, "Somebody's taking care of you – from God." I was telling him that I know now there's somebody with me here, I'm not alone. I must have got blessed. And now I'm never frightened. Now I never have any trouble of fear that anything will happen when I'm sleeping. I don't think about it, I go to bed and sleep.[47]

Walter, during a time of stress and illness, experienced increased powers of protection through a combination of Ojibwa and Christian ideology. His experience of a vision is clearly Ojibwa. At the same time, the idea that his visitor had been sent by the Christian God made sense to him and felt believable and good.

A few days before I met him, Fred Baptiste had attended the funeral of an old friend. What he did there is an example of syncretism, a fusion of cultural traditions:

F.B.   Like the other day I was looking at that picture on the wall there [points to a large colour print of the Last Supper]. I went to the last services for Alec McKay. And they say they represent this [the Last Supper]. I took a piece of cake in a piece of kleenex and I got up. They were talking about Jesus with this last supper he had with the Disciples before he goes to Heaven. "There's a piece of cake in this kleenex," I says "you're always talking about Jesus having the Last Supper. Now I'm going to put this cake where Alec can – inside his coffin. We're having the Last Supper with Alec – his body is going down into the grave." I know some didn't like it.

S.G.   You put that cake in his coffin because, in the Last Supper, Christ ate for a last time?

F.B.   Yes.... I was having the last supper with Alec before he goes down into the grave – he said when he goes home [to the afterlife] he's going to tell other people [spirits of the dead] that I did that.

S.G.   Where did you get the idea to do that?

F.B.   Through that [points to the picture] and from reading the
Bible. I was just thinking about this, you know. I did that
before, this was the second time I did that [Fred had placed
food inside a coffin at a previous funeral].[48]

The Christian idea of the Last Supper converged in his mind with
the Ojibwa custom of placing articles such as food and tobacco on
graves. A. Irving Hallowell speculated that "Indians who adhere
to the native concepts of life after death ... must feel much less
remote from the spirits of the dead than do most who have ...
capitulated to Christian notions."[49] Christianity does not (except
in the case of Catholics praying to saints) allow for communication
with the dead. Traditional Ojibwas, in contrast, held that food and
tobacco should be placed and replaced on graves subsequent to
burial, to aid the journey of the *djibai* or spirit of the dead person,
and to provide for continued visits from the living.[50]

By 1926, Christianity at Berens River had grown strong roots.
Yet as Leach wrote to his father provincial in St. Boniface, "We
say that the Indians are far more civilized than in years gone by.
It is true, but how they do cling to some of their old customs."[51]
The Ojibwa were clearly incorporating Christian elements into
their lives, hence the assessment that they were more "civilized,"
but Leach would have been even more impressed had he looked
harder for Christian elements integrated within the "cling[ing] to
old customs."

Percy Berens was sometimes frustrated at the limitations of
Euro-North Americans to think and believe in a wide scope. This
came out during a discussion about Thunderbirds.

P.B.   Well the white people don't believe in nothing at all! I
might just say that. They don't believe in nothing at all. Not
like we Indians – because our ancestors believed on all these
things. And then we're starting to see it's true – and then we
believe it. Like these Thunderbirds now, the Indians *believe*
from a long time that it's a bird.

S.G.   So they have the Thunderbirds *and* the Bible.

P.B.   Yeah! But the Bible is best. If you *really* explain it to an
       Indian, what the Bible really means and what's in the Bible,
       the Scriptures, like, then they'll be able to believe it, see?

S.G.   But it's okay to believe in the Bible *and* the Thunderbirds?

P.B.   Yeah! Sure!

S.G.   Why?

P.B.   Why not? If we didn't have Thunderbirds, maybe we would
       never have had no rain! And the whole earth would be
       just dried up. And then where are we going to be? Don't
       you know, you white people, don't you know enough that
       everything God created meant something to the people and
       to the beasts of the earth?

S.G.   Some white people say you should believe in the Bible
       but that you shouldn't believe in the ability to conjure or
       in Thunderbirds. But you say you can believe in the Bible
       and you can believe in the Thunderbirds. So how come the
       Indians are different from the white people that way?

P.B.   That's very easy to answer that question. Because the
       Indians are smart, clever – but the white man is stupid,
       ignorant. [Laughs.] Isn't that correct enough? Sure! *We*
       believe.[52]

Berens River Ojibwa flexibility about religion was early manifested
in willingness to partake of events in both Catholic and Protestant
churches. Once the two missions had earned some confidence and
acceptance among the people, these Saulteaux seem to have moved
fairly freely between the two, although they did maintain a loyalty
to the church in which they had been baptized. For example, the
Catholic John Edward Everett remembered the Methodist Niddrie
as "a big minister, a kind minister.... There's been many times since
that I've said 'God, I wish we had a minister like Mr. Niddrie.' A
kind natured person."[53] When asked whether he attended Niddrie's
church services, he replied "Yes! Don't you know there's one God?
It doesn't matter. I'm a Catholic. God, so love us – we have to
go!"[54]

Although Percy Berens was clearly partial to the United Church, he shows typical Ojibwa flexibility in explaining why the Berens River people attended the services of both denominations.

> Because the Indians know enough to know why Christ was born – so it didn't make no difference which church they go…. They wanted to celebrate the birth of Christ. See, it didn't matter where they go. Same with the Catholics – they could go to the United Church on Christmas service because that's what that minister did – not only on Christmas – also on ordinary Sundays.[55]

Virginia McKay, a Catholic, married Tom Boulanger, a Protestant Cree man from Oxford House, on 25 September 1925. Father De Grandpré officiated at the service which was held at the Berens River Roman Catholic Church.

S.G.   Although you were a Catholic, did you ever attend services in the Methodist church?

V.B.   Oh yes – to hear the Bible, you know?

S.G.   Why was it important to listen to the Bible?

V.B.   Because they wanted kids, like, to know about everything.

S.G.   Did you like attending services at the Methodist church?

V.B.   Oh yes – because my husband was Protestant.

S.G.   So you married a Protestant?

V.B.   He went to the Protestant church and got baptized there. He was not a Catholic but we got married at the Catholic church.

S.G.   How did your parents feel about you marrying a Protestant?

V.B.   They didn't want to let me, I guess. They wanted the children to go to the Catholic Church.

S.G.   Did they care that Tom, himself, wasn't a Catholic?

V.B.   No, they didn't care – there's only one God. There's only one door, too, in Heaven, they say.

S.G.   When you met Tom and then found out that he wasn't a Catholic, how did you feel about that?

V.B.   Nothing, I didn't feel nothing.

S.G.   So after you got married which church did you go to – did you go to both?

V.B.   Yeah, sometimes he would go with me to the Catholic Church, sometimes the other.[56]

In sum, Christian and Ojibwa beliefs still combine, to varying degrees, in the minds of many individuals influenced by the Berens River missions. The sincerity of their Christianity and the reality of their Ojibwa world view have remained in evidence and the presence of one has not detracted from the meaning or value of the other.

7   "I Will Fear No Evil"

Conclusions

....

When two religions met along the Berens
River, Ojibwa people accepted elements of Christianity and wove
selected Methodist or Roman Catholic threads into the rich cloth
of their world view. Which threads did they select? Which did
they reject, and why? How did they blend them? Along with
the Christianity that sustained them in their day-to-day life, the
individuals I met retained a belief in such Ojibwa beliefs as the
Thunderbirds and the power of medicine men and conjurors,
as well as in dreams as vehicles of prediction, guidance, and
foreshadowing. As well, many beliefs and ideas shared between
these two religions facilitated the integration of Christianity with
traditional Ojibwa concepts. Striving for honesty, being helpful, not
hurting others/doing unto others what an individual would have
done unto them, the power of belief, and the forgiveness of sins
in the face of confession and repentance are a few of the common
threads in both the teachings of Christ and the Ojibwa belief
structure.

Ojibwa people, upon conversion, had no intention of giving
up the power they already could receive as gifts from other-than-
human spirits. Rather, they often looked to Christianity as a
means of adding to their repertoire – of adding another layer of
armour that could protect them from evil and bring them closer
to a secure and happy life. When the missionaries dictated that
conversion to Christianity entailed complete transformation and
the casting off of old ways, Ojibwa people did not understand –

nor did they wish to understand – these imposed limitations. Why give up things that are already working well and are beneficial?

Belief in the powers of the shaking tent, a rite still practised at Little Grand Rapids during much of this period, is an excellent example of Ojibwa Christians retaining important elements of their traditional religion. This ceremony has curative and clairvoyant functions, as Hallowell learned, observing its use on the upper Berens River in the 1930s. In the case of healing, it has often been used to discover the hidden causes of illness as well as for producing a cure. For example, did the illness come about as a result of sorcery, or because of the moral transgressions of the ill person? If the latter is true, until the transgression is known and a confession is made to the shaman, no medicine can be of use.[1]

As well, the concept of personal relationships between individuals and the divine have provided a bridge between Ojibwa and Christian world views. Methodism embodies the principle of a personal relationship between God and the individual. Certainly, one of the primary social functions of the shaking tent is to personalize spirits and increase intimacy between them and the audience.[2] In these ways, both religions contain a mechanism that generates a sense of safety and confidence in facing life's dangers.

Conjuring may implicitly have reinforced the concept of a high god through its conspicuous absence in the shaking tent – this Being is the only other-than-human entity that is never present during these rituals; and it and other ceremonies shared as a premise the idea of life after death (through communication with the spirits of the dead). The shaking tent indirectly supports the Ojibwa social structure by exposing the dangers that befall people who violate societal mores.[3] These aspects make it possible to forge a link with Christianity which, of course, is centred on the idea of one God, is founded on the idea of an afterlife, and which serves, through its laws, to encourage individuals to confirm to the mores of their Judeo-Christian society.

As late as the 1930s, the Ojibwa saw all spirituality as medicine and power. Both candidates for chief at the signing of

the 1875 treaty at Berens River understood Ojibwa medicine
(one was actively practising and the other, upon conversion to
Christianity, had ceased practising) and their power and esteem
in the community shows the significance of spirituality in their
society. Religion and the protection that resulted with close
alliances with other-than-human spirits were critical for survival
and success. This view persists today, whether Ojibwa people
are discussing the concept of Christ dying for our sins or special
hunting powers granted to an individual by the *Memegwesiwag*, or
the Thunderbirds.

Berens River Ojibwa beliefs in Thunderbirds, the power of
medicine men, and the use of dreams were underpinned in their
frame of reference by empirical proof; indeed, for people living in
a tough physical environment and relying on hunting and trapping
skills for survival, experience and belief must be harmonized in
order for the latter to have credibility. Ojibwa people believed
because they saw, heard, and experienced. Personal testimony,
an instrument of validation in Saulteaux society, has served for
generations to provide corroborative evidence, especially in the
case of multiple testimonies. However, even personal testimony
has been critically weighed. Those people describing experiences
or sightings of things that existed outside the realm of recognized
tradition and mythology or claiming powers that were not
demonstrated, were given no credence.

Part of the Christian context in Berens River communities
was provided by Methodists caught up in an optimistic fervour
and striving to create the Kingdom of God on earth. Missionaries
throughout the world believed that their message could transcend
time, place, and circumstance. They believed their converts,
upon conversion, would take the moral high road and elevate
themselves to a new life.

Until the 1920s, Protestantism was a vital and formative
element in English Canadian culture and Methodists did
integrate new concepts of the day into their mission to
regenerate the world. This, coupled with a lack of understanding

and appreciation of their Cree/Ojibwa fields, made for mis-communication and misjudgements.

Around the world, Roman Catholics were as caught up in mission zeal as Protestants. With the advent of ultramontanism in the nineteenth century, the church experienced a tremendous surge of life and renewal with clerical expansion, an increased impact of the church on the lives of Catholics, a revitalization of its clergy, and an explosion of mission effort. Catholicism's vitality was part of the mosaic that made up the great influence of religion in nineteenth and early twentieth-century Canadian culture.

Like Protestant groups, Catholics believed that they had been chosen by God to fulfil an important mission. In Quebec, the clergy was much influenced by the ultramontane current that invigorated their theology and mission effort. It was this awakening that was manifest in the arrival of the Oblates of Mary Immaculate, an order devoted to mission work and which insisted on Roman supremacy and the opening of mission fields across Canada.

In encounters with Christianity, a number of factors influenced positive responses among native people along the Berens River. These included: a wish for literacy and Western education to assist survival in a world that was being continually affected and changed by Euro-Canadian institutions, a wish to understand the Bible as a source of potentially helpful and beneficial messages, added divine protection from illness or other crises, safety from bad medicine and harmful conjurors, access to Western medicine, and added dimensions and powers to existing ones derived from traditional Ojibwa venues such as rituals.

Where mission efforts were successful in these communities, we usually see the sustained presence of a devoted missionary who lived long enough in a community to achieve respect and earn trust among the people. By the late nineteenth century, many Ojibwa young people at the mouth of the Berens River were already second generation Christians. A tradition and loyalty had been established among individual families, and people wished to remain in the church where they and their parents before them had been baptized. Missionaries provided medical and spiritual aid that bolstered and often ran in tandem with that received from traditional sources such as medicine men. Social interaction between missionaries and parishioners as well as entertainment such as Christmas services or get-togethers at the ministers' homes for young people gave a vitality and presence of the church in the community.

A major theme in the conversion history of Berens River Ojibwa is their continual search for protection against their enemies. Percy Berens spoke with passion about his favourite Biblical Psalm, reciting from memory the verses which can be as meaningful within an Ojibwa context as in a Christian interpretation. The message of the twenty-third Psalm is one of protection from evil and a trust in God to lead a believer into the good life.

> The Lord is my shepherd; I shall not want.... Yea though I walk through the valley of the shadow of death, I will fear no evil; for thou art with me; thy rod and thy staff they comfort me. Thou preparest a table before me in the presence of mine enemies.... Surely goodness and mercy shall follow me all the days of my life; and I will dwell in the house of the Lord forever.

For Percy, the Christian God and his son, Jesus Christ, are powerful spirit helpers who care profoundly for his well-being. They protect him from evil. He will fear no evil.

Christianity, however, was not always accepted out of hand. Lack of support by missionaries (such as the Deer Lake Indians being left to fend for themselves at the time of the 1918 influenza epidemic), lack of agreement with the methods or lessons taught to children in schools, or lack of need to take on aspects of a new religion and lack of respect by a missionary for sacred Ojibwa rituals (such as the episode of a Methodist missionary kicking in the drum at Little Grand Rapids) could all yield cold responses. It is clear that the Berens River Ojibwa maintained considerable control over making choices – it was they who decided when and how they would or would not accept Christianity, when and if they would send their children to a new school, and whether or not they would allow baptism for themselves or their sick and dying relatives. Unlike the Little Grand Rapids community, however, Berens River was an important crossroads. General legislation made it impossible for these Ojibwa to participate in many rituals. Their northerly setting and relative distance from the Prairie conflicts of 1885, however, probably allowed them greater opportunity to maintain aspects of their world view.

Conversions and the taking on of Christianity had multi-dimensional meanings for Ojibwa people living along the Berens River between 1875 and 1940. They interpreted these meanings in myriad ways and incorporated Christian rituals and practices into the fabric of the Saulteaux world view. This they did in ways that were controlled by and meaningful to themselves as participants. Upon accepting Christianity, those Ojibwa whom I met and whom the missionaries knew best integrated it smoothly into their existing world view, striving to learn the Bible, attending church regularly at those times when they were at the mission, and deriving as much power and strength through this medium as possible. Christianity did not replace traditional ideas as much as it served to enhance possibilities and increase dimensions of the understanding and experiencing of life in this world. In listening to my Ojibwa friends, the theme of wanting to know and understand "everything" is as strong as it was when Jacob Berens told his son, William, that he must find a place in his mind for all that he would meet. This pivotal aspect of the Ojibwa world view contributes importantly to our understanding of mission efforts in North America from a native perspective. Essentially, Ojibwa people synthesized two philosophies that worked in concert to yield a flexibility and openness of spirit; on one hand, they realized that they did not know everything (when Jacob Berens told William that he must find a place in his mind for all things, he began by warning his son that he should not make the mistake of thinking he knew everything) and from that premise, they sought meaning and understanding.

It is especially crucial to listen to a multiplicity of voices and to try to hear both sides of the dialogue that occurred between Ojibwa and missionary. On their own, neither the oral nor the written narratives can be considered as the truth wherein the real facts lie. Neither still does the combination of the narratives yield "true history." Rather, as Julie Cruikshank explains, "both of them have to be understood as windows on the way the past is constructed and discussed in different contexts, from the perspective of actors enmeshed in culturally distinct networks of social relationships."[4] Ojibwa and missionaries alike perceived one another through the lenses of their own world view, lenses that were also tinted by the colours of individual experience and personality. These lenses continually overlay one another, yielding a myriad of shades and patterns.

Appendix

Cast of Characters

....

Bear (Maskwa): Yellow Legs's eldest son, Bear, was William
Berens's paternal grandfather. Born about 1790, he married Amo
(Bee) or Victoria. He died at Berens River circa 1873–74, without
converting to Christianity, just before the mission opened there,
although he did adopt the Christian surname Berens. Travelling
with Amo and his younger brother Cauwanas to the east side of
Lake Winnipeg, they brought his father's sacred stone and, in
the 1860s and 1870s, conducted the last Midéwiwin ceremonies
at Berens River. The three were pivotal in maintaining Ojibwa
traditions among subgroups that mingled along the river, reflecting
a variety of adaptations to life in a dynamic community. (A.
Irving Hallowell, ed., "Reminiscences of Chief William Berens,"
unpublished paper, 1940, p. 7.)

Berens, Jacob: A. Irving Hallowell dated Jacob's birth to 1832;
others, translating his name to "Something That Moves Across
the Sky" – a reference to Halley's comet – believe he was born in
1834. He married Mary McKaye [McKay], whose father, William,
was a Hudson's Bay Company trader at the Trout Lake post in
Ontario's Severn River drainage. He was born in Scotland and came
to Canada in 1818. Jacob Berens had four brothers, Joseph, James,
John, and Samuel. Betsey's mother, Victoria Keeper, was John's
daughter. Victoria's parents died when she was a young girl and she
was raised by Jacob. (Jennifer S. H. Brown, "Chief Jacob Berens"
Dictionary of Canadian Biography, vol. 14 [Toronto: University of
Toronto Press, 1998].)

De Grandpré, Joseph: De Grandpré was born at Isle du Pas,
Québec, on 26 March 1882 and died at Saint-Adolphe, Manitoba,
on 7 March 1973. He studied at Assumption College from 1896
to 1905 and entered the novitiate at Lachine on 14 August 1905.
He was ordained at Ottawa on 5 June 1909. He served in western
Canada at Camperville, Manitoba; Beauval, Saskatchewan and
Berens River; Bloodvein and Little Grand Rapids, Manitoba.
(Gaston Carriére, *Dictionnaire Biographique des Oblats de Marie
Immaculée au Canada*, vol. 1 [Ottawa: Éditions de l'Université
d'Ottawa, 1976], p. 261.)

Durkin, Douglas: Durken (1884–1968) was born and raised in
Parry Sound, Ontario. His mother, a strong Methodist, wanted
him to become a missionary in China and, while he had lost
interest in religious education by his early teens, her personality
and influence remained with him throughout his life. As a young
man, he worked with railway gangs and as a pianist for silent
movies in Winnipeg theatres. After graduating with a B.A. from
the University of Manitoba, Durkin lectured at a number of
schools in English and history, most notably Brandon College, until
1917 when he accepted a position as a lecturer in English at the
University of Manitoba where he later became assistant professor.
He moved to New York City in 1921 where he devoted his life
to writing his novels, the most notable of which is *The Magpie*
(1923), and teaching at Columbia University. Durkin married and
collaborated on a number of literary works with Martha Ostenso
who was also well known to the North American literati. His short
stories appeared in such popular magazines as *Harper's Magazine*,
Liberty, and *Century*. Durkin also composed a number of ballads
in collaboration with Carl Sandberg and wrote a screenplay, *Union
Depot*, with Gene Fowler. His mother's Methodist ideals manifested
themselves throughout Durkin's life; he was socialistic in outlook
and espoused progressive reforms regardless of public opinion. "His
hope for man's regeneration depended upon humanity's spiritual
salvation, not on political action." (Peter E. Rider's introduction to

Douglas Durkin, *The Magpie* [Toronto: University of Toronto Press, 1974], pp. xvi–xviii.)

Everett, John James: Everett was born in Berens River in 1894 and spent his life working in several other northern Manitoba and northwestern Ontario communities. A hunter and trapper, Everett also kept cows and horses. He and his wife, Alice, raised their own as well as many adopted and orphaned children. An elder in the Berens River Church for many years, he undertook full-time ministry work about 1960. Everett served as Lay Supply at Little Grand Rapids, Pikangikum and Berens River. He died in St. Adophe on 17 May 1976. As well as ministerial duties, Everett worked on translating the New Testament Scriptures and collaborated with Charles Fière, of Cross Lake, on translating the Gospel into Saulteaux. He lived to see the first copies of the Gospel of Mark published by the Canadian Bible Society. (Victoria University Archives, Biographical Files.)

Jones, Rev. Joseph: Joseph Jones (1881–1970) originally trained as a carpenter, was born in Lancashire, England, and arrived in Canada in 1902. He served as a carpenter and physical instructor at Brandon Industrial School between 1904 and 1907 and worked at Little Grand Rapids from 1907 to 1911 when he left to attend theological studies at Wesley College from whence he graduated in 1911. Between 1911 and 1914, the year of his ordination, Jones served as assistant principal at the Brandon School, designing a new school for Norway House where he served from 1914 to 1916. After overseas service in World War I, Jones served the rest of his career in Indian communities in northern Manitoba, building mission houses at Norway House, Cross Lake, Island Lake, and God's Lake, and serving as Principal of Portage la Prairie's Indian Residential School from 1934 to 1942. Jones married Florence Consterdine (1882–1988) who served as field matron at Cross Lake from 1926 to 1929 and matron at the Portage la Prairie school. (Victoria University Archives, Biographical Files.)

Jones, Rev. Percy Earl: Percy Earl Jones was born in Tunbridge Wells, England, in 1888. In 1908, he began his theological studies in Winnipeg's Wesley College. Jones served ten years in Methodist work at Poplar River and Berens River. He died in Melita, Manitoba, on 8 May 1940. Leach, Frederick: Leach was born in London, England on 14 July 1892. He joined the Oblates of Mary Immaculate on 9 March 1913 at Lachine, Québec, and took his perpetual vows on 9 March 1920 at Berens River. Leach also served at Bloodvein and Little Grand Rapids. He continued living in Berens River after his semi-retirement in 1965 until 1978 where he entered full retirement in St. Boniface. Leach died on 12 July 1982 at the residence of the Oblates of Mary Immaculate, St. Boniface. (Brother Frederick Leach, *Sixty years With Indians and Settlers on Lake Winnipeg* [Winnipeg: Oblates of Mary Immaculate, Manitoba Province, c.1983].)

McEwen, Annie E.: McEwen was a member of a prominent Red River settlement family. (PAM, A. E. McEwen Papers, MG8 B52, fos. 36–42, A. E. McEwen, Memoirs, "Four Years at Berens River.")

McKay, Mary: McKay (1836–1908) was the granddaughter of Donald McKay, a Scottish fur trader who was employed by the Hudson's Bay Company. Her father, William McKay, was the Hudson's Bay Company trader at Trout Lake in Ontario's Severn River drainage. Her parents and grandparents were of Scottish and Cree descent. Her skin was light and there did not exist among Berens River Ojibwa the intermediate racial term, *métis*. As well, she spoke English and possessed English cultural characteristics. This led the community to see her as white (A. Irving Hallowell, *The Ojibwa of Berens River, Manitoba: Ethnography into History*, edited with Preface and Afterword by Jennifer S.H. Brown [Fort Worth, Texas: Harcourt, Brace Jovanovich College Publishers, 1992], p. 15, n. 8).

McLachlan, James A.: McLachlan was born near Aylmer, Ontario, on 22 October 1855. After attending the Victoria and the Wesleyan Theological Colleges, he was ordained by the Conference in 1879. After twelve years in charge of the Victoria Indian Mission, he was transferred to Berens River in 1893. He and a boatload of six children, en route to the Brandon Industrial School, were drowned on Lake Winnipeg on 12 September 1903. McLachlan was buried at Berens River. (Victoria University Archives, Biographical Files.)

Niddrie, Annie: Niddrie was born in Morley, Alberta, on 18 February 1892 and died at Berens River on 19 February 1982. She worked at Berens River as organist, taught Sunday School and, in her words, "sat up with the dead when there was no one else available."

Niddrie, Rev. John: the Reverend Niddrie was born in Oban, Scotland, on 22 September 1863. After arriving in Canada in 1884, he was ordained in 1915 and was stationed at the McDougall Mission in Morley, Alberta, from 1889 to 1909. In Manitoba, he worked at Oxford House from 1910 to 1915 and Island Lake from 1915 to 1920. He then ministered at Berens River until his retirement in 1938. Niddrie died and was buried at Berens River on 4 May 1940. (Victoria University Archives, Biographical Files.)

Semmens, Rev. John: Semmens began his work in northern Manitoba as a Methodist missionary. In April 1901 he accepted the position of Indian agent at Berens River, replacing J. W. Short, who was retiring. He went on to become inspector of Indian agencies for the Department of Indian Affairs. He spoke highly of the first convert at Berens River, describing Jacob Berens as "a most thoughtful man, a good reasoner and a wise administrator." (United Church Archives, Conference of Manitoba and Northwestern Ontario, Personal Papers of John Semmens, PP34, File M, Rev. John Semmens, "Under Northern Lights: Notes on Personal History," p. 62.)

Yellow Legs: Yellow Legs, who married Mistamut, lived on the west side of Lake Winnipeg in the late 1700s. It is likely that his origins were in the Lake Superior area and if this is true, he would have been one of the first Ojibwa to move into the Lake Winnipeg area as the first major migrations there likely occurred between the 1780s and 1790s, a time when the Ojibwa and their Montreal-based fur trade counterparts expanded their territories westward. He died before 1830.

Bibliography

....

Archival Sources

American Philosophical Society, Philadelphia
A. Irving Hallowell Papers
> A. Irving Hallowell, ed. "Reminiscences of Chief William Berens." Transcribed
> by Jennifer S. H. Brown and Maurice Berens
Frank Speck Correspondence

Archives Deschâtelets, Ottawa
Oblates of Mary Immaculate, Berens River and Little Grand Rapids, Correspondence

National Archives of Canada, Ottawa
Records Relating to Indian Affairs
> Black Series
> School Records

Oblate Archives, Manitoba Province, Winnipeg
Frederick Leach, "Journal," 1923–1939

Provincial Archives of Manitoba, Winnipeg
Julia Asher (née Short) Reminiscences
W. M. Chapman Journal, 1912–1915
Lieutenant-Governor's Collection
Annie E. McEwen, "Four Years at Berens River"
United Church Registers (Little Grand Rapids, 1922–1939)

United Church Archives, Conference of Manitoba and Northwestern Ontario, University of Winnipeg, Winnipeg

Roscoe Chapin, "Memoirs of a Happy Journey Through Life"

J. A. C. Kell Papers

J. A. Lousley Papers

Luther Schuetze Papers

John Semmens Papers

F. G. Stevens Papers

"The Autobiography of Frederick George Stevens, Doctor of Divinity, Indian Missionary, Cree Scholar," 1950

Mrs. F. G. Stevens Papers

Victoria University Archives, Toronto

Biographical Files

John James Everett

Joseph Henry Lowes

Joseph Jones

Percy Earl Jones

James A. McLachlan

John W. Niddrie

Luther L. Schuetze

Board of Home Missions, General Files

James Endicott, Correspondence

T. E. Egerton Shore, Correspondence

Theses and Dissertations

Beckett, Kristen M. "Investigating Disease Experience in Aboriginal Populations in Canada: The 1918 Influenza Pandemic in Berens River and Poplar River, Manitoba." M.A. thesis, McMaster University, 1998.

Brooks, W. H. "Methodism in the Canadian West in the Nineteenth Century." Ph.D. diss., University of Manitoba, 1972.

Dueck, Susan Elaine. "Methodist Indian Day Schools and Indian Communities in Northern Manitoba, 1890–1925." M.A. thesis, University of Manitoba, 1986.

McCarthy, Martha. "The Missions of the Oblates of Mary Immaculate to the Athapaskans 1846–1870: Theory, Structure and Method." Ph.D. diss., University of Manitoba, 1981.

Pannekoek, Frits. "Protestant Agricultural Missions in the Canadian West to 1870." M.A. thesis, University of Alberta, 1970.

Miscellaneous Sources

Interviews: Susan Gray with Percy Berens; Walter Green; Betsey Patrick; Virginia Boulanger; Ida Green; Fred Baptiste; John Edward Everett.

Jennifer S. H. Brown and Maureen Matthews with Gordon Berens.

Flannery, Regina. "Thoughts on the Cree Concept of the Supreme Being in Response to Long's Interview with Preston: 'The Northern Algonquian Supreme Being Revisited.'" Unpublished paper, 1984.

Matthews, Maureen. "Thunderbirds." Transcript of a Canadian Broadcasting Corporation documentary for the series *Ideas*. 15, 16 May 1995.

Niddrie, Annie. "Annie Niddrie of Berens River." Edited by John Chalmers. 1940.

Niddrie, Rev. John W. "Niddrie of the Northwest: Memoirs of Rev. John W. Niddrie." Edited by John Chalmers. 1938.

Rundle, Robert Terrill. "Journal of Robert Terrill Rundle." MSS Glenbow Foundation, Calgary, Alberta.

Published Sources

Abel, Kerry. *Drum Songs: Glimpses of Dene History.* Montreal: McGill-Queen's University Press, 1993.

Abell, Arthur M. *Great Composers: Candid Conversations with Brahms, Puccini, Strauss and Others.* New York: Philosophical Library, Inc.,1955.

Adams, Howard. *Prison of Grass: Canada from a Native Point of View.* Saskatoon: Fifth House Publishers, 1989.

Airhart, Phyllis. *Serving the Present Age: Revivalism, Progressivism, and the Methodist Tradition in Canada.* Montreal: McGill-Queen's University Press, 1992.

Allen, Richard. *The Social Passion: Religion and Reform in Canada 1914–1928.* Toronto: University of Toronto Press, 1973.

Annual Report to the Church of the Methodist Missionary Society. 1875–1940.

Axtell, James. *After Columbus: Essays in the Ethnohistory of Colonial North America.* New York: Oxford University Press, 1988.

————.*The European and the Indian: Essays in the History of Colonial North America.* New York: Oxford University Press, 1981.

————. *The Invasion Within: the Contest of Cultures in Colonial North America.* New York: Oxford University Press, 1985.

————. "Some Thoughts on the Ethnohistory of Missions." *Ethnohistory* 29, no. 2 (1982), pp. 35–41.

Berkhofer, Robert F. *Salvation and the Savage: An Analysis of Protestant Missions and American Indian Response. 1787–1862.* Lexington: University of Kentucky Press, 1965.

Bishop, Charles A. *The Northern Ojibwa and the Fur Trade: An Historical and Ecological Study.* Toronto: Holt, Rinehart and Winston, 1974.

Bolt, Clarence. *Thomas Crosby and the Tsimshian: Small Shoes for Feet too Large.* Vancouver: UBC Press, 1992.

————. "The Conversion of the Port Simpson Tsimshian: Indian Control or Missionary Manipulation?" *B.C. Studies* 57 (1983), pp. 38–56.

Boon, T. C. B. *The Anglican Church from the Bay to the Rockies.* Toronto: Ryerson Press, 1973.

Boulanger, Tom. *My Life as a Trapper in Northern Manitoba.* Winnipeg: Pemmican Press, 1971.

Brown, Jennifer S. H. "'A Place in Your Mind for Them All': Chief William Berens." In *Being and Becoming Indian: Biographical Studies of North American Frontiers.* Edited by James A. Clifton. Chicago: Dorsey Press, 1989.

————. "Jacob Berens." In *Dictionary of Canadian Biography.* Vol. 14. Toronto: University of Toronto Press, 1998.

————. "Fields of Dreams: Revisiting A.I. Hallowell and the Berens River Ojibwa." Sergei Kan and Pauline Turner Strong, eds. *Native Americans: Histories, Cultures, and Representations.* Lincoln: University of Nebraska Press, 2006.

————. "The Track to Heaven: the Hudson Bay Cree Religious Movement of 1842–43." In *Papers of the Thirteenth Algonquian Conference.* Edited by William Cowan. Ottawa: Carleton University, 1982.

————. "'I wish to be as I see you': an Ojibwa-Methodist Encounter in the Fur Trade Country, Rainy Lake, 1854–55." *Arctic Anthropology* 24, no. 1 (1987), pp. 19–31.

———— and Robert Brightman. *"The Orders of the Dreamed": George Nelson on Cree and Northern Ojibwa Religion and Myth, 1823.* Winnipeg: University of Manitoba Press, 1988.

———— with Maureen Matthews. "Fair Wind: Medicine and Consolation Along the Berens River." *The Journal of the Canadian Historical Association* (1993), pp. 55–74.

———— and Elizabeth Vibert. eds. *Reading Beyond Words: Contexts for Native History.* Peterborough, Ont.: Broadview Press, 1996.

Bruno-Jofré, Rosa del C. "The Oblate Sisters, A Manitoban Order: Reconstructing the Early Years, 1904–1915." In *Issues in the History of Education in Manitoba: From the Construction of the Common School to the Politics of Voices*. Edited by Rosa del C. Bruno-Jofré. Queenston, Ont.: Edwin Mullen, 1993.

Buckland, A. R. *John Horden, Missionary Bishop: A Life on the Shores of Hudson's Bay*. London: Sunday School Union, 1895.

Canada Sessional Papers, (1875–1930). Annual Reports of the Department of Indian Affairs.

Canadian Catholic Historical Association: Annual Reports and Study Guides.

Careless, J. M. S. *The Union of the Canadas, 1841–1857*. Toronto: McClelland & Stewart, 1971.

Carriére, Gaston. "The Early Efforts of the Oblate Missionaries in Western Canada." *Prairie Forum* 4, no. 1 (1979), pp. 1–23.

———. *Dictionnaire Biographique des Oblats de Marie Immaculée au Canada*. 4 vols. Ottawa: Editions de l'Université d'Ottawa, 1976.

———. *The Oblates and the Northwest, 1845–1961*. Toronto: Canadian Catholic Historical Association, 1970.

Carroll, John. *Case and his Contemporaries*. 5 vols. Toronto: Wesleyan Office, 1867–77.

Carter, Sarah. *Lost Harvests: Prairie Indian Reserve Farmers and Government Policy*. Montreal: McGill-Queen's University Press, 1990.

Cayley, David. *Northrop Frye In Conversation*. Concord, Ont.: House of Anansi Press, 1992.

Champagne, Joseph Etienne, O.M.I. *Manual of Missionary Action*. Ottawa: University of Ottawa Press, 1948.

Choquette, Robert. *The Oblate Assault on Canada's Northwest*. Ottawa: University of Ottawa Press, 1995.

Christenson, Torben and William R. Hutchison. eds. *Missionary Ideologies in the Imperialist Era: 1880–1920*. Århus, Denmark: Bogtrykkeri, 1982.

The Christian Guardian, 1875–1920.

Chute, Janet Elizabeth. *The Legacy of Shingwaukonse: A Century of Native Leadership*. Toronto: University of Toroneto Press, 1998.

Colpe, Carsten. "Syncretism." In *The Encyclopedia of Religion*. Mircea Eliade, Editor in Chief. New York: Macmillan, 1987.

Comaroff, Jean. *Body of Power, Spirit of Resistance: The Culture and History of a South African People*. Chicago: University of Chicago Press, 1985.

Comaroff, Jean and John L. Comaroff. *Ethnography and the Historical Imagination*. Boulder, Colo.: Westview Press. 1992.

———. *Modernity and its Malcontents: Ritual and Power in Post-Colonial Africa*. Chicago: University of Chicago Press, 1993.

———— *Of Revelation and Revolution.* Chicago: University of Chicago Press, 1991.

Cook, Ramsay. *The Regenerators: Social Criticism in Late Victorian English Canada.* Toronto: University of Toronto Press, 1985.

DeCoccola, Raymond and Paul King. *The Incredible Eskimo: Life Among the Barren Land Eskimo.* Surrey, B.C.: Hancock House, 1986.

DeMallie, Raymond J., ed. *The Sixth Grandfather: Black Elk's Teachings Given to John Niehardt.* Lincoln: University of Nebraska Press, 1984.

DeMallie, Raymond and Douglas R. Parks. *Sioux Indian Religion: Tradition and Innovation.* Norman: University of Oklahoma Press, 1987.

Desmangles, Leslie G. "African Interpretations of the Christian Cross in Vodun." *Sociological Analysis* 38, no. 1 (1977), pp. 63–75.

Devens, Carol. *Countering Colonization: Native American Women and Great Lake Missions, 1630–1900.* Berkeley: University of California Press, 1992.

Dickason, Olive Patricia. *Canada's First Nations: A History of Founding Peoples From Earliest Times.* Toronto: McClelland and Stewart, 1992.

———— . *The Myth of the Savage: the Beginnings of French Colonialism in the Americas.* Edmonton: University of Alberta Press, 1984.

Dolphin, Frank J. *Indian Bishop of the West: the Story of Vital Justice Grandin, 1829–1902.* Ottawa: Novalis, 1982.

Duchaussois, Pierre. *Hidden Apostles: Our Lay Brother Missionaries.* Ottawa: University of Ottawa Press, 1937.

Dunning, R. W. *Social and Economic Change Among the Northern Ojibwa.* Toronto: University of Toronto Press, 1959.

Fiddler, Thomas. *Legends From the Forest.* Edited by James Stevens. Moonbeam, Ont.: Penumbra Press, 1985.

Fiddler, Thomas and James R. Stevens. *Killing the Shamen.* Moonbeam, Ont.: Penumbra Press, 1985.

Fienup-Riordan, Ann. *The Real People and the Children of Thunder: the Yup'ik Eskimo Encounter With Moravian Missionaries John and Edith Kilbuck.* Norman: University of Oklahoma Press, 1991.

Francis, Daniel and Toby Morantz. *Partners in Furs: A History of the Fur Trade in Eastern James Bay, 1600–1870.* Montreal: McGill-Queen's University Press, 1983.

Gagan, Rosemary. *A Sensitive Independence: Canadian Methodist Women Missionaries in Canada and the Orient 1881–1925.* Montreal: McGill-Queen's University Press, 1985.

Gaudin, S. D. *Forty-Four Years With the Northern Crees.* Toronto: Mundy-Goodfellow, 1942.

Gauvreau, Michael. *The Evangelical Century: College and Creed in English Canada From the Great Revival to the Great Depression.* Montreal: McGill-Queen's University Press, 1991.

———. "Beyond the Halfway House: Evangelicalism and the Shaping of English Canadian Culture." *Acadiensis* 20, no. 2 (1991), pp. 158–77.

General Conference Journals. "Report of the General Board of Missions." United Church Archives, Conference of Manitoba and Northwestern Ontario, Winnipeg, Manitoba.

Gilbert, Maurice and Normand Martel. *Dictionnaire Biographique des Oblats de Marie Immaculee au Canada.* vol. 4. Montreal: Missionnaires Oblats de Marie Immaculée, 1989.

Goulet, Jean-Guy A. *Ways of Knowing: Experience, Knowledge and Power Among the Dene Tha'.* Lincoln: University of Nebraska Press, 1998.

———. "Religious Dualism Among Athapaskan Catholics." *Canadian Journal of Anthropology* 3, no. 1 (1982), pp. 1–18.

Graham, Elizabeth. *Medicine Man to Missionary: Missionaries as Agents of Cultural Change Among the Indians of Southern Ontario, 1784–1867.* Toronto: Peter Martin Associates, 1975.

Grant, John Webster. *A Profusion of Spires: Religion in Nineteenth-Century Ontario.* Toronto: University of Toronto Press, 1988.

———. *The Moon of Wintertime: Missionaries and the Indians of Canada in Encounter Since 1534.* Toronto: University of Toronto Press, 1984.

Gray, Susan Elaine. "Methodist Indian Day Schools and Indian Communities in Northern Manitoba, 1890–1925." *Manitoba History* 30 (1995), pp. 2–16.

———. "'They Fought Just Like a Cat and a Dog!': Oblate-Methodist Relations at Berens River, Manitoba, 1920–1940." *Prairie Forum* 24, no. 1 (1999), pp. 51–64.

Gualtieri, Antonio R. *Christianity and Native Traditions: Indigenization and Syncretism Among the Inuit and Dene of the Western Arctic.* Notre Dame, Ind.: Cross Cultural Publications, 1984.

———. "Indigenization of Christianity and Syncretism Among the Indians and Inuit of the Western Arctic." *Canadian Ethnic Studies* 12, no. 1 (1980).

Gutierrez, Ramon. *When Jesus Came the Corn Mothers Went Away: Marriage and Sexuality in New Mexico 1500–1846.* Stanford, Calif.: Stanford University Press, 1991.

Halevy, Elie. *The Birth of Methodism in England.* Chicago: Clarendon Press, 1971.

Hallowell, A. Irving. *Contributions to Anthropology.* Chicago: University of Chicago Press, 1976.

———. *Culture and Experience.* Philadelphia: University of Pennsylvania Press, 1955.

———. *The Ojibwa of Berens River, Manitoba: Ethnography into History.* Edited with Preface and Afterword by Jennifer S. H. Brown. Fort Worth, Tex.: Harcourt, Brace Jovanovich, 1992.

———. *The Role of Conjuring in Saulteaux Society.* New York: Octagon Books, 1971.

———. "Some Empirical Aspects of Northern Saulteaux Religion." *Ethnohistory* 40, no. 1 (1934), pp. 389–404.

———. "Spirits of the Dead in Saulteaux Life and Thought." *Journal of the Royal Anthropological Institute* 70 (1940), pp. 29–51.

Hammond-Tooke, W. D. "The Aetiology of Spirit in Southern Africa," *African Studies* 45, no. 2 (1986), pp. 30–44.

Harkin, Michael. "Power and Progress: The Evangelistic Dialogue Among the Heiltsuk." *Ethnohistory* 40, no. 1 (1993), pp. 1–29.

Hefner, Robert. *Conversion to Christianity: Historical and Anthropological Perspectives on a Great Transformation.* Berkeley: University of California Press, 1993.

Herring, D. Ann. "'There Were Young People and Old People and Babies Dying Every Week': The 1918–1919 Influenza Pandemic at Norway House." *Ethnohistory* 41, no. 1 (1993), pp. 73–99.

Herring, Joseph B. "Kennekuk, the Kickapoo Prophet: Acculturation Without Assimilation." *American Indian Quarterly* 9, no. 3 (1985), pp. 295–307.

Hilton, Boyd. *The Age of Atonement: The Influence of Evangelicalism on Social and Economic Thought, 1795–1865.* Oxford: Clarendon Press, 1988.

Huel, Raymond J. A. *Proclaiming the Gospel to the Indians and Metis: The Missionary Oblates of Mary Immaculate in Western Canada, 1845–1945.* Edmonton: University of Alberta Press, 1995.

———. "Gestae Dei Per Francos: The French Catholic Experience in Western Canada." In *Visions of The New Jerusalem: Religious Settlement on the Prairies.* Edited by Benjamin G. Smillie. Edmonton: NeWest Publishers, 1983.

———, ed. *Western Oblate Studies*, 2. Lampeter, Wales: Edwin Mellen, 1992.

The Indian Missionary Record, 1938–1939. The Oblate Archives, Manitoba Province, Winnipeg, Manitoba.

Jolicoeur, Luis. *El cristianismo aymara: ¿inculturación o culturizacion?.* Cochabamba, Bolivia: Universidad Católica Boliviana, 1994.

Kan, Sergei. *Symbolic Immortality: the Tlingit Potlatch of the Nineteenth Century.* Washington: Smithsonian Institution Press, 1989.

———. "Shamanism and Christianity: Modern-Day Tlingit Elders Look at the Past." *Ethnohistory* 38, no. 4 (1991), pp. 363–87.

Kracht, Benjamin R. "The Kiowa Ghost Dance, 1894–1916: An Unheralded Revitalization Movement." *Ethnohistory* 39, no. 4 (1992), pp. 452–77.

Kugel, Rebecca. "Of Missionaries and Their Cattle: Ojibwa Perceptions of a Missionary as Evil Shaman." *Ethnohistory* 41, no. 2 (1994), pp. 227–44.

Landes, Ruth. *Ojibwa Religion and the Midewiwin*. Madison: University of Wisconsin Press, 1968.

Leach, Frederick. "Indian Medicine Men and Their Remedies." *The Moccasin Telegraph*, Winter (1966.)

———. "Fifty-Five Years With Indians and Settlers on Lake Winnipeg." (1973.)

Levasseur, Donat. *Les Oblats de Marie Immaculée dans l'Ouest et le Nord du Canada, 1845–1967*. Edmonton: University of Alberta Press, 1995.

Lindsay, Sandy. *Berens River: A Community Study, Teachers Guide*. Frontier School Division No. 48, 1992.

Long, John S. "*Manitu*, Power, Books and *Wiihtikow*: Some Factors in the Adoption of Christianity by the Nineteenth-Century Western James Bay Cree," *Native Studies Review* 3, no. 1 (1987), pp. 1–30.

———. "Rev. Edwin Watkins: Missionary to the Cree, 1852–1857." Pp. 91–117 in *Papers of the Sixteenth Algonquian Conference*. William Cowan, ed. Ottawa: Carleton University Press, 1985.

———. "The Reverend George Barnley and the James Bay Cree." *The Canadian Journal of Native Studies* 6, no. 2 (1986): 313–31.

———. "The Reverend George Barnley, Wesleyan Methodism, and the Fur Trade Company Families of James Bay." *Ontario History* 77, no. 1 (March 1985), pp. 43–64.

Lower, Arthur R. M. *My First Seventy-Five Years*. Toronto: MacMillan of Canada, 1967.

Lytwyn, Victor P. *The Fur Trade of the Little North: Indians, Pedlars and Englishmen East of Lake Winnipeg, 1760–1821*. Winnipeg: Rupertsland Research Centre, University of Winnipeg, 1986.

Maclean, John. *Vanguards of Canada*. Toronto: Mission Society of the Methodist Church, 1918.

Marano, Lou. "Windigo Psychosis: The Anatomy of an Emic-Etic Confusion." *Current Anthropology* 23, no. 4 (August 1982), 385–412.

Marshall, David B. *Secularizing the Faith: Canadian Protestant Clergy and the Crisis of Belief*. Toronto: University of Toronto Press, 1992.

———. "Canadian Historians, Secularization and the Problem of the Nineteenth Century." *Canadian Catholic Historical Association, Historical Studies* 60 (1993–1994), pp. 57–81.

McCarthy, Martha. *From the Great River to the Ends of the Earth: Oblate Missions to the Dene, 1847–1921*. Edmonton: University of Alberta Press and Western Canadian Publishers, 1995.

McColl, Frances. *Ebenezer McColl: "Friend to the Indians."* Winnipeg: Hignell Printing, 1989.

McGowan, Mark G. "The Catholic Restoration: Pope Pius X, Archbishop Denis O'Connor and Popular Catholicism in Toronto." *Canadian Catholic Historical Association, Historical Studies* 54 (1987), pp. 69–91.

———. "Rethinking Catholic-Protestant Relations in Canada: The Episcopal Reports of 1900–1901." *Canadian Catholic Historical Association, Historical Studies* 59 (1992), pp. 11–32.

McKillop, A. B. *A Disciplined Intelligence: Critical Inquiry and Canadian Thought in the Victorian Era.* Montreal: McGill-Queen's University Press, 1979.

The Missionary Bulletin. Toronto: The Missionary Society of the Methodist Church, 1903–1914.

The Missionary Outlook, 1881–1920.

Moir, John S. and C. T. McIntire, eds. *Canadian Protestant and Catholic Missions, 1820's-1960's: Historical Essays in Honour of John Webster Grant.* New York: Peter Lang, 1988.

Mol, Hans. *The Fixed and the Fickle: Religion and Identity in New Zealand.* Waterloo: Wilfrid Laurier Press, 1982.

Morice, A.G. *History of the Catholic Missions in Western Canada from Lake Superior to the Pacific, 1659–1895.* 2 vols. Toronto: Musson Book Company, 1910.

Morrison, Kenneth M. "Baptism and Alliance: The Symbolic Mediations of Religious Syncretism." *Ethnohistory* 37, no. 4 (1990), pp. 416–35.

Mulhall, David. *Will to Power: The Missionary Career of Father Morice.* Vancouver: University of British Columbia, 1986.

Murphy, Terrence and Gerald Stortz, eds. *Creed and Culture: the Place of English-Speaking Catholics in Canadian Society, 1750–1930.* Montreal: McGill-Queen's University Press, 1993.

Nute, Grace Lee, ed. *Documents Relating to Northwest Missions, 1815–1827.* St. Paul: Minnesota Historical Society, 1942.

Owens, Brian M. and Allan D. Ridge, eds. *The Diaries of Bishop Vital Grandin, 1875–1877.* vol. 1. Edmonton: Historical Society of Alberta, 1989.

Peers, Laura. *The Ojibwa of Western Canada, 1780–1870.* Winnipeg: University of Manitoba Press, 1994.

Pettipas, Katherine. *Severing the Ties that Bind: Government Repression of Indigenous Religious Ceremonies on the Prairies.* Winnipeg: University of Manitoba Press, 1994.

Pierce, Lorne. *James Evans* Toronto: Ryerson Press, 1926.

Polson, Gordon and Roger Spielmann. "'Once There Were Two Brothers . . .': Religious Tension in One Algonquin Community." Pp. 303–12 in *Papers of the Twenty-First Algonquian Conference.* William Cowan, ed. Ottawa: Carleton Univeristy Press, 1990.

Preston, Richard J. *Cree Narrative*, 2nd ed. Montreal: McGill-Queen's University Press, 2002.

Preston, Sarah. *Let the Past Go: A Life History.* Canadian Ethnology Service Paper No. 104. Ottawa: National Museums of Canada, 1986.

Ranger, Terence O., and John Weller, eds. *Themes in the Christian History of Central Africa.* Berkeley: University of California Press, 1975.

Rawlyk, George A., ed. *The Canadian Protestant Experience 1760–1990.* Burlington, Ont.: Welch Publishing, 1990.

Richter, Daniel K. "'Some of Them...Would Always Have a Missionary With Them': Mohawk Protestantism, 1683–1719." *American Indian Quarterly* 16, no. 4 (1992), pp. 471–84.

Riddell, J. H. *Methodism in the Middle West.* Toronto: Ryerson Press, 1946.

Rogers, E. S. *The Round Lake Ojibwa.* Toronto: Ontario Department of Lands and Forests for the Royal Ontario Museum, 1962.

———. and Mary Black Rogers. "Who Were the Cranes? Groups and Group Identity Names in Northern Ontario." In *Approaches to Algonquian Archaeology.* Edited by Margaret G. Hanna and Brian Kooyman. Calgary: University of Calgary, 1982.

Rogers, Mary Black. "Ojibwa Power Belief Systems." In *The Anthropology of Power: Ethnographic Studies From Asia, Oceana and the New World.* Edited by Raymond D. Fogelson and Richard N. Adams. New York: Academic Press, 1977.

———. "Ojibwa Power Interactions: Creating Contexts for 'Respectful Talk'." *Proceedings of the Conference on Native North American Interaction Patterns.* Edited by Regina Darnell. Ottawa: National Museums, 1985.

Ryerson, John. *Hudson's Bay; or, A Missionary Tour in the Territory of the Honourable Hudson's Bay Company.* Toronto: G. R. Sanderson, 1855.

Salisbury, Neal. *Manitou and Providence: Indians, Europeans and the Making of New England, 1500–1643.* New York: Oxford University Press, 1982.

Semmens, Rev. John. *The Field and the Work: Sketches of Missionary Life in the Far North.* Toronto: Methodist Mission Rooms, 1884.

Shipley, Nan. *The James Evans Story.* Toronto: Ryerson Press, 1966.

Smith, Donald B. *Sacred Feathers: The Reverend Peter Jones (Kahkewaquonaby) & the Mississauga Indians.* Toronto: University of Toronto Press, 1987.

Smith, T. Lynn. "Three Specimens of Religious Syncretism in Latin America." *International Review of Modern Sociology* 4, no. 1 (1974), pp. 35–50.

Stanley, Brian. *The Bible and the Flag: Protestant Missions and British Imperialism in the Nineteenth and Twentieth Centuries.* Leicester: Apollos, 1990.

Steinbring, Jack H. "Lake Winnipeg Saulteaux." In *Handbook of North American Indians.* Vol. 6: *Subarctic,* pp. 244–55. Edited by June Helm. Washington: Smithsonian Institution Press, 1981.

Thompson, E. P. *The Making of the English Working Class.* England: Penguin Books, 1981.

Tough, Frank. *"As Their Natural Resources Fail": Native Peoples and the Economic History of Northern Manitoba, 1870–1930.* Vancouver: UBC Press, 1996.

Townsend, W. J., H. B. Workman, and George Earys. *A New History of Methodism.* London: Hodder and Stoughton, 1909.

Turner, John Munsey. *Conflict and Reconciliation: Studies in Methodism and Ecumenism in England 1740–1982.* London: Epworth Press, 1985.

Van Die, Margaret. *An Evangelical Mind: Nathaniel Burwash and the Methodist tradition in Canada, 1839–1918.* Montreal: McGill-Queen's University Press, 1989.

Vescey, Christopher. *Traditional Ojibwa Religion and its Historical Changes.* Philadelphia: American Philosophical Society, 1983.

Westfall, William. *Two Worlds: The Protestant Culture of Nineteenth Century Ontario.* Montreal: McGill-Queen's University Press, 1989.

Western Oblate Studies: Proceedings of the Symposium on the History of the Oblates in Western and Northern Canada. Edmonton, Alta.: Western Canadian Publishers, 1990.

Whitehead, Margaret. *They Call Me Father: Memoirs of Father Nicolas Coccola.* Vancouver: UBC Press, 1988.

Young, E.R. *On the Indian Trail: Stories of Missionary Work Among the Cree and Saulteaux Indians.* New York: Young People's Missionary Movement, 1897.

———. *Oowikapun; or How the Gospel Reached the Nelson River Indians,* Toronto: William Briggs, 1895.

———. *The Apostle of the North: Rev. James Evans.* Toronto: William Briggs, 1900.

Notes

....

Notes to Preface

1 See, for example, Emma Larocque's "On the Ethics of Publishing Historical Documents" in Jennifer S. H. Brown and Robert Brightman, eds., *"The Orders of the Dreamed": George Nelson on Cree and Northern Ojibwa Religion and Myth, 1823* (Winnipeg: University of Manitoba Press, 1988), p. 201.

2 Jennifer S. H. Brown in collaboration with Maureen Matthews, "Fair Wind: Medicine and Consolation on the Berens River," in *Journal of the Canadian Historical Association* (1993), pp. 55–74.

3 For example, Carol Devens and Elizabeth Graham interpret native people as helpless or passively responsive to Euro-Canadian stimuli. Carol Devens, *Countering Colonization: Native American Women and Great Lakes Missions, 1630–1900* (Berkeley: University of California Press, 1992); Elizabeth Graham, *Medicine Man to Missionary: Missionaries as Agents of Cultural Change Among the Indians of Southern Ontario, 1784–1867* (Toronto: Peter Martin Associates, 1975).

4 Examples of church histories include: John Carroll, *Case and His Cotemporaries* (Toronto: Wesleyan Office, 1867–77) and Nan Shipley, *The James Evans Story* (Toronto: Ryerson Press, 1966). The following works, while offering more depth, still provide narratives generated solely from the perspectives of the missionaries: A. G. Morice, *History of the Catholic Missions in Western Canada from Lake Superior to the Pacific, 1659–1895* (Toronto: Mission Book Company, 1910); J. H. Riddell, *Methodism in the Middle West* (Toronto: Ryerson Press, 1946); T. C. B. Boon, *The Anglican Church from the Bay to the Rockies* (Toronto: Ryerson Press, 1973); Robert Choquette, *The Oblate Assault on Canada's Northwest* (Ottawa: University of Ottawa Press, 1995).

5 Howard Adams, *Prison of Grass: Canada from a Native Point of View* (Saskatoon: Fifth House Publishers, 1989).

6 Raymond J. DeMallie, *The Sixth Grandfather: Black Elk's Teachings Given to John Niehardt* (Lincoln: University of Nebraska Press, 1984); Raymond DeMallie and Douglas R. Parks, eds., *Sioux Indian Religion: Tradition and Innovation* (Norman: University of Oklahoma Press, 1987).

7 Jean-Guy Goulet, "Religious Dualism Among Athapaskan Catholics," *Canadian Journal of Anthropology* 3, 1 (1982), p. 1.

8 Ann Fienup-Riordan, *The Real People and the Children of Thunder: The Yup'ik Eskimo Encounter with Moravian Missionaries John and Edith Kilbuck* (Norman: University of Oklahoma Press, 1991), p. 7.

9 Ibid., p. 361.

10 Ibid., p. 363.

11 James Axtell, "Some Thoughts on the Ethnohistory of Missions," *Ethnohistory* 29, 1 (1982), pp. 35–41.

12 Clarence R. Bolt, "The Conversion of the Port Simpson Tsimshian: Indian Control or Missionary Manipulation?" *BC Studies* 57 (1983), p. 42.

13 Ibid., p. 39.

14 Ibid., pp. 45–46.

15 Sergei Kan, "Shamanism and Christianity: Modern-Day Tlingit Elders Look at the Past," *Ethnohistory* 38, 4 (1991) and his *Symbolic Immortality: The Tlingit Potlatch of the Nineteenth Century* (Washington: Smithsonian Institution Press, 1989).

16 For example, Maori charismatic religious movements in the nineteenth century blended Christianity with traditional beliefs. In Central Africa, Terence Ranger traced parallels in the transmission of ideas from missionary to African and subsequent African reinterpretations. See Hans Mol, *The Fixed and the Fickle: Religion and Identity in New Zealand* (Waterloo: Wilfrid Laurier Press, 1982); Ranger and John Weller, eds. *Themes in the Christian History of Central Africa* (Berkeley: University of California Press, 1975).

17 Jennifer S. H. Brown, "'A Place in Your Mind For Them All': Chief William Berens" in *Being and Becoming Indian: Biographical Sketches of North American Frontiers*, James A. Clifton, ed. (Chicago: Dorsey Press, 1989).

18 Percy Berens to Susan Gray, Winnipeg, Manitoba, 15 November 1994.

19 Walter Green to Susan Gray, Berens River, Manitoba, 1 December 1994.

20 Percy Berens to Susan Gray, Winnipeg, Manitoba, 15 November 1994.

21 Ibid.

22 Ibid.

23 John Edward Everett to Susan Gray, Berens River, Manitoba, 2 December 1994.

24 Ibid.

25 Percy Berens to Susan Gray, Winnipeg, Manitoba, 15 November 1994.

26 Julie Cruikshank, "The Discovery of Gold on the Klondike: Perspectives from Oral Tradition," Jennifer S. H. Brown and Elizabeth Vibert, eds., *Reading Beyond Words* (Peterborough, Ont.: Broadview Press, 1996), p. 452.

27 Maureen Matthews and Roger Roulette, "Fair Wind's Dream: Naamiwan Obawaajigewin," Brown and Vibert, pp. 330–59.

28 "The Journals and Voices of a Church of England Native Catechist: Askenootow (Charles Pratt), 1851–1884," Brown and Vibert, pp. 305–6.

Notes to Chapter 1

1 A. Irving Hallowell, *Contributions to Anthropology* (Chicago: University of Chicago Press, 1976), p. 333.

2 Susan Elaine Dueck, "Methodist Indian Day Schools and Indian Communities in Northern Manitoba, 1890–1925," M. A. Thesis, University of Manitoba, 1986, pp. 43–44.

3 Brown, "A Place in Your Mind For Them All," p. 210.

4 "Report of the Department of the Interior, 1875," *Sessional Papers* (1876), vol. 9, p. viii.

5 Jennifer S. H. Brown, "Chief Jacob Berens," *Dictionary of Canadian Biography*, vol. 14 (Toronto: University of Toronto Press, 1998).

6 Personal Papers of Rev. John Semmons (United Church Archives, Conference of Manitoba and Northwestern Ontario), p. 48.

7 A Hudson's Bay Company post had existed at Berens River since 1824, though records show occupation of the post as early as 1814 by men sent from the Jack River mouth. HBCA, District Reports, 1805–1825.

8 The Shaking Tent ceremony is described in detail in chapter 2. The Midewiwin is considered by many to embody the central tenets of the Ojibwa world view. It was a life-giving ceremony performed to cure illnesses and its teachings helped people to obtain health, a good life, and to prepare for the afterlife. See Laura Peers, *The Ojibwa of Western Canada, 1780 to 1870* (Winnipeg: University of Manitoba Press, 1994), pp. 23–24.

9 Brown, "Chief Jacob Berens," pp. 5–6.

10 "Report of E. McColl, Inspector of Indian Agencies, 1885," *Sessional Papers* (1886), vol. 18, p. 129.

11 "Report of A. MacKay, Indian Agent, 1885," *Sessional Papers* (1886) vol. 9, p. 110.

12 "Report of A. MacKay, Indian Agent, 1883," *Sessional Papers* (1884), vol. 17, p. 97; "Report of A. MacKay, Indian Agent, 1885," *Sessional Papers* (1886), vol. 19, p. 68; "Report of A. MacKay, Indian Agent, 1887," *Sessional Papers* (1887), vol. 21, p. 292; National Archives of Canada (hereafter NAC), Records Relating to Indian Affairs, RG10, vol. 3801, file 48638.

13 "Report of A, MacKay, Indian Agent, 1889," *Sessional Papers* (1890), vol. 23, p. 309.

14 James G. E. Smith, "Western Woods Cree," in *Handbook of North American Indians*, vol. 6, *Subarctic*, June Helm, ed. (Washington: Smithsonian Institution, 1981), p. 259.

184

15 "Report of E. McColl, Inspector of Indian Agencies, 1890," *Sessional Papers* (1892), vol. 24, p. 202.

16 "Report of A. MacKay, Indian Agent, 1890," *Sessional Papers* (1891), vol. 23, p. 131.

17 "Report of A. MacKay, Indian Agent, 1891," *Sessional Papers* (1892), vol. 25, p. 68.

18 "Report of A. MacKay, Indian Agent, 1893," *Sessional Papers* (1894), vol. 27, p. 71.

19 "Report of E. McColl, Superintendent Inspector, 1893," *Sessional Papers* (1894), vol. 27, p. 46.

20 "Report of A. MacKay, 1891," *Sessional Papers* (1892), vol. 25, p. 68. See also Sarah Carter, *Lost Harvests: Prairie Indian Reserve Farmers and Government Policy* (Montreal: McGill-Queen's University Press, 1990). Carter exposes the myths behind the standard view that agriculture failed on western Canadian reserves because Indian peoples could not be motivated to pursue or grasp the need for the enterprise.

21 "Report of A. MacKay, Indian Agent, 1894," *Sessional Papers* (1895), vol. 28, p. 73.

22 NAC, RG10, vol. 3946, file 123454.

23 "Report of A. MacKay, Indian Agent, 1896," *Sessional Papers* (1897), vol. 21, p. 260.

24 "Report of J.W. Short, Indian Agent, 1898," *Sessional Papers* (1899), vol. 33, p. 70.

25 *"As Their Natural Resources Fail": Native Peoples and the Economic History of Northern Manitoba, 1870–1930* (Vancouver: UBC Press, 1996), p. 180.

26 Ibid., p. 183.

27 Ibid., p. 237.

28 The term "Supply Missionary" refers to a missionary, usually inexperienced, who was temporarily placed in a community for a transitional period during which the Methodist Missionary Society searched for a permanent missionary placement.

29 "Report of J.A. McLachlan, 1897–8," *Annual Report of Missionary Society*, p. xlix.

30 *Annual Report of the Missionary Society of the Methodist Church*, 1893–1894, p. lviii; 1895–1896, p. xlix; 1896–1897, p. xlv; 1897–1898, p. xlviii; *Proceedings of the Sixteenth Session of the Manitoba and North-West Conference of the Methodist Church*, 1899, p. 332; *Proceedings of the Seventeenth Session*, 1900, p. 332; *Proceedings of the Eighteenth Session*, p. 27; *Proceedings of the Nineteenth Session*, p. 41, *Proceedings of the Twentieth Session*, p. 20. Copies in the United Church Archives, Conference of Manitoba and Northwestern Ontario.

31 Fred Baptiste to Susan Gray, Berens River, Manitoba, 1 December 1994.

32 "Report of Ebenezer E. McColl, Superintendent Inspector, 1895," *Sessional Papers* (1896), vol. 29, p. 210.

33 "Report of John Semmens, Indian Agent, Berens River Agency, 1901," *Sessional Papers* (1902) vol. 36, p. 73. Noting that most Ojibwa were connected with one or another of these pursuits, he listed the Dominion Fish Company, the Northern Fish Company, Ewing and Fryer and the J.K. McKenzie Company as dominating forces in the industry.

34 Annie E. McEwen was a member of a prominent Red River Settlement family. A.E. McEwen, Four Years at Berens River, A. E. McEwen Memoirs, Provincial Archives of Manitoba, MG8 B52, fos. 36-42.

35 Ibid., pp. 2, 6.

36 *Manitoba Conference Report*, 1908, p. 45. Copies in the United Church Archives, Conference of Manitoba and Northwestern Ontario. It is impossible to ascertain exactly what these "new methods" involved although it is likely that they centred around a "firmer stance" taken by the missionary. This may well have been expressed in intolerance, harsh judgements of behaviour and customs and, possibly, more public chastising of sinners.

37 *Annual Report of Missionary Society*, 1904–1905, p. xxii; 1905–1906, p. xxi; *Minutes of the Manitoba, Assiniboia and Alberta Annual Conferences of the Methodist Church*, 1907, p. 33; *Annual Report of Missionary Society*, 1908, p. 44; 1909, p. 224; 1910, pp. 176–77; *Minutes of the Thirteenth Session of the Manitoba Conference of the Methodist Church*, 1916, p. 231.

38 McEwen, Memoirs, p. 6.

39 Ibid., p. 6.

40 "Report of John Semmens, Indian Agent, Berens River Agency, 1903," *Sessional Papers* (1904), vol. 38, pp. 82–83.

41 McEwen, *Memoirs*, pp. 2–3, 7.

42 "Report of Duncan C. Scott, Deputy Superintendent-General of Indian Affairs, 1919," *Sessional Papers* (1920), vol. 56, p. 47.

43 D. Ann Herring, "The 1918 Flu Epidemic in Manitoba Aboriginal Communities: Implications for Depopulation Theory in the Americas," paper presented at the American Society for Ethnohistory meeting, Toronto, November 1990, p. 5. See also "'There were Young People and Old People and Babies Dying Every Week': The 1918–1919 Influenza Pandemic at Norway House," in *Ethnohistory* 41, no. 1 (1993), pp. 73–99.

44 Kristen M. Beckett, "Investigating Disease Experience in Aboriginal Populations in Canada: The 1918 Influenza Pandemic in Berens River and Poplar River, Manitoba," M.A. thesis, McMaster University, 1998, pp. 53–54.

45 Percy Berens to Susan Gray, Winnipeg, 15 November 1994.

46 Ibid.

47 "Report of Duncan C. Scott, Deputy Superintendent-General of Indian Affairs, 1919," *Sessional Papers* (1920), vol. 54, p. 47.

48 Annie Niddrie, "Annie Niddrie of Berens River" (unpublished manuscript edited by John W. Chalmers), p. 5.

49 Ibid.

50 Ibid., pp. 8, 12. The first policeman, Corporal Stewart, had arrived with his family in 1928.

51 Oblate Archives, Manitoba Province, Journal of Frederick Leach.

Notes to Chapter 2

1 *Contributions to Anthropology*, p. 357.

2 A. Irving Hallowell, *The Ojibwa of Berens River Manitoba: Ethnography into History*, ed. with preface and afterword by Jennifer S. H. Brown (Fort Worth, Texas: Harcourt, Brace and Jovanovich, 1992), p. 81.

3 Brown with Matthews, "Fair Wind,"pp. 55–74.

4 Ibid., p. 64.

5 Ibid.

6 Arthur M. Abell, *Talks with Great Composers: Candid Conversations with Brahms, Puccini, Strauss, and Others* (New York: Philosophical Library, 1955), p. 5.

7 Brown, "'A Place in Your Mind for Them All'," p. 208.

8 Percy Berens to Susan Gray, Winnipeg, Manitoba, 15 November 1994.

9 Walter Green to Susan Gray, Berens River, Manitoba, 1 December 1994.

10 Ruth Landes, *Ojibwa Religion and the Midéwiwin* (Madison: University of Wisconsin Press, 1968), p. 22.

11 A. Irving Hallowell, *Culture and Experience* (Philadelphia: University of Pennsylvania Press, 1955), p. 121.

12 James R. Stevens, ed., *Legends From the Forest: Told by Chief Thomas Fiddler* (Moonbeam, Ont: Penumbra Press, 1985), p. 42. Percy Berens provided an example of a shamanistic killing when he described how his brother had been killed by a conjurer. See later this chapter.

13 *The Ojibwa of Berens River.*

14 Writing to anthropologist Frank Speck on 19 July 1931, Hallowell explained that "The *pawaganak* are central in the active life of man, since they are the spiritual aspects of the concrete forces + objects of nature which he must use for a living while manitu is remote (cannot be a *pawagan*, by the way) and is only infrequently referred to (e.g., in the midewin) directly...." Accounts of Ojibwa cosmology from other areas refer to numerous manitous; however, Hallowell did not find these along the Berens River. On 1 August 1931, he told Speck that "... it's strange that aside from David Thompson I have nowhere [in written sources] run across the term *pawagan*. Yet that is the universal term among Cree + Saulteaux for dream-guardian and one of the 'keys.' *mantu* is never used in the plural and cannot be a *pawagan*." Correspondence of Frank Speck, Library of the American Philosophical Society, Philadelphia, Manuscript coll. 170 (2:F3). Transcribed by Jennifer S. H. Brown.

15   Hallowell, *The Ojibwa of Berens River,* p. 82.

16   Ibid., p. 82.

17   Ibid., p. 71.

18   Ibid., pp. 86, 91. Pawágan (dream visitor) was a generic term for a spiritual being, as was "grandfather" – a term conveying respect. A. Irving Hallowell, *The Role of Conjuring in Saulteaux Society* (New York: Octagon Books, 1971), p. 7.

19   A. Irving Hallowell, "Some Empirical Aspects of Northern Saulteaux Religion," *American Anthropologist* 36 (1934), p. 389.

20   Ibid., p. 392.

21   Ibid., p. 393.

22   Percy Berens to Susan Gray, Winnipeg, Manitoba, 15 November 1994. Interestingly, Percy's dichotomizing of evil versus righteous spirits suggests the influence of Christianity in his life.

23   For an excellent discussion on this, see Olive Patricia Dickason, *The Myth of the Savage: The Beginnings of French Colonialism in the Americas* (Edmonton: University of Alberta Press, 1984). All Amerindian societies led structured lives based on coherent belief systems and cyclical patterns. It was the Europeans' ignorance of this that led to the label "savage."

24   A. Irving Hallowell, ed., "Reminiscences of Chief William Berens," unpublished paper, 1940, A. Irving Hallowell Papers, American Philosophical Society, p. 7.

25   Fred Baptiste to Susan Gray, Berens River, Manitoba, 1 December 1994. The Thunderbirds are other other-than-human beings. These members of the hawk family manifest themselves through thunder and lightening.

26   John Edward Everett to Susan Gray, Berens River, 2 December 1994.

27   Percy Berens to Susan Gray, Winnipeg, Manitoba, 15 November 1994.

28   Percy Berens to Maureen Matthews, Winnipeg, Manitoba, 12 September 1994.

29   Gordon Berens to Maureen Matthews and Jennifer S. H. Brown, Fisher River Seniors Residence, 20 March 1995.

30   Ibid.

31   Ibid.

32   Ibid.

33   Percy Berens to Susan Gray, Winnipeg, Manitoba, 15 November 1994.

34   Rebecca Kugel, "Of Missionaries and Their Cattle: Ojibwa Perceptions of a Missionary as Evil Shaman," *Ethnohistory* 41, no. 2 (1994), pp. 228–29.

35   "Some Empirical Aspects," p. 395. See also, Hallowell's field notes held in the American Philosophical Society Library, Philadelphia, Ms. Coll. 26.

36   Ibid.

37   Ibid.

38   Percy Berens to Susan Gray, Winnipeg, Manitoba, 15 November 1994.

39   *Culture and Experience,* p. 199.

40 Hallowell, "Some Empirical Aspects," pp. 394–95.

41 Ibid., p. 398.

42 Thomas Fiddler and James R. Stevens, *Killing the Shamen* (Moonbeam, Ont.: Penumbra Press, 1985), p. 44.

43 Hallowell, "Some Empirical Aspects," p. 398.

44 A. Irving Hallowell, "The Ojibwa of Berens River," p. 89. The pawáganak could be seen through the eyes of the soul as opposed to the body. An integral part of reality, they have never been regarded by the Ojibwa as supernatural beings although their powers were indeed greater than those of the human, plant or animal entities under their control. If a man wished to hunt an individual animal, it was important for him to gain favour with that animal's "boss" or "owner. Once this had been done, it was equally important for him to avoid offending that entity. See Hallowell, "Some Empirical Aspects," p. 398.

45 Hallowell, "Some Empirical Aspects," p. 398.

46 Ibid., p. 398.

47 Ibid., p. 400.

48 Ibid.

49 An excellent discussion of this can be found in Jennifer S. H. Brown, "Going to School in Dreams: Ojibwa Conversations from Berens River, 1930–1940," paper presented at the Annual Edward S. Rogers Lecture in Anthropology, Royal Ontario Museum, 28 February 1997.

50 Betsey Patrick to Susan Gray, Berens River, Manitoba, 1 December 1994.

51 Walter Green to Susan Gray, Berens River, 1 December 1994.

52 A. Irving Hallowell, "Some Empirical Aspects," p. 402.

53 For an in-depth discussion, see *The Role of Conjuring in Saulteaux Society*.

54 Hallowell, "Some Empirical Aspects," p. 402.

55 *Culture and Experience*, p. 147.

56 Percy Berens to Susan Gray, Winnipeg, 15 November 1994. William related this experience to Hallowell in the 1930s, saying "About sundown, I could see a cloud rising in the west. It was calm.... Then I could hear the thunder ... just as something striking my body when I heard it. Then I knew what it meant. I thought I was going to be killed by the thunder that night.... you could see the lightning when it struck that rocky island ... running all over like snakes ... fearful. We hid our heads.... On the other side of the island when they saw the lightning they never expected us to live.... But I never gave up hope.... then she [Nancy] saw the day sky coming.... I jumped up and walked out then. I said "This old fellow did not kill us yet." See Jennifer S. H. Brown, "A Place in Your Mind for Them All," p. 216.

57 Ibid.

58 Fiddler and Stevens, *Killing the Shamen*, p. 22.

59 Gordon Berens to Maureen Matthews and Jennifer S. H. Brown, Fisher River Seniors Residence, 20 March 1995.

60   See Matthews and Roulette, pp. 354–55 and A. Irving Hallowell, "Spirits of
the Dead in Saulteaux Life and Thought," *Journal of the Royal Anthropological
Institute* 70 (1940), pp. 29–51.

61   Betsey Patrick to Susan Gray, Berens River, 1 December 1994.

62   Percy Berens to Susan Gray, Winnipeg, 15 November 1994. In an unpublished
paper on the Cree concept of the Supreme Being, Regina Flannery explains that
other-than-human spirits were given responsibility by a Being superior to them.
The Being, whom no-one has ever seen, is animate, non-anthropomorphic and
has no proper name. The Crees believe this spirit is concerned for humankind's
well-being and has ultimate control of the food supply (although day-to-day
activities were governed by spiritual Caretakers of the animals). Significant to
Flannery is the idea that the Supreme Being owns "everything on the earth,
but not man." The East Cree traditional Supreme Being is not worshipped, but
rather his presence "somewhere up there" is an omniscient given. Conjurors
derive their power through *pawáganak*, but ultimately from the Supreme
Being. In the case of the Ojibwa, Hallowell (quoted in Flannery's paper) states
definitively that "the ultimate controlling power of the universe is *kadabéndjiget*
(owner), the Supreme Being. His name is seldom uttered, 'he' remains unsexed
and extremely remote from any direct participation in human affairs." Regina
Flannery, "Thoughts on the Cree Concept of the Supreme Being in Response
to Long's Interview with Preston: 'The Northern Algonquian Supreme Being
Revisited,'" unpublished paper, 1984, in the possession of Jennifer S. H.
Brown. John Long provides an excellent discussion of the concept of Manitou
among nineteenth-century Western James Bay Cree in his 1987 article. See
his "*Manitu*, Power, Books and *Wiihtikow*: Some Factors in the Adoption of
Christianity by Nineteenth-Century Western James Bay Cree," *Native Studies
Review* 3, no. 1 (1987), pp. 1–30.

Notes to Chapter 3

1   *The Indian Missionary Record*, 1, no. 8 (September 1938).

2   Morice, *History of the Catholic Church in Western Canada*, vol. 2, p. 350.

3   "The Oblate Sisters, A Manitoban Order: Reconstructing Early Years,
1904–1915," Rosa del C. Bruno-Jofré ed., *Issues in the History of Education in
Manitoba: From the Construction of the Common School to the Politics of Voices*
(Queenston, Ont.: Edwin Mellen Press, 1993), p. 552.

4   Oblate Archives, Manitoba Province, Journal of Brother Frederick Leach.

5   Bishop Ignace Bourget had invited the Oblates of Mary Immaculate to Montreal
in 1841. This order was devoted expressly to mission work, steadfastly insisting
on supremacy and the opening up of mission fields across Canada. See John
Webster Grant, *Moon of Wintertime: Missionaries and the Indians of Canada in
Encounter Since 1534* (Toronto: University of Toronto Press, 1984), p. 184.

6   Archives Deschâtelets, Oblates of Mary Immaculate, Berens River, and Little
Grand Rapids Correspondence, box L581.M27L, no. 16.

7   United Church Archives, Conference of Manitoba and Northwestern Ontario, Rev. John Semmens Personal Papers, PP34, Semmens, "Under Northern Lights," p. 26.

8   Ibid., p. 39.

9   Ibid., p. 248. Undoubtedly, the Indians involved had a rather different view of what had been going on; however, the thing to note here is the perspective of the missionaries, who were on sincere, if shaky, ground.

10 Alexander Sutherland, "Address of the Toronto Conference of the Methodist Church," *Minutes of the Toronto Annual Conference of the Methodist Church, 1884* (Toronto: William Briggs, 1884), p. 248.

11 S. D. Gaudin, *Missionary Bulletin* 1, no. 3 (September 1903), p. 308.

12 "Annual Report of E. R. Young for Berens River, 1874–1875," *Annual Reports of the Wesleyan Methodist Missionary Society, 1873–1876* (Toronto: Wesleyan Conference Printing Office, 1876), p. xxix.

13 W. J. Townsend, H. B. Workman, George Eayrs, *A New History of Methodism* (London: Hodder and Stoughton, 1909), p. 496.

14 E. P. Thompson, *The Making of the English Working Class* (England: Penguin Books, 1981), pp. 441–44.

15 Oblate Archives, Manitoba Province, Journal of Brother Frederick Leach.

16 *The Indian Missionary Record* 2, no. 9 (November 1939).

17 Joseph Etienne Champagne, *Manual of Missionary Action* (Ottawa: University of Ottawa Press, 1948), pp. 277, 324.

18 *The Indian Missionary Record* 2, no. 1 (January 1939).

19 *The Indian Missionary Record* 1, no. 8 (September 1938).

20 *Manual of Missionary Action*, p. 564.

21 Ibid., p. 599.

22 Ibid., p. 600.

23 Ibid.

24 *The Indian Missionary Record* 1, no. 7 (July/August 1938).

25 J. R. Miller, "Denominational Rivalry in Indian Residential Education," in Raymond Huel, ed., *Western Oblate Studies 2* (Lampeter, Wales: Edwin Mellen Press, 1992). Religious enmity between Protestants and Catholics did not become rampant in the Canadas until the 1840s and 1850s. See J. M. S. Careless, *The Union of the Canadas, 1841–1857* (Toronto: McClelland & Stewart, 1971). Ultramontanism focused on centralization under papal direction and papal control of the church. The pope lived beyond the mountains in Rome (as opposed to the king who lived in France): hence the name ultramontanism. It was a reaction to the effects of the French Revolution with its liberal secularism. See Susan Elaine Gray, "The Ojibwa World View and Encounters With Christianity Along the Berens River, 1875–1940" (Ph.D. dissertation, University of Manitoba, 1996), chapter II.

26 Champagne, *Manual of Missionary Action*, p. 37.

27 Ibid., p. 40.

28 *The Missionary Bulletin* 1, no. 3 (September 1918), p. 315.

29 Mark G. McGowan, "Rethinking Catholic-Protestant Relations in Canada: The Episcopal Reports of 1900–1901," *Canadian Catholic Historical Association* 59 (1992), pp. 22–23.

30 Percy Berens to Susan Gray, Winnipeg, Manitoba, 15 November 1994.

31 Fred Baptiste to Susan Gray, Berens River, Manitoba, 1 December 1994.

32 Virginia Boulanger to Susan Gray, Berens River, Manitoba, 1 December 1994. Gordon Polson and Roger Spielmann, in their study of two competing Christian denominations within the Algonquin community of Winneway, quote an Algonquin person who makes the similar point that it was the missionaries, not the Aboriginals, who had rigid definitions of who is a Christian. "The Pentecostals figure if you're a Catholic you're not a Christian and vice versa. It's such a vicious circle. We don't have to put those kind of labels on who's right and who's wrong." Polson and Spielmann, "'Once There Were Two Brothers ...': Religious Tension in One Algonquin Community," in *Papers of the Twenty-First Algonquian Conference*, William Cowan, ed. (Ottawa: Carleton University Press, 1990), p. 308.

33 Victoria University Archives, T. E. Egerton Shore Correspondence, fonds 14, subseries 5, box 5, file 98.

34 Ibid.

35 Oblate Archives, Manitoba Province, Journal of Brother Frederick Leach.

36 Ibid.

37 Archives Deschâtelets (hereafter AD), Oblates of Mary Immaculate, Berens River and Little Grand Rapids, Correspondence, box L581.M27L, no. 14.

38 AD, box L581.M27L, no. 20. Cubby Green was Walter Green's father. Interestingly, William Berens himself got involved in this struggle, working with Green and Jones. He said that although he had received no official authority to return the children to Cubby, he was chief and had a right to rule his band. Leach wrote in exasperation, "The chief has not acted in an impartial manner as he should have done for he has admitted that he tried to influence the guardians to relinquish their rights of guardianship, especially Miss Sarah Shaw."

39 AD, box L581.M27L, no. 20, 1919.

40 AD, box L581.M27L, no. 21, June–July 1919.

41 AD, box L581.M27L, no. 110, 18 January 1929.

42 AD, box L581.M27L, no. 107.

43 AD, box L581.M27L, no. 23.

44 AD, box L581 .M27L 84.

45 Robert Choquette, "L'histoire de l'eglise de l'ouest: hier et aujourd'hui," paper presented at the Fourth Western Oblate Studies Conference, Winnipeg, 25 August 1995. As well, whether one wrote for a public as opposed to a private audience made a difference to both style and content.

46 See, for example, the account of the meeting between Robert Rundle and Jesuit Father De Smet in Glenbow Archives, Robert Terrill Rundle Fonds, Journal.

47 Choquette, *The Oblate Assault*, p. 178.

48 Kerry Abel, *Drum Songs: Glimpses of Dene History* (Montreal: McGill-Queen's University Press, 1993), p. 134.

49 Choquette, *The Oblate Assault*, pp. 183.

50 Oblate Archives, Leach Journal.

51 United Church Archives, Conference of Manitoba and Northwestern Ontario, Personal Papers of Luther L. Schuetze, PP36, p. 23.

52 Schuetze, Personal Papers, p. 33.

53 See Brown with Matthews, p. 67.

54 Schuetze, Personal Papers, p. 24.

Notes to Chapter 4

1 David Cayley, *Northrop Frye in Conversation* (Concord, Ont.: Anansi, 1992), p. 39.

2 *The Real People*, Introduction.

3 United Church Archives, Conference of Manitoba and Northwestern Ontario, Personal Papers of Frances G. Stevens, PP35, file A, p. 56.

4 Ibid.

5 There are three categories of windigos: a superhuman monster who may or may not have descended from human beings; human beings possessed by the spirit of the cannibal monster; and a "culture-specific psychotic syndrome" where the victims suffer a compulsive need to eat human flesh. The windigo concept is also associated with the fear of being lost in the bush. See Lou Marano, "Windigo Psychosis: The Anatomy of an Emic-Etic Confusion," *Current Anthropology* 23, no. 4 (August 1982): 386. John Long elaborates on how Western James Bay Crees used the power of Christianity, the Bible, and the other-than-human figure of Christ, to overcome other-than-human threats such as windigos. See Long's "*Manitu*, Power, Books and *Wiihtikow*."

6 F. G. Stevens Papers, p. 10.

7 Ibid.

8 Ibid., p. 11.

9 Rev. John Ryerson, *Hudson's Bay* (Toronto: G. R. Sanderson, 1855), p. 81.

10 Jennifer S. H. Brown, "A Place in Your Mind For Them All," pp. 209–10.

11 Jennifer S. H. Brown, "Fair Wind," p. 62.

12 A. Irving Hallowell ed., "Reminiscences of Chief William Berens," p. 1.

13 Jennifer S. H. Brown, "A Place in Your Mind," p. 204.

14 Ibid., p. 211.

15 Provincial Archives of Manitoba, Lieutenant-Governor's Collection, MG12 B1, no. 1443, 29 March 1877.

16 "Report of E. McColl, Inspector of Indian Agencies, 1881," *Sessional Papers* (1882), vol. 15, p. 107. Unfortunately, the sessional papers for this year do not contain any statistical material for attendance in the school; this data was not generated until 1885. McColl (1835–1902) acted first as inspector and then as superintendent of Indian Affairs for Manitoba and the Northwest Territories from 1877 to 1902. His agencies ranged from Cumberland House west to Lake Superior. (See Frances McColl, *Ebenezer McColl: "Friend to the Indians"* [Winnipeg: Hignell Printing, 1989]). Both Jacob and William Berens got along well with McColl; William told A. Irving Hallowell in 1940 that the inspector was "the best ... the Indians ever had since treaty was signed – a very clever speaker." When William was a young man, he and a friend had been hired by McColl to work for him, and at the end of the trip had given the pair "supper at his own table.... How many men can you find today to offer you that?" Not only had McColl paid the men all the money they had coming to them, he also gave each a present of a suit of clothes, and William Berens never forgot the kindness. See Hallowell, "Reminiscences of Chief William Berens," pp. 39, 41.

17 "Report of E. McColl, Inspector of Indian Agencies, 1882," *Sessional Papers* (1883), vol. 16, p. 142.

18 "Report of A. MacKay, Indian Agent, 1885," *Sessional Papers* (1886), vol. 19, p. 110.

19 Ibid.

20 NAC, RG10, vol. 3703, file 17665. Rev. A. W. Ross was stationed at Fisher River and visited Berens River occasionally.

21 NAC, RG10, vol. 3715, file 21257.

22 Ibid. According to MacKay in 1885, Jane Flett's school had six white children and seven treaty children on the roll; all were making excellent progress. MacKay commented that she was not receiving a salary for her efforts and suggested that, although she did not ask for financial compensation, she should be paid some sort of salary. Miss Parkinson stayed at the Methodist school until 1888 when her brother-in-law Rev. Enos Langford was transferred to Winnipeg. Although no teacher replaced her for two years, missionary J. W. Butler took over teaching duties when he could. MacKay reported to McColl on 23 May 1888, that Butler was "much esteemed by the Indians and greatly interested in the Mission work." NAC, RG10, vol. 3801, file 48638.

23 "Report of Rev. E. Langford for Berens River," *Sixty First Annual Report of the Missionary Society of the Methodist Church, 1884–85* (Toronto: Methodist Mission Rooms, 1885) p. xxix.

24 *Eighty-Sixth Annual Report of the Missionary Society of the Methodist Church,1909* (Toronto: Methodist Mission Rooms, 1910), p. 176.

25 *Minutes of the Fifteenth Session of the Manitoba Conference of the Methodist Church, 1918,* p. 300.

26 *Minutes of the Twentieth Session of the Manitoba Conference of the Methodist Church, 1923*, p. 322.

27 *The United Church of Canada Year Book* (Toronto: United Church of Canada General Offices, 1936), p. 399.

28 William Ivens went on to be active in the Social Gospel movement and found the Canadian Labour Churches. He ultimately left the Methodist Church for areas of activity which he believed held more scope and hope for societal change. Although the church, in 1918, had formally advocated social reconstruction by a shifting of emphasis from competition to cooperation, the emerging radical group (men like Ivens, J. S. Woodsworth and Salem Bland) differed in the extreme from Methodist leadership regarding the action required for this "reconstruction." While the outspoken Bland was dismissed, Woodsworth and Ivens chose to leave the church when they realized it would be impossible for them to carry out their work (concerning the plight of the "common man" and problems caused by the industrial revolution) within the structures that surrounded them. Both Ivens and Woodsworth were arrested for their participation in Winnipeg's 1919 General Strike. The Canadian Labour Churches were a variation of the "Labour Churches" founded in England in 1890 and were set up to appeal to those with whom the church had lost touch. By 1920, there were at least ten Labour Churches in Manitoba, each with its own flavour. See Richard Allen, *The Social Passion: Religion and Social Reform in Canada 1914–28* (Toronto: University of Toronto Press, 1971), pp. 66–85.

29 "Report of S. J. Jackson, Inspector of Indian Agencies, 1904," *Sessional Papers* (1905), vol. 39, p. 123.

30 *Minutes of the Manitoba Annual Conference of the Methodist Church, 1909*, p. 43.

31 "Report of Thomas Neville for Berens River, 1904–05," *Annual Report of the Methodist Missionary Society* (Toronto: Methodist Book Rooms, 1905), p. xxiv.

32 "The Indian Work: J. A. McLachlan's Report on Berens River," *Seventy Fourth Annual Report of the Missionary Society of the Methodist Church, 1897–98* (Toronto: Methodist Mission Rooms, 1898), p. xlix.

33 *Minutes of the Thirteenth Session of the Manitoba Conference of the Methodist Church, 1916*, p. 231.

34 *Minutes of the Sixteenth Session of the Manitoba Conference of the Methodist Church, 1919*, p. 327.

35 "Report of D. C. Scott, Deputy Superintendent General of Indian Affairs, 1919," *Sessional Papers* (1920), vol. 56, p. 47.

36 *The United Church of Canada Year Book* (Toronto: United Church of Canada General Offices, 1934), p. 458.

37 *The United Church of Canada Year Book* (Toronto: United Church of Canada General Offices, 1937), p. 380.

38 Antonio R. Gualtieri, *Christianity and Native Traditions: Indiginization and Syncretism Among the Innuit and Dene of the Western Arctic* (Notre Dame, Ind: Cross Cultural Publications, 1984), p. 1.

39 F. G. Stevens Papers, "The Sandy Lake Story," p. 1.

40 Ibid., p. 2.

41 Ibid., p. 3.

42 Fiddler and Stevens, *Killing the Shamen*, p. 122.

43 Ibid.

44 Ibid., p. 125.

45 F. G. Stevens Papers, "The Sandy Lake Story," p. 8.

46 Ibid.

47 "Annual Report of E. R. Young for Berens River, 1874–75," *Annual Reports of the Weslyan Methodist Missionary Society, 1873–76* (Toronto: Wesleyan Conference Printing Office, 1876), p. xxix.

48 "Report of J. A. McLachlan for Berens River," *Seventieth Annual Report of the Missionary Society of the Methodist Church, 1888–89* (Toronto: Methodist Mission Rooms, 1894), p. x.

49 United Church Archives, Conference of Manitoba and Northwestern Ontario, Personal Papers of John Semmens, PP34, "Notes on Personal History," p. 27.

50 There is a discrepancy in the sources here. While Young wrote that the Nelson House Cree brought the boy to him, Semmens said that Hartie was taken to Norway House by Young who had visited Sandy Hartie's camp and realized that the boy, with his injury, constituted a real burden on the family. See Egerton Ryerson Young, *On the Indian Trail: Stories of Missionary Work Among the Cree and Saulteaux Indians* (New York: Young People's Missionary Movement, 1897), pp. 96–99.

51 Semmens, "Notes on Personal History," p. 28.

52 Hallowell, ed., "Reminiscences of Chief William Berens," p. 46.

53 Ibid., p. 44. Richard Preston, in his study of the oral accounts of John Blackned, discusses a medicine man from the James Bay area who controlled the Shaking Tent (The-one-who's-kneeling-inside-here). This is the opposite situation that could exist when Aboriginal healers were also Christians. Here, this practising shaman studied the Bible, read it often, had a strong sense of being a Christian, and implied "that his conjuring [was] not in conflict with his Christianity." Richard J. Preston, *Cree Narrative*, 2nd ed. (Montreal: McGill-Queen's University Press, 2002), p. 96.

54 Percy Berens to Susan Gray, Winnipeg, Manitoba, 15 November 1994.

55 Ibid.

56 Hallowell, "Reminiscences of Chief William Berens," p. 7.

57 Semmens, "Notes on Personal History," p. 54.

58 Ibid.

59 "Annual Report of E. R. Young for Berens River, 1874–75," *Annual Reports of the Wesleyan Methodist Missionary Society, 1873–76* (Toronto: Wesleyan Conference Printing Office, 1876), p. xxx.

60 Ibid., p. xxii.

61 "Report on Indian Missions, 1877–78: J. Semmens: Berens River," *Fifty-Fourth Annual Report of the Missionary Society of the Methodist Church of Canada, 1877–78* (Toronto: Methodist Conference Office, 1878), p. xviii.

62 "Report of J. W. Short, Indian Agent, Berens River Agency, 1898," *Sessional Papers* (1899), vol. 33, p. 71.

63 "Report of E. McColl, Inspector of Indian Agencies, Lake Winnipeg Inspectorate, 1899," *Sessional Papers* (1900), vol. 34, p. 102.

64 "Report of John Semmens, Indian Agent, Berens River Agency, 1901," *Sessional Papers* (1902), vol. 36, p. 73.

65 "Report of S. J. Jackson, Inspector of Indian Agencies, 1904," *Sessional Papers* (1905), vol. 39, p. 119.

66 "Report of John Semmens, 1908," *Sessional Papers* (1909), vol. 43, p. 113.

67 NAC, RG10, vol. 3655, file 8977.

68 Ibid.

69 "Report of E. McColl, Superintendent Inspector, 1893," *Sessional Papers* (1894), vol. 27, p. 45.

70 United Church Archives, Conference of Manitoba and Northwestern Ontario, Julia Anna Asher, "Reminiscences," 1950, p. 89. The incidents involved a man named Musquomoat and his family. They had killed their mother who, they believed, was turning into a windigo. Musquomoat later converted and this, according to Asher, invoked in him an increasing sense of guilt throughout his life regarding his mother's death. The second case occurred over a "crazy woman" named Sarah Ross who was on the trapline when people in her midst perceived that she was becoming a windigo. She died before Short and McLachlan could get to her. While there was insufficient evidence to prosecute Thomas Bear and his wife who had been alone with her when she had died, the understanding was that she had been "killed as a wetigo."

71 "Report of A. W. Ross: Berens River and Little Grand Rapids," *Annual Report of the Auxiliary Missionary Society of the Toronto Conference, 1880–81* (Toronto: The Methodist Mission Rooms, 1881), p. xxiii.

72 PAM, MG1 C5, "Journal of W.M. Chapman," October 1912–November 1915.

73 Ibid., 2 August 1913.

74 Ibid., 18 September 1915.

75 Hallowell, ed., "Reminiscences of Chief William Berens," p. 54.

76 "Report of J. Semmens, Indian Agent, Berens River Agency, 1903," *Sessional Papers* (1904), vol. 38, pp. 82–83.

77 For an excellent example of syncretism among northern Manitoba Indians in the 1840s, see Jennifer S. H. Brown, "The Track to Heaven: The Hudson Bay Cree Religious Movement of 1842–1843," *Papers of the Thirteenth Algonquian Conference*, William Cowan, ed. (Ottawa: Carleton University Press, 1982).

78 Fiddler and Stevens, *Killing the Shamen*, p. 173.

79 Ibid.

80   Jennifer S. H. Brown with Maureen Matthews, "Fair Wind," p. 62.

81   Ibid.

82   Ibid., p. 67.

83   Jennifer S. H. Brown with Maureen Matthews, "Fair Wind," p. 62.

84   Maureen Matthews and Roger Roulette, "Fair Wind's Dream: Naamiwan Obawaajigewin," Brown and Vibert, pp. 354–55.

85   Hallowell, ed., "Reminiscences of Chief William Berens," p. 47.

86   Ibid., p. 50.

87   *The Invasion Within.*

Notes to Chapter 5

1   John Edward Everett to Susan Gray, Berens River, Manitoba, 2 December 1994. Here, Everett contrasts his experiences (which are grounded in the Ojibwa world view) regarding Thunderbirds with the Euro-Canadian scientific explanation of weather phenomena.

2   James Axtell, *After Columbus: Essays on the Ethnohistory of Colonial North America* (New York: Oxford University Press, 1988), pp. 49–52.

3   Jennifer S. H. Brown, "Afterword," in A. Irving Hallowell, *The Ojibwa of Berens River*, p. 113.

4   Susan Elaine Gray, "Methodist Indian Day Schools and Indian Communities in Northern Manitoba, 1890–1925," *Manitoba History* 30 (Autumn 1995), p. 5.

5   Percy Berens to Susan Gray, Winnipeg, Manitoba, 15 November 1994.

6   Susan Elaine Gray, "Methodist Indian Day Schools," p. 5.

7   A. Irving Hallowell Papers, MS Coll. 26, APS, Philadelphia.

8   Ibid.

9   Ida Green to Susan Gray, Berens River, Manitoba, 1 December 1994.

10   Percy Berens to Susan Gray, Winnipeg, Manitoba, 15 November 1994.

11   Ibid.

12   Fred Baptiste to Susan Gray, Berens River, Manitoba, 1 December 1994.

13   Walter Green to Susan Gray, Berens River, Manitoba, 1 December 1994. Annie Niddrie, speaking of Berens River in the 1920s, also mentioned the respect held by the people for the Sabbath. "The older Indians were so honest and truthful and the very soul of honor … no drinking and no working on Sundays. It was a hallowed day." See Annie Niddrie, "Annie Niddrie of Berens River."

14   Percy Berens to Susan Gray, Winnipeg, Manitoba, 15 November 1994.

15   Ibid.

16   Ibid.

17 Fred Baptiste to Susan Gray, Berens River, Manitoba, 1 December 1994.

18 Ibid.

19 Ibid.

20 Betsey Patrick to Susan Gray, Berens River, Manitoba, 1 December 1994. Gordon Green (Ida's husband) and Harry Everett were likely the boys who lived with Rev. Niddrie. Niddrie sent Harry, Betsey's cousin, to college to be trained as a minister. Betsey does not know what happened to him after he left Berens River.

21 Ibid.

22 Ibid.

23 Virginia Boulanger to Susan Gray, Berens River, Manitoba, 1 December 1994.

24 Ibid.

25 *Culture and Experience*, p. 147.

26 Ida Green to Susan Gray, Berens River, Manitoba, 1 December 1994.

27 John Edward Everett to Susan Gray, Berens River, Manitoba, 2 December 1994.

28 Ibid.

29 *The Real People*, ch. 1.

30 AD, L581, M27L, 130.

31 *Minutes of the Sixteenth Session of the Manitoba Conference of the Methodist Church* (1919), p. 327.

32 *The United Church of Canada Year Book* (Toronto: United Church of Canada General Offices, 1934), p. 458.

33 *The United Church of Canada Year Book* (Toronto: United Church of Canada General Offices, 1936), pp. 400, 424.

34 Luther L. Schuetze Personal Papers, p. 24.

35 Ibid., p. 37.

36 *The Role of Conjuring*, pp. 53–55.

37 Luther L. Schuetze Personal Papers, p. 38.

38 Ibid., p. 39. This drum has disappeared. When Schuetze moved from Little Grand Rapids, he gave it to a Mr. Davidson who was the credit manager of Ashdown's Wholesale and the Sunday school superintendent in a Winnipeg church.

39 "Dans une premiere visite faites au Petit Grand Rapide l'automne 1924, vingt-trois enfants ont été baptisté catholiques, dont treize de l'âge a l'école.... Douze autre enfants plus jeunes ont aussi été baptisé et plusieurs d'entre eux auront dans un an ou deux l'age de ecole. Tous devront avoir une instruction en rapport avec leur religion et leur foi. C'est pourquoi les conseilluers et les parents demandent avec instance une ecole catholique sur la Reserve du Petit Grand Rapide." AD, L1001, M27L, 2.

40 Brother Frederick Leach, O.M.I., *Fifty-Five Years with Indians and Settlers on Lake Winnipeg* (Winnipeg: The Order of Mary Immaculate, Manitoba Province, 1973), p. 32.

41 "Journal of Brother Frederick Leach."

42 Ibid.

43 Ibid.

44 *Sixty Years*, p. 31.

45 Ibid., p. 25.

46 "Journal of Brother Frederick Leach."

47 Ibid.

48 Ibid.

49 Ibid., p. 31.

50 Ibid.

51 "Beaucoup de monde est venu à l'église le dimanche. C'est dire que Boniface [Guimond] fait bon travail par la et ... je souhaite qu'il y reste encore." AD, L581, M27L, 161.

52 Roscoe Tranner Chapin, "Memoirs of a Happy Journey Through Life," p. 44.

53 F. G. Stevens Papers, "The Sandy Lake Story," p. 12.

54 Hallowell, *The Ojibwa of Berens River*, p. 62.

55 Walter Green to Susan Gray, Berens River, Manitoba, 1 December 1994.

56 Fred Baptiste to Susan Gray, Berens River, Manitoba, 1 December 1994.

57 John Edward Everett to Susan Gray, Berens River, Manitoba, 2 December 1994.

58 Ibid.

59 Virginia Boulanger to Susan Gray, Berens River, Manitoba, 1 December 1994.

60 *The Sixth Grandfather*, Introduction to Part I.

61 F. G. Stevens Personal Papers.

62 Ibid., p. 12. John S. Long also presents interesting accounts of missionaries whose failures were the result of contempt for Aboriginal cultures, an unwillingness to compromise, and inflexibility. See, for example, his "The Reverend George Barnley, Wesleyan Methodism, and the Fur Trade Company Families of James Bay," *Ontario History* 77, no. 1 (March 1985), pp. 43–64 and "Rev. Edwin Watkins: Missionary to the Cree, 1852–1857," pp. 91–117 in *Papers of the Sixteenth Algonquian Conference*, William Cowan, ed. (Ottawa: Carleton University Press, 1985).

63 "Journal of Brother Frederick Leach." It is interesting that this girl had the Christian name Mary. It is possible that the Methodists had been influential here.

64 Ibid. We do not learn exactly when Mary died but can assume it was fairly soon after 27 May when Leach noted that he was spending most nights at her bedside; she was never baptized.

65 John Edward Everett to Susan Gray, Berens River, Manitoba, 2 December 1994.

66 Jennifer S. H. Brown, "Fields of Dreams: Revisiting A. I. Hallowell and the Berens River Ojibwa," in Sergei Kan and Pauline Turner Strong eds., *Native Americans: Histories, Cultures, and Representations* (Lincoln: University of Nebraska Press, 2006), p. 11.

67 "[U]n peu trop tranquille, l'en serait ennuyeux s'il n'y avait pas les travaux manuels pour nous occuper. Le travail du ministère est bien peu de chose il ne sufferait pas pur [*sic*] occuper un père et nous sommes deux. Depuis quatre mois que je suis [ici] je n'ai entendu en tout qu'une quinzaine de confessions. Excepté à Noel ou il y a un grand concours. Celors [*sic*] j'ai en sept confessions." AD, L581, M27L, 29.

68 "[D]ans notre pauvre mission, les jours s'écoulent monotones et tranquilles." AD, L581, M27L, 50.

69 "[J]e ne crois pas que l'acquisition de la langue soit la plus grande difficulté que je rencontrerai dans le travail des missions. Ce sera plutôt, je crois, de parvenir à aimer les sauvages, car je les trouve bien independants [orgueilleux] (?), dissimulés et hypocrites, sans parler de leur malpropreté. Cela fait que je n'ai pas beaucoup de sympathie pour eux. Je crois que le [voisinage ?] des méthodistés les rendus pires qu'ailleurs. Mais j'espère qu'avec le temps, je parviendrai à trouver quelque qualité dans ces êtres qui sont pourtant du monde. Je termine ... avec l'espoire que sur ma prochaine lettre, je pourrai nous écrire en toute verité: j'aime mes sauvages, et je commence à parler avec eux dans leur langue." AD, L1001, M27L, 2.

70 Leach, *Sixty Years*, p. 49.

71 Jean Comaroff and John L. Comaroff, *Of Revelation and Revolution* (Chicago: University of Chicago Press, 1991), p. 247.

72 Ibid., p. 245.

73 Jean and John L. Comaroff, *Ethnography and the Historical Imagination* (Boulder, Colorado: Westview Press, 1992), p. 5.

74 Robert Hefner, "Introduction: World Building and the Rationality of Conversion," in Robert W. Hefner, ed., *Conversion to Christianity: Historical and Anthropological Perspectives on a Great Transformation* (Berkeley: University of California Press, 1993), p. 4.

75 Jean-Guy A. Goulet, *Ways of Knowing: Experience, Knowledge and Power Among the Dene Tha'* (Lincoln: University of Nebraska Press, 1998), p. 209.

76 Ibid., p. 200.

77 Ibid., p. 207.

78 Ibid., p. 211.

79 Hans Mol, *The Fixed and the Fickle*, Conclusion.

80 Ibid., Introduction and ch. II.

81 Sergei Kan, "Shamanism and Christianity," p. 380.

82 *Ways of Knowing*, pp. 216–17.

83   See Katherine Pettipas, *Severing the Ties that Bind: Government Repression of Indigenous Religious Ceremonies on the Prairies* (Winnipeg: University of Manitoba Press, 1994), p. 156.

Notes to Chapter 6

1   Gualtieri, *Christianity and Native Traditions*, p. 71.

2   Ibid., p. 71.

3   Hallowell, *The Role of Conjuring*, p. 7.

4   Brother F. Leach, "Indian Medicine Men and Their Remedies," *Moccasin Telegraph* (Winter 1966), pp. 36–37.

5   Specifically, Leach was concerned about misdiagnosis and improper doses of medicines administered to sick people by medicine men – although he did acknowledge the usefulness of Indian medical roots and herbs and retained a lifelong interest in these things.

6   A. Irving Hallowell Papers, MS Coll. 26, APS, Philadelphia.

7   Walter Green to Susan Gray, Berens River, Manitoba, 1 December 1994.

8   Percy Berens to Susan Gray, Winnipeg, Manitoba, 15 November 1994.

9   Virginia Boulanger to Susan Gray, Berens River, Manitoba, 1 December 1994.

10   Tom Boulanger, *An Indian Remembers: My Life as a Trapper in Northern Manitoba* (Winnipeg: Pemmican Press, 1971), pp. 63–64.

11   Fred Baptiste to Susan Gray, Berens River, Manitoba, 1 December 1994.

12   Percy Berens to Susan Gray, Winnipeg, Manitoba, 15 November 1994.

13   Sergei Kan, "Shamanism and Christianity."

14   Percy Berens to Susan Gray, Winnipeg, Manitoba, 15 November 1994. At Poplar River, explains Percy, there is a high place where one can see the Thunderbirds' nests.

15   Transcript from Maureen Matthews, "Thunderbirds," a Canadian Broadcasting Corporation *Ideas* documentary broadcast, 15,16 May 1995.

16   Ibid., pp. 4,5.

17   Ibid., p. 13.

18   Ibid., p. 14.

19   Percy Berens to Jennifer S. H. Brown and Maureen Matthews, Winnipeg, Manitoba, 12 September 1994.

20   Brown with Matthews, p. 59.

21   Gordon Berens to Jennifer S. H. Brown and Maureen Matthews, Fisher River Seniors Residence, 20 March 1995.

22   Rev. John Niddrie, "North of the Northwest," p. 109.

23 Leach, *Sixty Years With Indians*, p. 30.

24 Ibid., p. 31.

25 Personal Papers of Luther Schuetze, p. 11.

26 Ibid.

27 Ibid., p. 24.

28 Ibid.

29 United Church Archives, Conference of Manitoba and Northwestern Ontario, Personal Papers of Rev J. A. C. Kell.

30 Stevens Papers, F. G. Stevens, "The Sandy Lake Story," p. 12.

31 Personal Papers of Rev. J. A. C. Kell, "Wetigoes – Or What?" (1928).

32 Ibid.

33 Ibid.

34 Kell Papers, J. A. C. Kell, "The Social Organization of the Northern Cree," Oxford House, 1928, p. 8.

35 *Ethnography and the Historical Imagination*, p. 5.

36 Donald B. Smith, *Sacred Feathers: The Rev. Peter Jones and the Mississauga Indians* (Toronto: University of Toronto Press, 1987), ch. 6.

37 *Sioux Indian Religion*, Introduction.

38 John S. Long, "The Reverend George Barnley and the James Bay Cree," *The Canadian Journal of Native Studies* 6, no. 2 (1986): 322–23. Gordon Polson and Roger Spielmann present an insightful description of what they term "ethno-Christianity." They quote an Algonquin member of the Catholic Church who says, "I believe what the church teaches, but I still have my own beliefs, too." Polson and Spielmann suggest that there is "a distinctly native, in-group view of understanding the Christian message, perhaps even a kind of religious dualism." Polson and Spielmann, "Once There Were Two Brothers," p. 306.

39 Ranger and Weller, *Themes in the Christian History*, Introduction.

40 Gordon Berens to Jennifer S. H. Brown and Maureen Matthews, Fisher River Seniors Residence, 20 March 1995.

41 Ibid.

42 Ibid.

43 Hallowell Papers.

44 Sarah Preston documents a similar situation when Cree woman Alice Jacob describes a dream with Christian overtones. About this dream, she says she "went away someplace." Preston notes that dreams are very significant to Cree people as a source of knowledge and/or a sign of the dreamer's spiritual power. Both Alice's and Walter's dreams had strong culture-specific bases overlain with Christian elements. See Sarah Preston, *Let the Past Go: A Life History*, Canadian Ethnology Service Paper No. 104 (Ottawa: National Museums of Canada, 1986), pp. 21, 33.

45 Walter Green to Susan Gray, Berens River, Manitoba, 1 December 1994.

46 Ibid.

47 Ibid.

48 Fred Baptiste to Susan Gray, Berens River, Manitoba, 1 December 1994.

49 Hallowell, *Culture and Experience*, p. 157.

50 Ibid., pp. 157–58.

51 AD, L581, M27L, 86, 1926.

52 Ibid.

53 John Edward Everett to Susan Gray, Berens River, Manitoba, 2 December 1994.

54 Ibid.

55 Percy Berens to Susan Gray, Winnipeg, Manitoba, 15 November 1994.

56 Virginia Boulanger to Susan Gray, Berens River, Manitoba, 1 December 1994.

Notes to Chapter 7

1 *The Role of Conjuring*, p. 54.

2 Ibid., pp. 85–86.

3 Ibid., p. 86.

4 Julie Cruikshank, "The Discovery of Gold on the Klondike," p. 435.

Index

CPSIA information can be obtained
at www.ICGtesting.com
Printed in the USA
LVOW01s0738260116

471610LV00012B/75/P